D0874781

Books also by William A. Cook and Sunbury Press

*Diamond Madness Classic Episodes of Rowdyism,
Racism and Violence in Major League Baseball*

The Lindbergh Baby Kidnapping

LADY MOGULS

A HISTORY OF WOMEN WHO HAVE OWNED
MAJOR LEAGUE BASEBALL TEAMS

WILLIAM A. COOK

Mechanicsburg, Pennsylvania USA

Published by Sunbury Press, Inc.
50 West Main Street
Mechanicsburg, Pennsylvania 17055

www.sunburypress.com

For information about special discounts for bulk purchases, please contact Sunbury Press Orders Dept. at (855) 338-8359 or orders@sunburypress.com.

To request one of our authors for speaking engagements or book signings, please contact Sunbury Press Publicity Dept. at publicity@sunburypress.com.

ISBN: 978-1-62006-636-2 (Trade Paperback)
ISBN: 978-1-62006-637-9 (Mobipocket)

Library of Congress Control Number: 2015951596

FIRST SUNBURY PRESS EDITION: October 2015

Product of the United States of America
0 1 1 2 3 5 8 13 21 34 55

Set in Bookman Old Style
Designed by Crystal Devine
Cover by Lawrence Knorr
Edited by Janice Rhayem

Continue the Enlightenment!

For
Anita Bolce.
A wonderful sister

CONTENTS

INTRODUCTION

Women have been part of the tradition and lore of the game of baseball for more than 150 years. Endless stories abound about women's participation in the grand old game in almost every capacity. The first organized women's team in the United States was started at Vassar College in 1866.

The All-American Girls Professional Baseball League (AAGPBL) was created by Chicago Cubs owner Philip K. Wrigley, who wanted to fill seats in his ballpark during the World War Two era. The league was a resounding success, continued in the post-war era, and by 1948 the league had drawn more than one million paying customers and produced such notable lady players as the Grand Rapids Chicks' Sophie Kuries, who had 202 stolen bases in 204 attempts and Dorothy Kamenshek, who played first base for the Rockford Peaches. Legendary Philadelphia Athletics owner and manager Connie Mack remarked that Dorothy Kamenshek would be worth $100,000 if she were a man and were able to play in the Major Leagues.

In the front offices of both major and minor league teams, women have played important roles for over 100 years. Margaret Donahue became the secretary for the Chicago Cubs in 1927 and helped to run the team well into the 1940s. Also in the 1940s, Grace Kelly was a vice president of the Class AAA Minneapolis Millers. One of the most memorable of the early ladies in the front office is Nona Seeds, who ran the Amarillo Gold Sox in the West

Texas League in the 1930s while her husband Bob, who owned the team, was pursuing a Major League career.

Women have also been involved with scouting. In the 1920s and 1930s, Bessie Largent and her husband Roy traveled around the country on behalf of the Chicago White Sox seeking talented players. Among those they are credited with finding are Zeke Bonura, Art Shires, and Hall of Fame shortstop Luke Appling.

In the MLB central office in 2012 there were ten women in senior vice president positions and eleven women in vice president roles, including Katy Feeney, senior vice president for scheduling and club relations, who has the complex responsibility of creating the master schedule.

While stories of women in baseball are substantial and have been well documented over the years in many published works, this book is about an exclusive group of women in baseball history. Some of them are well known, some not, they are women who have experienced the game from the very top as Major League team owners and co-owners while enduring the subtle displeasure of their solidly entrenched male colleagues.

The history of women who have owned Major League teams is more than a mere curiosity; in fact the stories of these ladies form an anthology of a struggle for acceptance and recognition as entrepreneurs and sports-minded individuals that understand the tradition of the game of baseball and it's ingrained connection to American culture.

It all began in 1911 when Helene Hathaway Robison Britton inherited the St. Louis Cardinals, and continued through the ensuing decades with various women gaining control of Major League teams through subsequent inheritances. However, a few women such as Joan Whitney Payson of the New York Mets and Marge Schott of the Cincinnati Reds, both of whom had a strong independent interest in baseball, gained majority control of a Major League team with their own finances. More recently Linda Alvarado became a co-owner of the Colorado Rockies through her own investment.

In 1985 a watershed event occurred for women in Major League baseball: Marge Schott gained majority control of the Cincinnati Reds, joining Jean Yawkey of the Boston

Red Sox and Joan Kroc of the San Diego Padres, thereby bringing the number of women at that time to three who owned Major League teams.

The degree to which the lady moguls have taken an active role in running their ball clubs is varied. Some, such as Eleanor Hempstead who inherited the New York Giants, chose to turn the reigns of leadership over to their husbands. Others, such as Grace Comiskey of the Chicago White Sox and Florence Dreyfuss of the Pittsburgh Pirates, while not day-to-day hands-on owners, made their presence felt and were often involved with major decisions affecting their ball clubs.

Also, today after decades of indifference and neglect, Negro Leagues players are enshrined in the National Baseball Hall of Fame, and the statistics of some of the leagues' most talented players appear in *The Baseball Encyclopedia.* Therefore, to bridge the gap between the period of exclusion and today, I have chosen to include in this work two women who were involved with ownership and administration of Negro Leagues teams; Olivia Taylor of the Indianapolis ABC's and Effa Manley of the Newark Eagles. In 2006 Effa Manley became the first woman elected to the National Baseball Hall of Fame.

Collectively, the remarkable women mentioned in this work have added colorful, enriching, and sometimes controversial experiences to the history of Major League baseball. It is my hope that their legacy will continue to expand and to inspire more women to make further inroads into both ownership and management of big league teams.

I would like here to acknowledge the assistance of the following libraries and archives in making this work possible: the New York Public Library, Public Library of Cincinnati & Hamilton County, St. Louis Public Library, and the National Baseball Hall of Fame & Museum.

1

HELENE HATHAWAY ROBISON BRITTON

ST. LOUIS CARDINALS

Helene Hathaway Robison was born in 1879. She grew up in the Cleveland suburb of Bratenahi near the shores of Lake Erie and was educated at Hathaway-Brown School. Helene's father, Frank De Hass Robison, and his brother, Martin Stanley Robison, owned a streetcar company and the National League Cleveland Spiders baseball franchise.

In addition, in 1899, the Robison brothers purchased the St. Louis Browns National League franchise from legendary Chris Von der Ahe after his corporation went bankrupt following a fire at the New Sportsman's Park and the owner not having any insurance.

The Robison brothers renamed the ballpark League Park, and the team was named the St. Louis Perfectos. Then they sent most of the better players from their 1898 Cleveland team to St. Louis, including two twenty game winning pitchers, Cy Young and Jack Powell. Consequently, in 1899, the Cleveland Spiders, playing in the twelve-team bloated National League, experienced one of the most miserable seasons in Major League history finishing with a record of 20-134 with a winning percentage of .130.

For the 1900 season, the National League restructured into an eight team circuit and dropped four franchises including the Cleveland Spiders. That same year, the St. Louis National League team was renamed the Cardinals.

In 1901, Helene Hathaway Robison married Schuyler Pearson Britton, a Cleveland attorney employed by a printing company. The couple quickly had two children, a boy (Frank) and a girl (Marie).

In 1908, Helene's father, Frank De Hass Robison, died, and the St. Louis Cardinals ownership passed on to her uncle, Martin Stanley Robison. Shortly before the start of the 1911 Major League Baseball season on March 11, her uncle died. As Martin Stanley Robison did not have any children, in his will, he left 75 percent of the stock in the St. Louis Cardinals to his niece, Helene. The remaining shares were left to Helene's mother.

Earlier in the year in Cleveland, Helene Britton had sued for divorce from her husband, but they had reconciliation. At that moment, an air of uncertainty seemed to surround the St. Louis Cardinals and the baseball moguls were left guessing and wondering what the new ownership structure of the franchise would be. It was unprecedented in Major League history for a woman to be in complete control of a team. The answer came quickly. After considering an offer to sell the Cardinals to Charles Weeghman of Chicago, Helene and her mother decided to keep the team.

Helene, her husband Schuyler, and their children moved from Cleveland to St. Louis. They moved into a mansion on the 4200 block of Lindell Boulevard; popularly known as "Millionaires Row." Their home directly faced Forrest Park, the setting for the 1904 World's Fair.

The fact that the St. Louis Cardinals were legally under the control of a thirty-two-year-old woman sent shock waves through the close fraternity of Major League moguls. The American League moguls, more than their National League brethren, were absolutely smitten by Helene's status and reluctance to sell the team. Collectively, they agreed on an informal, non-written policy that no woman would ever be left in control of an American League franchise through matters of probate.[1] Also, following the death of John T. Brush, owner of the National League New

York Giants on November 26, 1912, the ball club let it be known that neither his wife nor daughters that had inherited the team would play any active role in conducting the affairs of the team.

National Commission chairman and president of the Cincinnati Reds, August Garry Herrmann, was philosophical about Helene Britton's entry into Major League baseball, "I imagine that some time ... there will be a change in ownership, or at least, in active management, that will result in a man becoming president of the St. Louis club."[2]

Helene Britton, an active suffragette, was far from indifferent to the sexism displayed by various Major League team owners. She said in an interview "that if ever a woman was left with a white elephant upon her hands, she is that woman."[3] Openly, she stated that her male colleagues were mean to a degree and lacking in chivalry. Nonetheless, while it was suggested in the press that she lacked enthusiasm for baseball, she immediately went forward with gusto in the discharge of her duties.

Helene renamed the rickety old fire trap of a ballpark the Cardinals played in to Robison Field as a tribute to her late father and uncle. Edward A. Steininger, a local building contractor, was appointed president and remained in the position until the 1912 season when he left to head up the St. Louis entry into the Federal League. So Helene asked her legal advisor James C. Jones to succeed Steininger. He served briefly before she appointed her husband as temporary president of the team.

Some members of the press began referring to Helene Britton as "Lady Bee" and regarded her simply as a novelty. However, when Helene quickly let it be known through her actions as well as words that she would have the final say in any matter that was of serious concern to the welfare of the St. Louis Cardinals, her persona quickly faded as the butt of jokes by the writers.

The game of baseball was not unfamiliar to Helene Britton. In an interview with *Baseball Magazine* she stated:

> I can honestly say that I have always loved baseball. My father and uncles talked baseball ever since I

can remember. My father early insisted that I should keep score and he didn't have to use any coercion. I was only eager to do so once I had mastered the details of the game and learned to comprehend the mysterious symbols with which the official scorers at our park designated the plays which were transpiring before our eyes.

I grew up, as I say, in a very atmosphere of baseball. I even played it when a girl and I am glad to know that the game is played in a somewhat modified form in hundreds of girl camps and elsewhere by young ladies all over the United States. Played in that way, I believe it is as a healthful and interesting diversion though I realize that anything which resembles a professional type is distinctly a man's game.[4]

In Helene Britton's first year as the owner of the St. Louis Cardinals in 1911, the club, piloted by player/ manager Roger Bresnahan, finished in fifth place with a record of 75-74, twenty-two games behind the pennant winning New York Giants. Nonetheless, the Cardinals had been in the race until fading in August and drew a record home attendance of 450,000 fans and made a profit of $150,000. For his efforts, Bresnahan was rewarded by Helene Britton with a raise and a new long-term contract extension.

Roger Bresnahan, known as the "Duke of Tralee," had been a legendary catcher with the New York Giants from 1902 to 1908, playing on two National League championship teams under manager John McGraw with the battery mate of Christy Mathewson. He came to St. Louis as the player/manager in a trade for three players following the 1908 season and would a few years later have the distinction of being the first manager in the Major Leagues to work for a female owner and the first manager to be fired by a woman. Bresnahan was an innovator and is credited with being the first catcher to wear shin guards in 1907. He would play in the Major Leagues for seventeen years (1897-1915), manage for five years (1909-1912, 1915), and be elected to the Baseball Hall of Fame in 1945.

With Bresnahan back at the helm, the Cardinals' fans were anticipating the beginning of the 1912 season with huge enthusiasm. Determined to expand the Cardinals female fan base, prior to the season, Helene Britton had announced that every Monday would be Ladies Day at Robison Field. Women accompanied by male escorts would be admitted to the ballpark free.

On Thursday April 11, 1912, an estimated 20,000 delighted fans attended the opening game at Robison Field, including club owner Helene Britton and her two children, as the Cardinals defeated the Pittsburgh Pirates 7-0. Player/manager Roger Bresnahan had injured his knee in the pre-season City Classic game with the rival American League St. Louis Browns and could not play.

The Friday game between the Cardinals and Pirates was rained out. However, on Saturday before 10,000 fans, the Cardinals again beat the Pirates, this time by a score of 6-5 in ten innings. Then on Sunday, before a crowd of 25,000, the Cardinals defeated the Chicago Cubs 5-4 in twelve innings in a classic mound dual between the Cardinals' lefty Harry "Slim" Salee and the Cubs' Mordecai "Three-Finger" Brown, both hurlers going the distance.

Without Roger Bresnahan in the lineup, the St. Louis Cardinals opened the 1912 season 3-0. For Helene Britton, it was a monumental start to the season with more than 55,000 fans going through the turn-styles of Robison Field. But the magic didn't last long.

The troubles began when Roger Bresnahan offered to buy the Cardinals and Robison Field from Helene Britton for $500,000. When she rejected his offer, he was smitten. The rejection of his offer was so shocking to Bresnahan that it sent him to the hospital with what he claimed was an attack of tonsillitis.

While Bresnahan was hospitalized, the Cardinals fell apart. By May 9, the Cardinals had fallen into last place with a record of 5-16. During this period, there were days when the attendance at Cardinals home games was less than 800. Everyone was attempting to explain the ball club's collapse. Some blamed it on a lack of trying or playing in sympathy with Bresnahan's failed attempt to gain control of the team.

As the Cardinals struggled, Helene Britton began to clash with Roger Bresnahan on how to best run the team. She accused Roger Bresnahan of being careless in the way he directed the management of the team. The *St. Louis Post-Dispatch* had stated in its April 14 edition that Helene had "changed from the demure, housewifely little person of a year ago."[5]

On May 22, from his hospital bed, Roger Bresnahan appealed to National Commission Chairman Garry Herrmann to protect him from attacks on his management of the Cardinals. Herrmann was perplexed on what to do about the matter. It was clear that Bresnahan didn't like being criticized by a woman. So just what was Herrmann supposed to do about it? Helene Britton owned the team, and Roger Bresnahan was her subordinate.

By August 22 the Cardinals had climbed in the standings to sixth place with a record of 50-64. But the troubles between Helene and Bresnahan escalated further in August when he wanted to trade popular second baseman Miller Huggins and outfielder Rube Ellis to the Cincinnati Reds for outfielder Mike Mitchell and infielder Tex McDonald. There had been talk that Reds president Garry Herrmann wanted to acquire Huggins, a native of Cincinnati and a graduate of the University of Cincinnati law school, for the purpose of naming him manager of the Reds. But Helene Britton would not allow the trade to go through.

The Sporting News, reporting on the matter, stated, "Mrs. Britton could not see where the trade would benefit her team and put her French heel down on it. There is some argument on her side when man for man is considered, but there is an angle she may well ponder upon. That is in the block to Huggins opportunity to become a manager. And yet she has a right to the view that if Cincinnati wants a manager it should pay a manager's price, for managers these days are at a premium."[6] Furthermore, *The Sporting News*, sensing the building tension between Helene and Roger Bresnahan, was questioning if she had come to the conclusion that perhaps it was wise to keep Huggins as managerial material in reserve.

The St. Louis Cardinals finished in sixth place with a record of 63-90. In an effort to plan for the 1913 season, Helene Britton invited Roger Bresnahan to her home for a sit-down on the matter. However, Bresnahan was in a far different frame of mind. He proceeded to insult Helene by asking her "what the hell any goddam woman can tell me about baseball?"[7]

On August 17, 1912, Horace Fogel, the outspoken and eccentric owner of the Philadelphia Phillies, alleged in a telegram sent to National Commission Chairman Garry Herrmann and National League president Thomas J. Lynch, that the St. Louis Cardinals under the leadership of Roger Bresnahan had laid down to let the New York Giants win the pennant in 1911. When Helene Britton questioned Bresnahan about the accusations during the meeting at her home, he went into a tirade laced with foul language defending himself. By late October, Helene Britton had enough of Roger Bresnahan, and to the shock of the baseball world—she fired him.

Later that fall, Horace Fogel would deny the charge he had made against Bresnahan stating that his telegrams were privileged communications that one executive might freely write to another. Nonetheless, Fogel's indiscretion had been responsible for further damaging the relationship between Helene Britton and Roger Bresnahan.

Roger Bresnahan had a five-year contract with the Cardinals approved by Helene Britton that called for $10,000 a year, plus 10 percent of the gate. Bresnahan approached Helene with a buyout proposal whereby he would be paid his $50,000 salary, surrender his claim to 10 percent of the gate, and resign. But the proposal fell apart, because Helene could not agree to the $50,000 salary payment.

Immediately, Bresnahan charged that Helene had compromised his five-year contract and filed a claim against her with the National Commission and in court for $40,000. Garry Herrmann and The National Commission pushed the matter to the back burner of its agenda, hoping that the two would find common ground on the issue. Helene realized that she had painted herself into a corner, so attorneys for both parties entered into negotiations on the matter. In early January 1913, a compromise settlement was agreed to, and Helene bought out Bresnahan's contract for $20,000.

Now that Bresnahan was a free agent, several clubs made offers for his services as a player rather than a manager, including Cincinnati, Pittsburgh, and Chicago. He signed for the 1913 season to become a catcher for the Chicago Cubs where he would wind up his seventeen-year Major League career in 1915 once again as a player/manager.

On February 8, 1913 Helene Britton removed the temporary tag from her husband's status as president of the Cardinals and appointed Schuyler P. Britton officially to the position. In reality, Schuyler was more of an honorary president than functional one—it was clear to everyone that Helene was calling the shots.

Miller Huggins was appointed to succeed Bresnahan as manager. Immediately, Huggins was introduced to the fact that he was working for Helene Britton. During the National League's annual meeting in New York in December 1912, the Pittsburgh Pirates wanted to make a trade for Cardinal Ed Konetchy, one of the better first baseman in the National League. In the 1912 season, Konetchy had batted .314 with 81 RBIs. However, he was unhappy with his contract and was threatening to be a holdout for more money in the 1913 season. Pittsburgh manager Fred Clarke was willing to trade four players for Konetchy and Rebel Oakes. While Miller Huggins was in favor of the trade, Helene Britton vetoed it.

On opening day, Helene Britton gave each woman entering Robison Field a carnation. The Cardinals finished the 1913 season under Huggins in eighth place with a dismal record of 51-99.

Entering into the 1914 season, not only were Helene Britton's Cardinals confronted with competition at the gate from the American League's St. Louis Browns, who played only a few blocks away in Old Sportsman's Park, but now a new entity had entered the game in the presence of the Federal League's St. Louis Terriers. Federal League teams had also snatched up a few of Helene Britton's ballplayers, such as starting outfielders Steve Evans and Rebel Oaks.

Despite it all, the St. Louis Cardinals, managed by Miller Huggins, finished in third place with a record of 81-72. It was the highest in the standings the team had finished in since being purchased by the Robison brothers in 1899. Furthermore, the Cardinals had a higher season attendance (256,099) than the Browns (244,714). The Terriers' attendance figures for the season were not announced, but the record shows that the team finished last in the Federal League.

The 1915 season was Helene Britton's fifth year as majority owner of the St. Louis Cardinals. While no critical decision affecting the ball club could be made without her input, Helene left the voting on league matters to her husband, the managing of the Cardinals to Miller Huggins, and scouting of prospects to her two scouts, Bob Connery and Eddie Herr.

It was Huggins's third year as manager, and the club finished in sixth place with a record of 72-81. The fact that the Cardinals played mediocre ball hardly deterred Helene's enthusiasm for the game; she attended as many home games as possible, sitting in her private box, cheering them on enthusiastically.

On August 12 following a thirteen inning, 6-3 loss to the Chicago Cubs at Robison Field, Helene was visibly upset. She quickly left her box and confronted umpire Bill Byron, who was quite aware of her status. For fifteen minutes, Helene audaciously questioned the umpire on why he had thrown a few of her players out of the game. The press took notice that she had grilled Byron and caught up with her. When asked about the incident, she stated, "Really I am disgusted with the work of the umpires against my ball club and I decided to secure a personal explanation. I asked Byron if Mr. Huggins or Mr. Hetzel used bad language to him when the players were put off the ball field. He said no, and then I asked him why he put them out of the game. I asked Mr. Byron if he did not think he was favoring the other club. He smiled and denied it."[8]

Toward the end of 1915, a player destined to become the greatest right handed hitter of all time would put on a St. Louis Cardinals uniform—Rogers Hornsby. He would play in the Major Leagues for twenty-three years (twelve for the Cardinals), and when he retired as a player in 1937 he had a lifetime batting average of .358, second only to Ty Cobb.

Helene Britton did not favor making trades to improve her ball club. She was confident that good players could be developed within the club's minor league affiliates. Elaborating on that belief, she stated:

> It has been the fortune, good or bad, for the Cardinals to depend largely upon the development of young players. This policy, which has prevented the more sensational methods of trades and deals, has its drawbacks and its compensations. Personally I believe that a successful ball club is one of the many things that money alone cannot purchase. The expenditure of a fortune may indeed procure high salaried stars but the experience of owners who have made the costly experiment has shown that teams composed of stars do not as a usual thing become pennant winners.[9]

The bottom line of Helene's philosophy of winning was that star players could not guarantee success in the standings. More important was the level of harmony among all the players, regardless of their marquee status. For playing in eighteen games and hitting .246 in the 1915 season, Rogers Hornsby was paid $1,500.

At the close of the 1915 season, the Federal League moguls were waiting for adjudication in a pending law suit in Federal Court before Judge Kenesaw Mountain Landis. Nonetheless, the Federal League had lost between three and five million dollars in its two-year existence and the owners decided to come to terms with the National and American Leagues and disband.

One of the major issues blocking a settlement of the dispute with the Federal League was that there were three teams in St. Louis. So it was determined by the National League moguls that one of the teams would have to be sold as part of the agreement. Helene Britton had quietly announced that she would be willing to sell the Cardinals.

The value on the team and Robison Field had been estimated at $500,000.

In December the National and American Leagues held their annual meetings in New York, and it seemed promising that the negotiations for a peace agreement with the Feds could begin. But at the National League meeting at the Waldorf-Astoria Hotel, the situation hit a major obstacle when out of the blue one of the National League owners arrogantly demanded that Mrs. Britton "must sell" her team. Furthermore, the other owners and National League president, John Tenner, were advancing their collective belief that it was for the good of the game for Helene Britton to get out of baseball. They were even so bold as to suggest a selling price of $250,000.

But Helene Britton was of the opinion that the other owners and Tenner were attempting to auction off her team. The haughtiness and male chauvinism of her colleagues deeply offended Helene, and she pulled down the "for sale" sign on the Cardinals, while letting it be squarely known that no man, nor group of men, could tell her what she must do. Infuriated, she left the meeting and told the press, "I have not sold the Cardinals and I'm not going to sell the Cardinals."[10]

In late December, a peace meeting between the National and American Leagues and the Federal League was held at the Sinton Hotel in Cincinnati. The St. Louis situation was solved in the agreement with the Federal League by permitting Philip DeCatesby Ball, owner of the Federal League's St. Louis Terriers, to buy the American League's St. Louis Browns from John Galvin and his partners, then merge the two teams' rosters on to the Browns.

The 1916 St. Louis Cardinals, despite having the brilliant rookie Rogers Hornsby on the team, who hit for an average of .313 (fourth highest in the National League), were a bad team. They lost the last twelve games of the season and finished in a tie for seventh place with Cincinnati with a record of 60-93. Still, Helene Britton did not ignore the contributions of Hornsby to the ball club and approved a $500 bonus for him.

In August Charles Weeghman, former Federal League owner of the Chicago Whales that had acquired the

Chicago Cubs in the peace agreement, sent a telegram to Helene Britton offering to buy Rogers Hornsby for an undisclosed sum. Also, the Brooklyn club was offering to trade the Cardinals shortstop Ollie O'Mara and outfielder Casey Stengel for Hornsby and $20,000 cash. Helene Britton and husband Schuyler turned down both offers. The Brittons let it be known that they might trade a player, but were against the outright sale of any player.

At that time, the Brittons' marriage was falling apart. Schuyler Britton had taken to the bottle and began to stay away from home most nights out carousing. According to the charges of Helene Britton, Schuyler had returned home on November 7, 1916 at 2:00 a.m. to discover that she had locked him out of their stately mansion on Lindell Boulevard. In a drunken rage, Schuyler attempted to break down the door. When Helene finally admitted him to the house he "nearly set fire to the house"[11] with his careless use of a cigar. Then a heated argument ensued between the couple; Helene packed some of Schuyler's things, he left and never came back.

On November 17, 1916, for the second time, Helene Britton filed a petition for divorce from Schuyler P. Britton. In her petition, Helene asked for custody of the couple's two children. She alleged that Schuyler had mentally abused her and "frequently struck"[12] her.

Miller Huggins was forced to leave his home in Cincinnati and testify in the divorce proceedings. The divorce would be granted on February 12, 1917.

Later that same day, Helene Britton assumed the title of president of the St. Louis Cardinals. Her self-appointment made her the first woman to hold such a title in Major League Baseball history. Also, in a complete turnabout, she announced that anyone on the Cardinals, except Rogers Hornsby, was for sale or trade.

The fact that Helene had protected Hornsby didn't deter the efforts of Charles Weeghman. He offered $75,000 cash for Hornsby. Weeghman's intrepid attempts to buy Hornsby were beginning to appear tantamount to tampering with one of her players, and it bothered Helene. While Helene and Miller Huggins turned down the offer, Helene supposedly stated that she would not trade

Hornsby for the entire Chicago Cubs team. But there was speculation that if Weeghman had offered the Cardinals pitcher Jim "Hippo" Vaughn and another hurler, that Helene and Huggins may have made the deal.

As the National League club owners gathered at the Waldorf Astoria in New York for their annual winter meeting in December 1916, Helene Britton stopped before entering the meeting room to address the press and speak about her duties as president and owner of the St. Louis Cardinals, as well as her goals for the club:

> You can reach me here most any morning at 9:30 and frequently I make it as early as 9:00 o'clock. Unless I have an important appointment downtown in the afternoon you will find me here until past sundown. I want to succeed–why shouldn't I? I am not looking to success for personal prosperity. I am not so narrow-minded. Just look what it means to all of us to have a winning ball club. It will push St. Louis to the front line. Cleveland is my original home but I'm in St. Louis and I'm proud to be here. My father and my uncle tried, and I will not give up. I know it can be done. Probably not today, maybe tomorrow; and I only ask the fans not to pass snap judgment. I could have sold years ago. But I love this game, just like my father and uncle. I could have sold last winter, and I could have sold last summer, but I have refused all the offers. A prosperous business is one that moves without a hitch. If there are any flaws in my club I hope to eliminate the defects, and then once operating successfully, I know that it will be an easy position for me.[13]

Upon concluding her remarks, Helene Britton entered the meeting room and took her seat among her male colleagues.

The National League owners and league president, Tenner, were still smitten by their unsuccessful attempt the previous year to force Helene Britton to sell the Cardinals and reinstate their fraternity with all male ownership. What they would learn is that it wasn't necessary to humiliate Helene to get what they so desired; it was simply a case of just letting matters take a natural course of events.

The fact was that Helene Britton wanted out of Major League Baseball. She had grown weary with baseball during the war with the Federal League. She was tired of losing on the field and tired of losing money. In the 1916 season, the Cardinals had only played before a sparse 224,308 fans at home, and the team was near bankrupt. Having rid herself of her husband Schuyler, Helene Britton was now ready to sell the Cardinals and move on. She asked her attorney James C. Jones to start looking for a buyer for the ball club and Robison Field. Helene was asking for $375,000 with a $75,000 down payment.

Manager Miller Huggins was interested in buying the team and was attempting to arrange a deal primarily financed by former Cincinnati Reds majority stock holder and yeast magnate Julius Fleischmann.

But Helene was in a hurry to rid herself of the Cardinals, and when she started to make overtures that she would be willing to sell the ball club to buyers in another city, a group of local merchants, headed up by Sam Breadon, a local automobile dealer, and her attorney, James C. Jones, raised $50,000. Helene agreed to accept the reduced down payment, and the club was sold in February 1917.

Following the sale of the Cardinals, Helene remarked, "Being a woman owner of a baseball club was difficult at first. It was also new to me, even though I had heard and talked baseball all my life. I loved it, though, and regretted selling it."[14]

Philip DeCatesby Ball, owner of the St. Louis Browns, was a rather brash person with an aggressive obnoxious personality. Branch Rickey, the business manager for the St. Louis Browns, didn't like working for Ball. He found him uncouth and lacking in baseball knowledge. So he quit and was named president of the Cardinals.

Miller Huggins was hugely disappointed that Helene Britton had sold the Cardinals before he could arrange the necessary financing with his investors. Nonetheless, Huggins stayed on with the new owners as manager of the

Cardinals for one more year. The 1917 St. Louis Cardinals finished in third place with a record of 82-70 while continuing to play to a lot of empty seats, as only 288,491 fans ventured through the turnstiles of the renamed Cardinal Field (previously Robison Field).

The following season, Miller Huggins moved on becoming the manager of the New York Yankees. He would pilot the legendary Bronx Bombers teams of Babe Ruth and Lou Gehrig in the "roaring twenties" that would take him all the way to the Baseball Hall of Fame.

In 1918 Helene remarried. Her husband was Charles Sulyard Bigsby, a Cleveland widower, who was an electrical appliance distributor originally from Boston.

Also in 1918, through a near default by the Breadon group, Helene Britton nearly wound up in control of the St. Louis Cardinals again. The full amount due her from a year ago had not yet been paid and there was an outstanding amount of $165,000. On June 22, a hasty letter was sent to all the Cardinals stockholders by Branch Rickey informing them that $40,000 needed to be raised immediately for a note due to Helene Britton on July 1. In addition, another $20,000 was needed for current liabilities. The issue was solved when the Board of Directors authorized a new issue of $100,000 in stock to pay off the remaining debt.

Helene's second husband died in 1935. On January 8, 1950, Helene Britton died in West Philadelphia after an illness of three months. She had been living with her daughter Marie. Her son Frank also lived nearby as did her four grandchildren. Her remains were taken back to Cleveland and buried in Lake View Cemetery.

2

EFFA MANLEY

NEWARK EAGLES

Standing alongside Leroy Satchel Page, Cool Papa Bell, Buck O'Neil, and Josh Gibson as being among the most famous persons to have ever been associated with Negro Leagues baseball, is Effa Manley. Along with her husband Abe Manley, the two ran one of the most successful Negro Leagues teams of all time—the Newark Eagles. Attempting to be assimilated into the historically male dominated business of baseball, Effa Manley competently ran the business operations for the Eagles. Her name was on all the correspondence, she made decisions at board meetings, advised and sometimes negotiated player contracts, hired stadium vendors, and handled the cash. There were even rumors that when Effa sat in the stands at Ruppert Stadium and crossed and uncrossed her legs, it was a signal for a player to steal a base or take a pitch.

In the era of segregation, notwithstanding the life insurance business, Negro Leagues baseball was among the largest of black owned enterprises in America. Effa Manley attempted to strengthen the Negro Leagues; she fought for the elimination of booking agents, better schedules, better salaries, improved travel conditions, and attempted to convince the team owners to build their own ballparks. Also, she was a player's advocate that attempted to treat everyone fairly. While newspaper reporters didn't like the fact that Effa tried to tell them what to write, they never avoided interviewing her, because they knew she was good copy.

Born Effa Brooks on March 27, 1897, in Philadelphia, Pennsylvania, her racial background has been a matter of huge speculation and debate by historians and filled with ambiguity. But Effa attempted to set the record straight in an interview for an oral history project by the University of Kentucky in 1977 in which she emphatically stated that she was white. According to Effa, her mother Bertha Ford Brooks, a seamstress, was a white woman of German descent. Her father John M. Bishop, a financier, was a white man. Her birth was a result of an extra-marital affair between the couple while her mother was employed by Bishop. Her grandparents were of German and Native American descent.

Effa Brooks' mother was married to a black man and had four children with her black stepfather. Later, Effa's mother had two more children with another black man. So Effa grew up in a black community in Philadelphia, in a biracial home environment with six biracial siblings and was raised by a white mother and black stepfather.

Effa was blond with hazel eyes. Light-skinned, she could have easily passed as white if part of her heritage had actually been black. According to Effa, "The Negro thing is what I always knew,"[1] and her personal identification would be linked to the black experience her entire life. Larry Lester, one of the panel members who voted to enshrine Negro League players and executives in the National Baseball Hall of Fame in 2006, remarked in regard to Effa Manley, "I guess you could say she's the blackest white woman in the world."[2]

Effa simply felt a strong conviction to live her life as a black woman in a white world. It was an extremely bold decision to make in a society, which at the time in the early part of the twentieth century, was overwhelming in its racial intolerance. In fact, Effa would become a black activist and participate in the civil rights movement of the 1930s.

Following graduation in 1916 from William Penn High School in Philadelphia, Effa moved to New York City where she became employed in a hat shop. Later, she moved to Harlem and became involved with civil rights issues and followed the preaching of Marcus Garvey, who stressed that whites would always be racist and advocated wholesale migration of American blacks back to Africa where they could develop a distinct type of racial civilization of their own.

Effa Brooks met Abraham (Abe) Manley, a black man, while attending a World Series game at Yankee Stadium in 1932. Soon after, Abe took Effa to Tiffany's to buy her a ring. Effa recalled, "When we went back to pick it up, every salesgirl in the store was there to take a peep at us. They had heard this old Negro man had bought a five-carat ring for the pretty young white woman. I got a kick out of that."[3] The couple would be married the following year. Abe was forty-eight years old and Effa was thirty-six. Effa's marriage license listed her race as "colored."

It was the second marriage for both. Previously, Effa had a whirlwind marriage to a man by the name of Bush, whom she had met on the beach in Atlantic City.

Born on December 22, 1885, Abraham Lincoln Manley was originally from Hertford, North Carolina. He had come north to seek better economic opportunity and had established successful enterprises in Camden, New Jersey and New York City.

While Abe Manley was successful in real estate ventures, his major source of income was gained through running numbers racketeering operations in Camden and Harlem. However, Abe abandoned his Camden numbers operation in the mid-1920s after white mobsters fire-bombed his Rest-A-While Club in that city. So Abe left Camden and moved his number's game to Harlem.

The fact that Abe Manley was involved in the rackets was hardly an anomaly among Negro Leagues team owners. In fact, running numbers games almost seemed like a prerequisite to being a Negro Leagues team owner. Gus Greenlee was the owner of the Pittsburgh Crawfords, and for a time, president of the Negro National League (NNL). Greenlee, a big man known as "Big Red," stood 6'3" and weighed 210 pounds. Among his other endeavors was being the owner of a speakeasy in Pittsburgh, being a boxing promoter, and operating in the numbers game in the Steel City.

Alex Pompez, flamboyant owner of the New York Cubans, was raking in an estimated $7,000 to $8,000 a day in his Harlem numbers racket. But he was eventually forced to surrender control of his piece of the action in Harlem to gangster Dutch Schultz. One day, Schultz paid a visit to Pompez, laid his gun on the table in front of him, and announced that he was going to be his partner. Schultz told Pompez if he refused, "You are going to be the first nigger I am going to make an example of in Harlem."[4]

Effa Manley was in the forefront of the civil rights movement of the time. In June 1934, working with the Citizens League for Fair Play, Effa assisted the Reverend John H. Johnson in organizing a boycott of Blumstein's Department store in Harlem. Their campaign was called "Buy-Where-You-Can-Work." Blumstein's had been hiring blacks as elevator operators and porters since 1929, but like most other businesses along 125th Street, the owners refused to hire black sales clerks or cashiers. At the time, it was estimated that 75 percent of Blumstein's sales were to black customers. In a sit-down meeting with William Blumstein and Louis Blumstein, the store owners, Effa told them that the only employment available to black woman in Harlem was either to be a domestic worker or a prostitute.

After six weeks of well-organized protest and picketing and one-on-one meetings with Effa Manley, the Blumstein's capitulated and agreed to hire thirty-five black sales clerks and clerical employees by the end of September. As a result of the Blumstein's boycott, by one year later over 300 stores on 125th Street in Harlem employed blacks. By 1943, Blumstein's featured a black Santa Claus and were using black mannequins.

Later, Effa Manley became the treasurer of the Newark, New Jersey chapter of the NAACP. She often used Newark

Eagles games to promote civic causes. In 1939 at Ruppert Stadium, she held an "Anti-Lynching Day."

At the time Effa met Abe Manley, she knew very little about baseball, but Abe was an avid fan, mostly of Negro Leagues baseball. In fact, in 1929 Abe had started his own semi-pro team called the Camden Leafs. In November 1934 the Negro National League, hoping to make stronger inroads into the New York market, voted to add a new team in Brooklyn. Abe and Effa Manley obtained the franchise, named them the Eagles after a Brooklyn newspaper, and planned to play their home games at Ebbets Field. At the insistence of Effa, Abe hired Ben Taylor, a well-known veteran of black baseball, to manage the club.

Ben Taylor started looking for players to sign for the Eagles roster. Most of the established players were not available and most of the players signed were past their prime. However, the Eagles were able to sign a young pitcher from the defunct Baltimore Black Sox by the name of Leon Day, who would become a Negro Leagues star and be with the Eagles until they disbanded thirteen years later.

Ben Manley took the Brooklyn Eagles to Jacksonville, Florida for spring training. On opening day at Ebbets Field in 1935, the Eagles played the Homestead Grays, and New York Mayor Fiorello LaGuardia threw out the first ball. But only 3,000 fans were in attendance. Other than a large turnout of 7,500 for a Memorial Day doubleheader, crowds were very sparse throughout the season.

The 1935 season proved to be unprofitable for the Brooklyn Eagles. So Abe Manley boughtout the struggling Newark Dodgers from Charles Tyler, merged their roster with his Brooklyn Eagles, and moved the franchise to New Jersey, thus becoming the Newark Eagles. The Eagles would play their home games in Ruppert Stadium situated near the Passaic River in an industrial area called the "Ironbound," due to its borders being defined by railroad tracks. Ruppert Stadium was the home of the New York Yankees, the Newark Bears farm team. The stadium, built in 1926 and named after Yankees beer baron owner Jacob Ruppert, could seat 12,000 fans.

One of the players that Abe Manley acquired in the purchase of the Newark Dodgers was third baseman Ray Dandridge, generally believed to be one of the best at his position ever. In 1937, Dandridge hit .407, and over the course of eight Negro Leagues seasons, Dandridge hit .335.

Effa Manley began attending the NNL meetings rather than Abe and immediately acquired a reputation as brash and forthright. She pulled no punches in asserting that a great future was possible for Negro Leagues baseball if the owners would conduct themselves in a businesslike manner and cease all the showmanship and petty one–up-manship taking place.

Booking agents, mostly white men, for decades had exclusively been doing the Negro Leagues scheduling. While the team owners, such as Cumberland (Cum) Posey, were reticent to challenge the status quo, Effa Manley immediately stressed that the NNL teams should do their own booking. While a power struggle for leadership in the NNL between Cumberland Posey and Gus Greenlee existed, Effa Manley refused to ally with either side. By 1936 Effa Manley was learning baseball quickly and was elected vice president of the six-team Negro National League. In 1937 she filled the treasurer's post.

Effa's outspoken manner was getting the Newark Eagles noticed. In 1938 *The New York Post* ran a metaphoric photo of Effa with one of her high-heeled feet on the top dugout step, wearing an Eagles jacket and looking out across the field. There were even rumors circulating that Effa was overruling the Eagle's manager's calls from her box seat in the stands.

Pitcher Terris (The Great) McDuffie joined the Eagles in 1936 and soon became the ace of the staff. An eccentric player, the black press started to refer to McDuffie as "Negro baseball's Dizzy Dean."[5] On July 4, 1938 in the first game of a doubleheader, McDuffie pitched a complete game against the New York Black Yankees. Then he entered the second game with one out in the first and proceeded to pitch 8 2/3 innings of the nightcap, winning his second game of the day.

Some who knew Effa Manley well considered her an imposing woman who had a penchant for fur coats, manners, and extra-marital sex with young black ballplayers. There was countless gossip taking place among the Eagles about Effa's trysts. One of Effa's favorite young black ballplayers, in a literal sense, was Terris McDuffie. It has long been believed that in early summer 1938, when Abe Manley was made aware of McDuffie being involved with Effa, he traded him to the New York Black Yankees for two old bats and a pair of used sliding pads.

After the 1938 NNL season was concluded, twenty-year-old outfielder Lenny Pearson left the Eagles to play in the Puerto Rican winter league. Pearson's departure for the winter was painful for Effa Manley. Despite the twenty-one year difference in their ages, Effa had been having an affair with Pearson during the season.

By 1937 Effa and Abe Manley had put together a highly competitive Eagles team that featured what they billed as their "Million-Dollar-Infield," consisting of Ray Dandridge, Willie Wells, Dick Seay, and Mule Suttles.

Almost from the time that they acquired the Eagles franchise, the Manley's had coveted having Satchel Paige pitch for their team. In 1935 they offered Gus Greenlee, who owned the Pittsburgh Crawfords, $5,000 for Paige, but he turned them down.

Prior to the 1938 season, Greenlee wanted Paige to accept a 50 percent salary cut for the coming season. When Paige refused the cut and returned his contract unsigned, Greenlee sold Paige to the Manleys for $5,000. But allegedly, Paige jumped the team and accepted an offer to pitch in Venezuela for $2,000 a month. Paige always maintained that he never saw a contract from the Eagles. "I never did see no contract," Paige later said, "so when folks say I jumped away from Newark ask them to show you the contract."[6]

The Manleys knew Paige was in Venezuela and left a ticket for him at the Pan American Airlines office to fly to Newark if he decided to come home. But according to Effa, South American promoters refused to let him leave.

Nonetheless, Effa Manley reasoned that since Abe had offered Gus Greenlee $5,000, Satchel Paige was now property of the Newark Eagles. So it was agreed that if Paige singed a contract with the Eagles, then Greenlee would be paid $5,000 for him. Furthermore, to protect the Eagles baseball territory, Effa got a limited court injunction that forbade Paige from playing for any other team in New York or New Jersey.

In 1939 Satchel Paige returned to the United States. Although Effa Manely offered Paige a contract calling for $1,000 a month, an unprecedented sum in Negro Leagues baseball, he signed a contract to pitch for the Kansas City Monarchs of the Negro American League (NAL). The Monarchs were owned by John L. Wilkinson, a white man and an astute baseball executive, who had formerly owned the Kansas City Blues of the American Association. However, with Effa Manley accusing Wilkinson of tampering with Paige, he could not officially join the Monarchs. So he joined a barnstorming team with a roster filled with players whose contracts were owned by Wilkinson, called the Satchel Paige All-Stars.

In 1940 the Manleys attempted to sign Paige again. Paige informed Effa in a letter he would only consider joining the Eagles if she would sleep with him. Effa said that she didn't know if he was serious, or what to say in response, so she threw Paige's letter away. So Paige continued to barnstorm with the All-Stars.

The whole Satchel Paige affair was troublesome for Effa Manley, and she used the situation to stress the fact that neither the Negro National League nor Negro American League were organized strongly enough to force John Wilkinson to toe the line and live up to the regulations and laws of the leagues.

Effa believed that what was needed was a commissioner for black baseball. She advocated that the commissioner's office could be financed with taking 10 percent of the booking fees received by Ed Gottlieb, a white booking agent from Philadelphia. Effa Manley refused to allow the Newark Eagles to play at Yankee Stadium, because Ed Gottlieb received 10 percent of all bookings in the place except for the first doubleheader of the season between the Black Yankees and Cuban Stars. So the Newark Eagles did not play in Yankee Stadium.

As for her concerns over the fact that John Wilkinson had signed Satchel Paige, Effa said:

That Wilkinson has underwritten the team Satchel
is playing with and to date nothing has been done
about it. On May 16, when I found that Paige was
back in Kansas City and that he was playing with
the Wilkinson club, I immediately wrote Dr. J. B.
Martin, president of the Negro American League
telling him that Satchel is my property and advising
him of the situation. We exchanged a lot of
correspondence, but Paige has yet to show up in
Newark this season. Dr. Martin did order his league
clubs to cancel all games between Paige's team and
member clubs and both Dr. Martin and Tom Wilson,
president of the Negro National League, agree that
Paige is Newark property. I was dumbfounded when
my husband, Abe Manley and I went to Richmond
to find Wilkinson there with the club. He told me
that no one had given Paige a contract last year and
for that reason, he had picked him up.[7]

The bottom line in the Satchel Paige affair for Effa
Manley was that she believed the Eagles had bought him
fair and square from Gus Greenlee's Pittsburgh Crawfords
in 1938. She stated, "If I don't get Satchel Paige within the
next few days, I might take steps to get a few of those star
players with the Monarchs—especially such a pitcher as
Hilton Smith." Effa Manley also threatened to leave the
NNL if the Paige affair was not settled at the joint meeting
of the NNL and NAL in New York on June 18, 1940.

In 1939 the Pittsburg Crawfords became the Toledo
Crawfords. While the issue of who had the rights to Satchel
Paige, the Crawfords, the Eagles, or if he was a free agent
played out, once again in the 1940 season, Satchel Paige
was out barnstorming with the Paige All-Stars.

After a very heated and protracted dispute, the Manley's dropped their claim on Satchel Paige and claimed two
players off the Toledo roster, Buster "Bus" Clarkson and
Spoon Carter.

Satchel Paige was now officially property of the Kansas
City Monarchs. Within a few years, Paige was the biggest
star in the Negro Leagues. He appeared in *Time Magazine*
and *The Saturday Evening Post*. For America's black

community at that time, Satchel Paige became to baseball what Joe Louis had become to boxing. Now Paige began to honor his contracts, concentrated on pitching, and his legend grew enormously each time he took the mound.

Following a disastrous 1940 season at the gate, the Manleys gave serious consideration to disbanding the Newark Eagles. The Philadelphia Stars were also considering withdrawing from the NNL. For the 1940 season, Cumberland Posey decided to split his home schedule for Homestead Grays between Pittsburgh and Washington. But there was some optimism; the defense industry was starting to produce large amounts of war materials, although not particularly hiring large numbers of black workers, still both league presidents, Tom Wilson (NNL) and Dr. J. B. Martin (NAL) where confident that black attendance would increase at games in 1941.

At the league meeting in January 1941, Ed Gottlieb agreed to give up 20 percent of his booking fee profits to the NNL treasury, and the team owners agreed to expand interleague play with the NAL for the coming season. The fact that Ed Gottlieb was Jewish, as were several of the other more well-known promoters for black baseball, such as Abe Saperstein of the Harlem Globe Trotters fame and William Leuschner, created a whiff of anti-Semitism among a few of the Negro League team owners. Effa Manley stated in 1941, "These Jews would be stopped in their tracks,"[8] if she or her husband were made league chairman. To Effa, the NNL was a colored organization, and she wanted all the money kept within that group. On the other hand, Cumberland Posey pointed out that Jews "put their money into Negro Baseball when it was at its lowest ebb."[9]

Still, a strategy for the bigger threat to NNL solvency in 1941 went unresolved, the defection of black players from both the NNL and NAL to play in Mexico. Although Cumberland Posey had offered Josh Gibson a contract calling for $3,000 to play for the Homestead Grays in 1941, Gibson accepted an offer of $6,000 to play in Mexico. It was the second tour of service for Josh Gibson in Latin America. In 1937 he had accepted $2,200 from Dominican Republic dictator Rafael Trujillo to play on his personal team for seven weeks.

Effa Manley attempted to offer a suggestion to ease the financial loss of the player defections to Mexico. She suggested that the wealthy owners of the Mexican League teams should be contacted and that the NNL team owners ask for restitution for the loss of a player who jumped his contract. Effa felt that having a financial stake in the Mexican League would suggest that the NNL was operating as a farm system for them. However, the other NNL team owners failed to act on her suggestion.

Nonetheless, Negro League baseball's popularity did rebound to a degree in the summer of 1941, and evidence of it was demonstrated by two events.

On May 11, 1941 Satchel Paige, under contract to the Kansas City Monarchs of the NAL, was given permission by the NNL to pitch an exhibition game in a doubleheader for the Philadelphia Stars vs. New York Black Yankees at Yankee Stadium. *Life Magazine* sent photographers to cover the game and attendance was 20,000. Effa Manley, still upset about being snubbed by Paige when he wouldn't sign with the Newark Eagles, bitterly opposed the game.

Then on Sunday, July 27, 50,256 fans jammed Comiskey Park in Chicago for the 9th Annual Negro East vs. West All-Star Game. The fans, who were only 2 percent white, came by excursion trains, cars, and buses from as far away as Alabama, Mississippi, Ohio, New York, New Jersey, Oklahoma, South Carolina, and Missouri.

Prior to the game, "The Star-Spangled Banner" was sung by LaJulia Rhea, the first Negro woman to sing in the title role of "Aida" with the Chicago Civic Opera Company.

The East defeated the West 8-3 led by Buck Leonard of the Homestead Grays with a home run and a single in three at bats. Terris McDuffie of the Homestead Grays was the starting pitcher for the East. Monte Irvin of the Manley's Newark Eagles started at third base for the East and went two for three at bat.

Satchel Paige had been injured in a game against the Cuban Stars at Yankee Stadium just prior to the All-Star Game. Nonetheless, Paige had not pitched in the All-Star Game for five years and every fan in the park wanted to see him take the mound. *The New York Amsterdam-Star News* reported that when Paige dragged himself out to the mound to pitch the eighth inning, "he got an ovation usually reserved for Babe Ruth or Joe DiMaggio or Carl Hubbell."[10]

Each player was paid $50.00 to play in the All-Star Game. Publicity for the game had been handled by Abe Saperstein. However, in a move to appease Effa Manley and get her off their backs, the owners took away Saperstein's $1,100 promotional fee.

Looking back at all the hoopla bestowed on Satchel Paige, years later, Effa Manley stated that, in her opinion, Smokey Joe Williams, who pitched for the Homestead Grays in the 1920s and early 1930s, was a better pitcher than Paige.

In 1941 the Homestead Grays won a $10,000 judgment in court against Josh Gibson for contract jumping. In order to settle the legal problems with the Homestead Grays, Josh Gibson returned home to play in Pittsburgh for the 1942 season. The ruling was a landmark decision for the Negro Leagues as it sent a message to all concerned that Negro Leagues contracts had the same validity as did white Major Leagues contracts.

The United States was now actively fighting in World War Two and local draft boards were keeping players in the country. Effa Manley seized the opportunity to restrict the movement of some of the Newark Eagles top talent by notifying the draft board in Essex County, New Jersey, that Monte Irvin and Lenny Pearson were planning to leave the country to play in Mexico.

The Negro Leagues, just like the white Major Leagues, struggled during the World War Two years. Star players were in the service and attendance dropped. In all, forty-five Negro Leagues players were either wounded or killed in action during World War II. Effa Manley tried to do her part for the war effort by wearing a uniform and serving on the gas rationing committee in Newark.

Monte Irvin was making $125 a month playing for the Eagles. In 1942 he went to Effa Manley and told her that he would like a $25 a month raise, because he was getting married. Although she emphasized that Abe set the salaries, Effa turned him down. So Irvin went to Mexico to play in 1942 and was drafted before the 1943 season began.

To supplement the Eagles income during the war, the Manley's decided to take the Eagles on the road. The team proved to be a big attraction in Washington, D.C., where they played the opening game of the 1942 season at Griffith Stadium to a crowd of 27,000. Because of the good gate receipts on the road, the Newark Eagles finished the 1942 season with a modest profit.

Effa Manley was convinced that following World War Two, integration of the Major Leagues was going to occur. In an attempt to make a pre-emptive strike at protecting the Negro Leagues from decimation, at the NNL meeting in 1944 at Washington, D.C., Effa pleaded with her colleagues to approach the Major League owners about taking NNL clubs in as farm teams. When she attempted to contact Major League owners, no one would speak with her.

On November 25, 1944, baseball commissioner Judge Kenesaw Mountain Landis died. Gone was one of the stalwarts of keeping Major League Baseball a segregated game. During the 1944 season the Philadelphia Phillies were for sale. Bill Veeck, Jr. wanted to buy the team and sign players from the Negro Leagues to play on the Phillies. When Landis was informed of Veeck's intentions, he ordered the franchise to be taken off the market.

Landis would be succeeded as commissioner by former U.S. Senator from Kentucky, A. B. "Happy" Chandler, who was open to the integration of Major League Baseball. Chandler told a black sportswriter, "If a black boy can make it on Okinawa and Guadalcanal, hell he can make it in baseball."[11]

In January 1945 disgruntled former NNL president and team owner Gus Greenlee announced that he was going to form a new Negro league—the United States League (USL). Facing heavy financial losses in 1939, Greenlee disbanded the Pittsburgh Crawfords and put together a semi-pro team. By the end of the war, Greenlee wanted back in the NNL, but the other owners didn't want him back and turned down his application for reinstatement. Then NAL did the same. So the forming of the USL was Greenlee's attempt to have revenge against the Negro Leagues.

Branch Rickey, part owner and general manager of the Brooklyn Dodgers, was eager to integrate Major League Baseball. So in May he announced that he was going to form a team he called the Brown Dodgers and have them compete in the USL. Rickey's intent was for the Brown Dodgers to become a farm team for the white Brooklyn Dodgers playing at Ebbets Field when the team was on the road.

But the United States League soon folded. According to Effa Manley, the reason that the league could not be organized was because none of the team owners in the NNL or NAL would let any of the proposed USL teams play in their parks. Furthermore, Effa stated that when Branch Rickey attempted to contact the Negro Leagues through John G. Shackleford, a black Cleveland attorney who had formerly played in the Negro Leagues, to see if any of the teams were interested in joining the USL, the president of the NAL said he wasn't interested and the president of the NNL did not respond. Also, promoter Abe Saperstein, who had a stake in the Birmingham Black Barons of the NAL, blocked Gus Greenlee's attempts to schedule USL exhibition games in other venues. So, with the United States League figuratively DOA, Effa Manley says that Branch Rickey started talking directly to players.

Since leaving the U.S. Army in 1944, Jackie Robinson, a former star athlete at UCLA, was given a brief tryout by the Boston Red Sox in April 1945 at Fenway Park and rejected. Robinson was then signed to play shortstop for the Kansas City Monarchs for the remainder of the 1945 season.

Wendell Smith, a black Pittsburgh sportswriter, then recommended Jackie Robinson to Branch Rickey as having all the qualities needed to integrate Major League Baseball. On August 29, 1945 Branch Rickey met with Jackie Robinson in Brooklyn. Two months later on October 23, 1945 Branch Rickey announced that Jackie Robinson had been signed to play for the Brooklyn Dodgers AAA farm team, the Montreal Royals in 1946.

While Effa Manley never met Jackie Robinson personally, she believed that Monte Irvin would have been a better selection to integrate baseball. Prior to the 1946 season, Irvin was again ready to play ball in Mexico. But Effa passionately pleaded with him to stay and play for the Eagles. She felt that if Branch Rickey's experiment with Jackie Robinson worked out, big league scouts would be looking for additional black players, and by playing in Newark rather than Mexico, Irvin would have a good chance of being signed by a Major League team.

As the Newark Eagles were preparing to leave for spring training in 1944 held on the campus of Virginia Union University in Richmond, a tall, gangling kid of about eighteen years showed up at the team's front office and begged Effa Manley to take him along. It was Don Newcombe. Effa told him to come back the following day and speak with Abe. So he did and somehow convinced Abe Manley to allow him to get on the bus and go to spring training with the Eagles. Effa stated that Newcombe needed a lot of work, but he showed promise. With the war still ongoing and the Eagles needing players, Newcombe made the team, compiling a season record of 1-3 for the 1944 Eagles. However, after Newcombe gave up a home run to Roy Campanella at Ruppert Stadium, Eagles manager Mules Suttles told him, "You'll never make a big league pitcher because you're too goddamn dumb."[12]

The following season in 1945, under a pair of new Eagles managers, Willie Wells and Biz Mackey, Don Newcombe did better and finished with a record of 8-4.

In October 1945 Branch Rickey organized a subterfuge Major League tryout series for black players by scheduling exhibition games between Negro players and returning white war veteran Major League players such as Virgil Trucks, Frank McCormick, Goody Rosen, Eddie Stankey, Ralph Branca, Whitey Kurowski, and others, playing games at both Ruppert Stadium in Newark and Ebbets Field in Brooklyn.

Neither Effa nor Abe Manley opposed the contests and even agreed to have Eagles manager Biz Mackey both select players and manage the Negro Leagues' team. Among the players selected by Mackey were Monte Irvin and Don Newcombe of the Eagles and Roy Campanella of the Baltimore Elites. Cumberland Posey, who owned the Homestead Grays, refused to let Josh Gibson play and he urged returning war veteran Buck Leonard of the Kansas City Monarchs to not play in the games.

With a less than All-Star Negro Leagues squad, the Major League war veterans won all four games convincingly. It was stated in the *New Amsterdam News* that, "The White boys bore down all the way. The idea was to prove once and for all that Negroes aren't ready for the big leagues. There is speculation as to whether, even with Gibson, Leonard, Sammy Bankhead and Wellmaker, the Negro team would have been 'in' the series, the way those Major League players put on the heat."[13]

Regardless, after Branch Rickey watched Don Newcombe have a mediocre pitching effort in one of the exhibition games at Ebbets Field, he offered him a contract to pitch for the still to be organized Brown Dodgers. Then, as soon as Rickey signed Jackie Robinson, he re-signed Newcombe to a Brooklyn Dodgers contract to play Class-A ball. At the time, Newcombe was making $250 a month pitching for the Manley's Eagles. Rickey had given Newcombe a $500 signing bonus when he signed his contract to play for the Brown Dodgers. Now he gave him an additional $1,000, and his contract for the coming season called for $1,700.

Effa Manley didn't protest when Rickey signed Newcombe. She knew it would be wrong to do so. She would have been accused of attempting to block integration and advancement opportunities for blacks. However, that did not preclude her from expressing her displeasure personally to Branch Rickey over the Newcombe signing.

On July 4, 1946, while Effa was at Yankee Stadium for a doubleheader between the Newark Eagles and Black Yankees, she was informed that Rickey was also in the stadium. So Effa found her way to his box and scolded him, "Mr. Rickey, I hope you're not going to grab any more of our players. You know, Mr. Rickey, we could make trouble for you on the Newcombe transaction if we wanted to."[14]

Going forward, Effa Manley continued to maintain a negative opinion about Branch Rickey. She was to state that Branch Rickey took a million dollars' worth of ball players from the Negro Leagues and never bothered to say thanks.[15]

In early April 1946 just prior to the start of the season, Negro League baseball suffered a devastating loss when Cumberland Posey died. Posey had been a guiding force in the organization of the leagues, development of players, and promoting national marque attention on his Homestead Grays.

The 1946 Newark Eagles, led by returning war veterans Larry Doby, who hit .386; Monte Irvin, who hit .333; and Leon Day, who pitched a no-hitter against the Philadelphia Stars on opening day, won the NNL pennant. That September, the Eagles faced off against the NAL pennant winning Kansas City Monarchs featuring Buck O'Neil and Satchel Paige in a playoff for the Negro Leagues championship.

The first game of the series was played at the Polo Grounds in New York on September 17, drew 19,423 fans, and saw the Monarchs beat the Eagles 2-1.

Two nights later on September 19, the second game of the series was played at Ruppert Stadium in Newark. Effa Manley arranged for heavyweight champion Joe Louis to throw out the first ball, and the Eagles rebounded before nearly 10,000 fans winning 7-4. In the game, Larry Doby hit a two-run homer off Satchel Paige, who was ineffective pitching in relief giving up four runs.

Game three and four were played at the Monarchs home park in Kansas City, and saw the Eagles and Monarchs split the games.

Then the series shifted to Comiskey Park in Chicago for game five. The Monarchs won 5-1 to give them a three game lead over the Eagles in the series.

The series then returned to Ruppert Stadium on September 27 for game six, and saw the Eagles on the strength of two home runs by Monte Irvin to tie the series at three games all with a 9-7 win. The deciding seventh game was played on Sunday. After the Monarchs' Buck O'Neil tied the game at 1-1 in the sixth inning with a home run, the Eagles came back to win 3-2 in front of 7,200 screaming fans at Ruppert Stadium. The Manley's had finally got their championship and were the reigning king and queen of the Negro Leagues.

The crowds for the series would have been much better, maybe 30,000-40,000 in the Polo Grounds had the Kansas City Monarchs not came east and lost convincingly in exhibition games against the Philadelphia Stars and Black Yankees just days before the playoff series with the Eagles began. The Black Yankees had finished last in the NNL and pounded Satchel Paige in one of those games played at Yankee Stadium.

The following season in 1947, Negro Leagues baseball would begin to die a slow death when Jackie Robinson joined the Brooklyn Dodgers and became the first black player to play in the Major Leagues in the modern era. There were those, like NNL attorney Louis F. Carroll, that were optimistic that Negro Leagues baseball would survive, because its teams had national followings rather than regional and whites made up only 2 percent of the gate at any given time.

But according to Effa Manley, the handwriting was on the wall for the Negro Leagues before Robinson even joined the Dodgers. She stated that when Jackie Robinson joined the Brooklyn Dodgers farm team in Montreal in 1946, black fans stopped coming to Negro Leagues games and went to Montreal and Baltimore in droves to see him play.

Even before opening day in Brooklyn in 1947, there was a large number of black fans that turned out at Ebbets Field to see Jackie Robinson play in an exhibition game. Robinson was wildly cheered by those fans even when he hit into a double play. It was a scene that would be repeated in every ballpark in the National League during the 1947 season and continue for several years. When Robinson made his Midwestern debut, black fans came to Chicago, Cincinnati, and St. Louis from every direction to see him play by every mode of transportation possible. Many made the trip the same day to avoid lodging problems with "whites only" hotels. On May 18 a sellout crowd of 46,572 were on hand at Wrigley Field in Chicago and another 20,000 had to be turned away. It was the largest crowd at Wrigley Field since the Cubs abolished crowds on the field in 1936.

During a Negro Leagues game at Yankee Stadium in 1947, there was suddenly a huge ovation from the fans on an ordinary play. Moments later it was learned that the fans in the stands were listening to the Brooklyn Dodgers on portable radios and the ovation was for Jackie Robinson, who had just hit a home run. Total attendance for Negro League games at Yankee Stadium in 1947 would be 63,000, less than half of what it had been in 1946.

By 1947 Bill Veeck had bought the Cleveland Indians, and he still wanted to be on the forefront of integrating Major League baseball. To that end, he wanted to integrate the American League that summer and wanted a black player with a similar personality and playing ability as Jackie Robinson. The player he felt that best matched Robinson's attributes was Newark Eagles second baseman Larry Doby. So on July 1 Veeck contacted Effa Manley and offered $10,000 for Doby and an additional $5,000 if he was still on the Indians Major League roster thirty days after he bought his contract.

Effa and Abe Manley were very fond of Larry Doby and had even become the godparents of his first-born child. At the time, Doby was hitting .458 with the Eagles, and the Manleys knew that his departure could be devastating to the team and also be another severe blow to Negro Leagues baseball's popularity. Nonetheless, Effa knew it would be wrong to try to hold on to Doby, and she told Veeck she would agree to sell him to the Indians on one condition— that he never give him a contract calling for less than $5,000. Veeck agreed.

Larry Doby played his final game for the Newark Eagles on July 4, 1947, hitting a home run in his final at bat—his fourteenth of the season. His batting average at the time was .414. The next day, Doby took a cab with Bill Veeck to Newark Airport for a flight to Chicago to join the Indians for a game at Comiskey Park against the White Sox. On July 5, 1947 when Larry Doby stepped to the plate wearing number 14 on his Indians jersey, he became the first black player to play in the American League and second to play in the Major Leagues in the modern era. In 1994 the Cleveland Indians would retire Larry Doby's number.

Despite the profit made on the sale of Larry Doby to the Cleveland Indians, the Newark Eagles lost $22,000 in 1947 as attendance dropped by 50 percent from the 1946 season total of 120,092. It was estimated that the six teams in the NNL had lost a total of $100,000 and only three teams in the NAL, Chicago, Indianapolis, and Memphis, made a profit. Effa Manley said that at the end of the 1947 season she begged Abe to quit and sell the team, but that he was a born gambler and wouldn't do it.

Jackie Robinson finished the 1947 season with the Brooklyn Dodgers being named the National League's first Rookie of the Year and playing in the World Series against the New York Yankees. Then he immediately gave the Negro Leagues a verbal cold slap in the face telling a reporter from the *Atlanta Daily World* that Negro Leagues baseball needed a housecleaning from top to bottom.

Then Robinson took his criticism of the Negro Leagues a step further stating in a widely publicized article in *Ebony Magazine*:

> Players have to make the jump between cities in uncomfortable buses and then play in games while half asleep and very tired. Umpiring is unsupervised and quite prejudiced in many cases. The umpires are quite often untrained and favor certain teams.
>
> When players are able to get a night's rest, the hotels are usually of the cheapest kind. The rooms are dingy and dirty, and the rest rooms in such bad condition that the players are unable to use them ... [16]

Furthermore, Robinson stated that while he was with the Kansas City Monarchs, he saw no one controlling off field behavior of the players. There were some nights players would not get to bed at all, staying out all night drinking while management looked the other way. Robinson even vented his dislike of Satchel Paige's character, saying he refused to comply with white standards for baseball players, coming to the park late, drinking, and engaging in philandering night life.

Robinson's criticism of Satchel Paige's lax attitude toward team rules has credibility. This part of his

personality even followed him from the Negro Leagues into
the Major Leagues. On several occasions after joining the
Cleveland Indians in the summer of 1949, Paige was called
on the carpet by manager Lou Boudreau for violating club
rules. In one instance, he failed to show up for the final
game of a series with New York at Yankee Stadium. The
game was eventually rained out so the Indians caught an
earlier train to Boston. Paige, not knowing of the new
arrangements, missed the train. So Boudeau fined him
$100. When the Indians manager asked Paige why he was
a no-show at Yankee Stadium, he replied that he knew it
was going to rain. Boudreau then asked Paige how he knew
that and he stated, "My feet told me. I always know when
it's gonna rain."[17]

The popular Jackie Robinson's criticism of the Negro
Leagues was tantamount to throwing water on a drowning
man. Effa Manley refused to allow Robinson's diatribe to go
unchallenged. She was deeply agitated by the fact Jackie
Robinson had formed such strong opinions and expressed
them after only playing in the Negro Leagues for a few
months. Effa stated that Robinson "was ungrateful and
more likely stupid. No greater invasion of the good sense of
the American people could have been attempted," she said.
"No greater ingratitude was ever displayed ... How could a
child nurtured by its mother turn on her within a year
after he leaves her modest home for glamour, success and
good fortune? Jackie Robinson is where he is today
because of organized Negro baseball."[18]

In 1977, years later, aware of Jackie Robinson's legacy,
Effa Manley tempered her remarks in regard to him stating
she "didn't know Jackie Robinson and when he was
playing in the Negro Leagues, he was never spoken of as s
superstar." While Jackie Robinson said the only contract
he had was a handshake, Effa stated that unlike Robinson,
"all the Newark Eagles had legal contracts." Furthermore,
"Negro Leagues ball players enjoyed their work; they loved
what they were doing."[19]

Prior to the 1948 season, the Negro Leagues would seek
admittance to the Minor Leagues, but be turned down. The
reason for the rejection was the issue of territorial rights.
All the NNL and NAL teams used various Major League and

Minor League parks, which would pose a direct conflict for organized ball. Also, commissioner Happy Chandler had concerns over alleged gambling at Negro Leagues games, i.e., betting by fans in the stands.

Still, the NNL attempted to get by for another season, but by September the New York Black Yankees had permanently disbanded. The Newark Eagles had lost another $25,000, and the Manleys decided it was time to call it quits. On September 9, 1948 at a press conference held at her home in Newark, Effa Manley announced the Eagles were for sale. Effa's deep frustration showed as she blasted everyone for the loss of her team, the press, the Negro fans, Branch Rickey, Jackie Robinson ...

Black journalist Wendell Smith took exception with Effa writing, "She blamed everyone for the demise of her dream world and refused to recognize ... that nothing was killing Negro baseball but Democracy."[20]

In the fall of 1948, Effa Manley went to Cleveland to see Larry Doby play for the Indians in the World Series against the Boston Braves. She checked into a black hotel and was given a room with bathroom accommodations being at the end of the hall. Effa says that heavyweight champion Joe Louis was staying in the same hotel, and when he heard about her sub-par lodging he demanded that she use his suite.

During the fall, the Homestead Grays also left the NNL and became a barnstorming team. In 1949 the remaining three NNL teams, the Baltimore Elite Giants, Philadelphia Stars, and New York Cuban Stars merged into the NAL. The Manleys sold the Eagles to Dr. William Young, a Memphis dentist and an associate to Hugh Cherry. Then the franchise was transferred to Houston.

While the Newark franchise sale was in progress, the last of the Eagles' star players, Monte Irvin, was signed to a contract by the Brooklyn Dodgers and assigned to St. Paul of the American Association. Branch Rickey thought that the Eagles had disbanded and therefore Irvin was a free agent. Effa Manley quickly filed a protest with MLB Commissioner Happy Chandler stating that while she had announced her intention of withdrawing from the NNL, the Eagles franchise remained intact.

When Happy Chandler balked at assisting Effa, she hired Newark attorney Jerry Kessler to represent her interest in Irvin against the Dodgers. Kessler advanced the mandate that Irvin's contract was the same as that which covered the operation of Major League and Minor League Baseball. Not wanting to see a test case on the reserve clause occur, the Dodgers released their claim on Irvin.

Effa Manley then began to shop Irvin's contract around to various teams. The New York Yankees had no interest in Monte Irvin or integrating their team. However, the New York Giants jumped at the chance to acquire Irvin and his contract was subsequently purchased for $5,000.

The price paid for Irvin's contract was considerably more than the $1,000 Effa had asked from Bill Veeck in 1946. The proceeds from the sale of Irvin's contract were evenly divided between the Manleys, the Eagles' new owners, and Jerry Kessler for his legal fees. Abe Manley allowed Effa to keep their share of the Irvin contract proceeds, and she used it to buy a mink stole. Years later, Effa Manley still remained curmudgeon, stating that if Monte Irvin had been white, she would have got $100,000 for him.

Within a few years, the remaining Negro League teams were all selling their star players at discount rates to remain in business. The Kansas City Monarchs sold Hank Thompson to the New York Giants for $5,000, and the Philadelphia Stars sold Harry Simpson to the Cleveland Indians for $6,500. In 1950 Willie Mays's contract was purchased by the New York Giants from the Birmingham Barons for $15,000. On June 12, 1952 the Boston Braves bought the contract of nineteen-year-old Hank Aaron from the Indianapolis Clowns for $10,000, and in 1953 the Chicago Cubs bought the contract of twenty-two-year-old Ernie Banks for $10,000 from the Kansas City Monarchs. But by the mid-1950s the gold rush was over for Negro Leagues team owners and black players, such as Curt Flood, Frank Robinson, John Roseboro, Vada Pinson, Maury Wills, and others as they were going directly from high school into organized ball.

Following the 1976 season, Hank Aaron would retire with 755 career home runs. At that time, it was the all-time record. In addition, he would finish with 3,771 career hits, third highest in Major League history. Hank Aaron would be the last player in the Major Leagues to have played in the Negro Leagues.

By 1960 the Negro Leagues would be gone. The last game played was an All-Star game at Yankee Stadium on August 20, 1961. Satchel Paige, who was then fifty-four years old and had in addition to pitching for several decades in the Negro Leagues also pitched five years in the American League with the Cleveland Indians and St. Louis Browns, pitched three scoreless innings in the game.

On December 9, 1952 Abraham Manley died. His funeral was held in Catholic Church in the Germantown section of Philadelphia. The lead pallbearers were Larry Doby and Monte Irvin, who placed his casket in a hearse for the trip back to Newark and burial at Fairmont Cemetery.

Effa decided to leave Newark and move back to Philadelphia to be near her family. Later, she would move to Los Angeles. While cleaning out the house that she had shared with Abe, she decided to abandon two five-drawer file cabinets that contained a treasure of Negro National League records and documents. She came to the conclusion that she was out of baseball and didn't see any further need for keeping them.

Effa would not remain a widow very long, as she would marry twice more; the first would be Charles Alexander, an old friend. Both of her succeeding marriages would be to musicians, but neither husband could measure up to Abe's standards, and in retrospect, Effa called the marriages "stupid."[21]

Out of baseball and living in Los Angeles, Effa Manley would occasionally make an appearance at a reunion of Negro Leagues players. Eventually, Effa began a letter writing campaign to get former Negro Leagues stars elected to the Baseball Hall of Fame sending much correspondence to the museum in Cooperstown and to *The Sporting News*.

Then the conciseness of America was raised by former Boston Red Sox slugger Ted Williams in his National Baseball Hall of Fame induction speech at Cooperstown on July 25, 1966. Williams stunned the crowd when he asked that former Negro Leagues players be included among the Hall's inductees with the following statement:

> Inside the building are plaques to baseball men of all generations. I'm proud to join them. Baseball gives every American boy a chance to excel. Not just to be as good as someone else, but to be better than someone else. This is the nature of man and the nature of the game. And I've been a very lucky guy to have worn a baseball uniform, and I hope some day that names of Satchel Paige and Josh Gibson in some way can be added as a symbol of the great Negro players who are not here only because they weren't given a chance.[22]

It would take five more years, but finally, in 1971 Satchel Paige would be the first former Negro Leagues player to be enshrined at Cooperstown selected by the Hall of Fame's Special Committee on the Negro Leagues whose members included Monte Irvin and Negro Leagues team owners Ed Gottlieb and Alex Pompez. The Committee also selected Josh Gibson.

By 2012 thirty-five other former Negro Leagues players would have plaques hanging in the Hall of Fame including four players that played for Effa and Abe Manley's Newark Eagles: Ray Dandridge (1987), Leon Day (1995), Larry Doby (1998), and Monte Irvin (1973).

At the age of eighty-four on April 16, 1981, Effa Manley died. She was buried at Holy Cross Cemetery in Culver City, California. Her gravestone reads, "She loved baseball."

In an attempt to further recognize the accomplishments of Negro Leagues players, the Eighth edition of *The Baseball Encyclopedia*, published in 1990, added a new section that listed more than 130 Negro Leagues stars, including nicknames and pitching and hitting statistics.

While the black press of the 1920s had good coverage of Negro Leagues games, the Great Depression years caused steep cutbacks in coverage. The fact that any later official statistics of Negro Leagues players exist at all can be attributed to Effa Manley. She was an advocate of keeping uniformed statistics in the Negro National League. But most of the other owners objected on the basis that it was too expensive to do. But through the advocacy of Effa, by 1944, both the Negro National League and the Negro American League were employing established bureaus (Elias Bureau in the NNL) and (Howe News Bureau in the NAL) to keep statistics. While it was a huge step forward, the games still lacked official scorers, thereby making the leagues' statistics suspect.

On August 12, 1991 seventy-five members of the defunct Negro Leagues gathered in Cooperstown, New York for a three-day reunion organized by the National Baseball Hall of Fame, Major League Baseball, and Southern Bell.

At that time, only eleven former Negro League players were enshrined in the Hall of Fame. Addressing the players attending the reunion, baseball commissioner Fay Vincent stated, "As the eighth commissioner of baseball, I say to you with sorrow and regret, I apologize for the injustice you were subjected to. Every decent-thinking person in this country agrees. Your contribution to baseball was the finest kind because it was unselfish."[23]

As the former Negro Leagues players, such as Buck O'Neil, Lorenzo (Piper) Davis, and Albertus A. (Cliffie) Fennar, wandered past the exhibits, faded jerseys, old gloves, wrinkled programs, etc., a few of them expressed mixed feelings about the tribute as perhaps being a little too late.

As Clinton H. (Butch) McCord, a former player on the Nashville Cubs, was viewing a display dedicated to "Women in Baseball," which featured owners such as Jean Yawkey (Boston Red Sox) and Marge Schott (Cincinnati Reds), as well as women players such as Toni Stone, who played second base for the Indianapolis Clowns in the Negro Leagues, he was concerned that the display did not feature Effa Manley. "She should be in there too. She ran a good team,"[24] said McCord.

It would take another decade and a half, but in 2006, Effa Manley became the first woman elected to the National Baseball Hall of Fame.

3

GRACE REIDY COMISKEY

CHICAGO WHITE SOX

Grace Elizabeth Reidy was born on May 15, 1893 on Chicago's west side. She was the daughter of Thomas and Elizabeth Reidy. She attended Erickson School and Marshall and St. Mary High schools. On September 29, 1913 Grace Reidy married J. (John) Louis Comiskey. The couple had three children: Dorothy (born in 1917), Grace Lou (born in 1921), and Charles A. II, known as Chuck (born in 1925).

J. Louis Comiskey was the son of Charles A. Comiskey, Chicago White Sox owner and Major League legend. Charles Comiskey (i.e. Commy, The Old Roman) had been a player/manager for thirteen years between 1882 and 1894 in the American Association, Player's League, and National League with the St. Louis Browns, Chicago Pirates, and Cincinnati Reds. When Ban Johnson formed the Western League (forerunner to the American League) in 1894, Charles Comiskey resigned as manager of the Cincinnati Reds. He was given the Sioux City Minor League franchise and transferred it to St. Paul. Then in 1900 when the American League was formed, Comiskey moved his St. Paul team to Chicago and renamed them the White

Stockings. In 1901 the American League was recognized as a Major League and the Chicago White Stockings won the circuit's first pennant. In 1906 Comiskey's Chicago White Sox (name changed in 1904) won the American League Pennant again. The 1906 White Sox were referred to as the "hitless wonders" due to the fact that they had the lowest team batting average (.230) of any team in the league. Comiskey would build one of the first all reinforced steel and concrete ballparks in the Major Leagues at 35th and Shields on Chicago's Southside that would be named Comiskey Park. The new ballpark would be dedicated on St. Patrick's Day March 17, 1910 with the laying of green cornerstone, be in use, and carry the Comiskey name until the 1990s.

From the time of her marriage to J. Louis Comiskey until her death, the Chicago White Sox and baseball would occupy center stage in Grace Comiskey's life. For years, Grace and J. Louis would live in Charles Comiskey's home where she would be constantly surrounded with talk about the White Sox and baseball. It was there that Grace Comiskey was educated in the fine points of the business of Major League Baseball through the tutelage of the Old Roman himself, Charles Albert Comiskey. Also, she was an avid reader of *The Sporting News* and could judge the quality of players based on their statistics. By the time that it would become Grace Comiskey's turn to run the Chicago White Sox, she had the background to instantly grasp any situation.

Following the 1913 World Series played between the Philadelphia Athletics and New York Giants, Charles Comiskey and John McGraw, manager of the New York Giants, had planned to take their teams on a world tour. So the newlyweds, Grace and J. Louis, joined Charles Comiskey and his wife and went along on the junket. After a brief American exhibition tour, the teams left Vancouver, B.C. on November 19 aboard the *R.M.S. Empress of Japan* bound for Yokohama, Japan. During the tour, the two teams would play thirty-one games in faraway places such as London, Cairo, Tokyo, Ceylon, Shanghi, Manila, and Sydney.

As the teams and their entourage sailed aboard the *St. Albans* on Christmas Eve, December 24, 1913 through the Torres Straights between New Guinea and Australia, everyone seemed a bit homesick and despondent. To lift the spirits of the touring party, some of the women on the voyage, including Blanche McGraw (wife of John McGraw), Josephine Callahan (wife of White Sox manager Jimmy Callahan), and Nancy Comiskey (wife of Charles Comiskey), summoned everyone on deck to decorate a Christmas tree that had been purchased in Manila.

Then on Christmas night following a feast, the tourists were entertained with a concert performed by Josephine Callahan and Della Wiltse (wife of New York Giants pitcher George "Hooks" Wiltse) alternating on the piano and Grace Comiskey on her violin. While all the women's performances drew raves, it was the consensus that Grace Comiskey was the most accomplished musician.

The touring teams and entourage would sail home on the ill-fated *Lusitanian* arriving in New York harbor on March 7.

By 1914 Major League Baseball found itself in a conundrum. During the next few years it would be confronted with a strong challenge from the Federal League, and growing concerns about the expanding war in Europe and the possible entry of the United States looming ever large. By 1918 the United States was involved in the conflict and baseball faced an uncertain future. While Major League Baseball would survive the Great War, immediately following the conflict it was to face an internal challenge to its integrity that had the power to tear it apart as the national game.

Charles Comiskey had, over the second decade of the twentieth century, built a powerful Chicago White Sox team. Just prior to the United States entry into the war in 1917, the White Sox had won the American League pennant and defeated John McGraw's New York Giants in a legendary World Series. In 1919, the Chicago White Sox would once again reign as American League champions, but lost the World Series to the Cincinnati Reds. However, a year later, it would be alleged that eight White Sox players had conspired with gamblers to throw the 1919 World Series to the Reds.

The taint of a crooked World Series would prove to be catastrophic to the Chicago White Sox franchise and Charles Comiskey. In September 1920 the White Sox were well on their way to defending their title as American League champions when the scandal of the 1919 World Series was revealed to the public, and eight White Sox players were indicted on conspiracy charges. It left Charles Comiskey with no other alternative but to suspend the eight Chicago players, including legendary Shoeless Joe Jackson, a slugger in the prime years of his career. With a weakened lineup, the White Sox collapsed in the standings during the final week of the season. Although seven of the indicted players (the indictment against one player was dropped) were acquitted of a conspiracy to throw the series at a trial held in 1921, a few days following the not-guilty verdict, all eight players named in the original indictment would be banned from Major League Baseball by new commissioner Judge Kensaw Mountain Landis.

Some baseball moguls and sportswriters blamed the crooked events of the 1919 World Series on Charles Comiskey and his frugal management style: denying players raises, promising players bonuses for winning the 1917 World Series and never paying up, and pinching pennies on team amenities, including laundering uniforms. In contrast to this penny-pinching, Comiskey would flaunt his wealth by inviting sportswriters and sportsmen to lavish outings in the Michigan woods, a practice that his underpaid players deeply resented. However, Charles Comiskey blamed American League president Ban Johnson for not following up on rumors of a conspiracy during the World Series.

Nothing Charles Comiskey tried to rebuild his team worked, and the Chicago White Sox fell on hard times. Following the 1920 season, the White Sox never finished higher in the standings than fifth place between 1921 and 1931. For the next decade, Charles Comiskey attempted to rebuild his team throwing good money after bad, while at the same time returning to his frugal ways denying players raises.

Following the 1925 season, Comiskey released future Hall of Fame outfielder Harry Hooper when he refused to take a pay cut. Bibb Falk, an outstanding left handed college pitcher who hit .400, was signed by Comiskey off the University of Texas campus in 1920 for a $2,500 salary and $1,000 bonus. Falk was converted to an outfielder and did an outstanding job replacing Shoeless Joe Jackson. In the 1924 season while the White Sox finished in last place, Bibb Falk hit for an average of .352, third highest average in the American League. So Falk asked Comiskey for a bonus. Comiskey refused Falk's request, telling him in a letter that "they'd never heard of a player giving them a refund after he had a bad year."[1]

On October 26, 1931 Charles Comiskey passed away at his estate in Eagle River, Wisconsin. Until the day he died, Comiskey still believed that he had been cheated out of the 1919 World Series Championship and remained bitter at Ban Johnson. Nonetheless, it was a fact that Charles A. Comiskey, who had received a ball club for free, had over the course of forty years turned it into an enterprise worth over $2,000,000. In 1939 Charles A. Comiskey was elected posthumously to the National Baseball Hall of Fame.

Grace Comiskey's husband, J. Louis Comiskey, his father's only heir, was named to succeed him as owner of the Chicago White Sox. Now it was up to him to reverse the fortunes of the team in the depression era.

Beginning in 1934, J. Louis brought Jimmy Dykes aboard to manage the team and followed by bringing up some talented players such as Luke Appling, Zeke Bonura, and Ted Lyons. Over the decade of the 1930s J. Louis spent lavishly, attempting to improve the ball club. While the White Sox finished in third place in 1936 and 1937, they simply lacked the fire power to overcome the powerful New York Yankees and Detroit Tigers and continued to remain non-competitive in the pennant race.

On July 18, 1939, J. Louis Comiskey died in the same house as his father had in Eagle River, Wisconsin. He was only fifty-four years old and seemed to have had a great future in baseball ahead of him. Unfortunately, J. Louis was grossly overweight and had a history of heart disease.

The estate of J. Louis Comiskey was valued at $2,325,000. In his will he left half of his shares (3,725) in the Chicago White Sox to his widow, Grace Reidy Comiskey, and the other half were to be divided in equal shares among his three children: Dorothy, twenty-two; Grace Lou, eighteen; and Charles A. II, thirteen.

Net income from the shares left to Grace Comiskey was intended to provide income for her until Charles A. II reached twenty-one years of age. One third of each trust left by J. Louis to his children was to be delivered to each upon reaching the ages of twenty-one, thirty, and thirty-five.

There were 7,450 shares of existing Chicago White Sox stock at par value of $100 each. All but fifty shares had been owned by J. Louis Comiskey. The other shares were owned by vice president and secretary of the White Sox, Harry Grabiner, who had been with the ball club for the past thirty-six years and directed it in times when Charles Comiskey was periodically ill.

The will directed the First National Bank of Chicago to act as trustee and direct the running of the ball club. Furthermore, the will directed that Harry Grabiner be retained for ten years at a salary of $25,000 annually and Joseph Barry, traveling secretary, be retained for a similar period at an annual salary of $6,000. Also, it was stipulated in the will that no shares of the stock in the White Sox be sold until Chuck turned thirty-five years old, unless the sale of said shares should be deemed prudent and desirable by the trustees.

The most important thought to J. Louis Comiskey was that the Chicago White Sox remain in his family's ownership as it had since the formation of the American League. To that end, Comiskey stated in his will:

> It is my present opinion and desire that the trustees shall not sell said shares of the capital stock of the American league baseball club of Chicago prior to the time when my youngest surviving child attains the age of 35 years, but if circumstances should arise after my death which in the opinion of the trustees would render a sale of shares prudent and

desirable, then it shall have power to sell all or any part of such shares of stock held by it as trustees.[2]

There are those who hold the historic view that this language in Comiskey's will was vague in regard to expressing his firm intention that eventually his son Chuck would rise to the right of succession as head of the White Sox, setting up a family feud that would cripple the White Sox administration for the next twenty years.

While the First National Bank of Chicago immediately appointed two bank officers as trustees, Roy C. Osgood and John C. Meachem, it was slow on setting up a board of directors and appointing a president to run the White Sox. The facts were that the bank really had no interest in running a Major League team.

On January 18, 1940, completely ignoring the last wishes of J. Louis Comiskey and tradition and connection of the Chicago White Sox to the people of Chicago, the First National Bank of Chicago, acting as the executor of the estate of J. Louis Comiskey, filed a petition in Cook County Probate Court asking for permission to sell the team. It was the bank's opinion that the operation of a Major League team involved many financial uncertainties. Consequently, since the Comiskey family was dependent on income from the team, it would be to their best interest in the estate to sell.

The sale of the Chicago White Sox would still require the approval of the American League, which stipulated in its constitution that it would have the right to pass on eligibility of would-be purchasers.

However, the outright arrogance of the First National Bank of Chicago in suggesting that it was for the good of the heirs to rid itself of the White Sox, immediately got ire of Grace Comiskey. She was deeply aware of the tradition and historical connection inherent in the Comiskey family's ownership of the Chicago White Sox and was bound and determined to save for her family what she considered a Chicago institution. Immediately, she hired attorney Thomas J. Sheehan to challenge the bank in asking for permission to sell the team.

Sheehan quickly demonstrated the absurdity in the notion that the White Sox were a liability upon the trust by pointing out that the White Sox property was clear and not a dollar was owed on anything. In fact, in the 1939 season, the Chicago White Sox had drawn 592,003 at the gate, a pretty fare attendance figure considering the depression still loomed over the nation. Some of that attendance was attributed to the fact that lights had been installed in Comiskey Park and eight night games had been played. Sheehan stated, "We are prepared to fight this move to the utmost. The Comiskey family wants to retain possession of the White Sox."[3] Nonetheless, a long bitter court battle on the matter between the Comiskey heirs and the bank was expected.

When interviewed at her apartment at 5555 Everett Avenue, Grace Comiskey told the press that it had been the expressed wish of her late father-in-law, Charles A. Comiskey, that the White Sox would be passed on to her son, Charles A. Comiskey II. "My father-in-law formed it (the ball club), he often told me as a monument to his grandson, and it was his greatest wish that he some day would become president of it. And certainly Lou, my husband, thought of nothing else."[4] Also, Grace took the bank to task. "One thing is obvious," she said, "a bank doesn't know how to run a ball club. Of course I couldn't run a bank—but I know baseball."[5] For twenty-seven years Grace Comiskey had rarely missed a White Sox home game. She stated that she had been her father-in-law's confidant, and he had discussed crowds, players, trades, and contracts with her daily when he was active with the club.

In existence in probate matters in Illinois law at the time was a provision known as the "widow's award." Under the law, a widow was entitled to one-third of her husband's estate outright. On February 21, 1940, in an attempt to take a preemptive strike against any sale of the Chicago White Sox by the trustees, Grace Comiskey appeared in Probate Court and filed a petition renouncing her interest in the will of her husband. Subsequently, she asked that she be given outright her dower rights of one-third of the estate as required by law. In addition, Dorothy Comiskey petitioned the court for her payment of the estate due her when she attained the age of twenty-one. At that time, Dorothy was twenty-three years old.

If the court agreed with their petitions, Grace and her daughter Dorothy would immediately assume 40 percent control of 7,450 shares of the Chicago White Sox. Of course, fifty other shares were owned by Harry Grabiner. Nonetheless, this would allow the Comiskey's to remain as sizeable stockholders in the White Sox and any prospective bidders for the ball club would not be bidding for full ownership.

Meanwhile, on February 28 Dorothy Comiskey and her children through their attorney, Thomas J. Sheehan, filed an answer with the Probate Court to the petition filed by the First National Bank of Chicago. The family's answer stated that the bank, in seeking authority to sell the Chicago White Sox, had violated the trust and disregarded the wishes of the late J. Louis Comiskey. They also elaborated in their answer on the fact that the name Comiskey and White Sox had been synonymous with Chicago baseball for forty years.

The following day on March 1, Probate Judge John F. O'Connell, after a two hour hearing, ruled in favor of the Comiskey heirs and denied the petition by the First National Bank of Chicago for the right to solicit bids for sale of White Sox stock.

The bank stated it was pressed for cash to pay estate taxes and once again reaffirmed its belief that Major League Baseball was too risky a gamble to be a suitable trust for Grace Comiskey and her children. The bank contended that taxes would run from $117,000 to $1,000,000. In order to reinforce their contention that running a baseball club was a risk, attorneys for the bank cited the following:

1. The White Sox lost $675,000 in the eleven years since 1929. In 1932 alone, the club lost $242,000.
2. At one time, White Sox stock was valued at $144.50 per share, now an estimated $60 per share.

3. Box-office value of a Major League team depends upon the production of its stars, on the weather and on the quality of opposing teams.[6]

In response to the bank's concerns over the tax obligation, attorney Thomas J. Sheehan stated the Comiskey family would produce the money for the taxes if other assets proved to be inadequate.

While Judge O'Connell agreed that in his ruling hazards were involved with owning a Major League team including, the weather, injuries to players, and the outcome of the pennant race, he stressed that more important was that the bank had an obligation to watch for dangers to the estate. Therefore, it directed the bank should present a definite plan to preventing such dangers. But the key to Judge O'Connell's ruling was that when the will of J. Louis Comiskey was placed in the trust of the First National Bank, it was obligated to insure that an income for minor heirs (namely Charles A. Comiskey II) be commensurate with present values.

In his ruling Judge O'Connell stated in part:

It is difficult to estimate what the future values of the White Sox stock would be if it were sold to strangers now," stated Judge O'Connell. "The White Sox have been and are a definite part of the fiber of Chicago life. Charles A. Comiskey was a national figure. The Sox are recognized as Comiskey property, and his grandson Charles II, bears his name. If this asset (the Sox property) can be conserved in its entirety and the Comiskey name continues to be associated with it down the years, it may be of even greater value than it is at present.[7]

While Judge O'Connell denied the bank's petition, he refused to rule on the petitions of Grace Comiskey and her daughter Dorothy seeking outright grant of approximately four-ninths of the 7,450 White Sox shares in the estate.

While the courtroom had been packed with spectators, including many Cubs fans, neither Grace Comiskey nor any of her children were present. When informed of the court's decision, Grace was elated. "We're satisfied that the Sox are going to stay in the Comiskey family, right where they belong,"[8] she said.

Later in 1940, Grace Comiskey was awarded her dower rights in renouncing the will. She was awarded 2,158 shares of White Sox stock and $60,000 by the Probate Court. Previously in June, she had been awarded $100,000 which was considered a maintenance award, which was customary practice while the matter was in Probate Court.

During the First National Bank of Chicago's season of trusteeship in 1940, the Chicago White Sox under the direction of vice president Harry Grabiner and manager Jimmy Dykes finished, in a tie for fourth place in the American League with the Boston Red Sox, eight games behind the pennant winning Detroit Tigers. Shortstop Luke Appling led the team in hitting with an average of .348, second best in the league. The team drew a home attendance of 660,336 (fifth of eight) and made a profit of $200,000.

On December 29, 1940 it was announced that Dorothy Comiskey, now twenty-three years old, was engaged to marry John Rigney, a pitcher for the White Sox. During the 1940 season Rigney had tied for the lead among White Sox pitchers in wins with fourteen.

In mid-January 1941 the First National Bank of Chicago asked the court to relieve it of its responsibilities as trustee of the Chicago White Sox. It based its decision on preferring not to handle the White Sox stock unless it could do so as a complete unit. Two weeks later, the bank was retired as trustee in a friendly court action.

At the same time, the Probate Court gave the bank the right to sell to Grace Comiskey a total of 916 shares of White Sox stock for not less than $125 per share. The added stock shares increased Grace's interest in the ball club to 3,094 shares.

To complete the matters, under the Probate Court the children under the terms of the will would receive one-third of their holdings upon attainting majority twenty-one years of age. The remainder would not be released from trusteeship until Charles A. II, reached the age of thirty-five.

Of course Dorothy had reached the age of twenty-one prior to the death of her father, so she received 484 shares of White Sox stock or one-third of her baseball inheritance. Grace Lou was to receive her shares on March 7, 1942 and Chuck his initial portion six years later.

On March 5, 1941, the board of directors of the Chicago White Sox held a special meeting to complete steps necessary to return ownership of the team to the Comiskey family from the bank trustees. Once again, all but fifty shares of stock in the ball club were in the hands of the Comiskey family. Both Grace and Dorothy were named trustees.

But more impressive was that Grace Comiskey had been elected president of the White Sox and thereby became the second woman in Major League history to serve as a ball club's chief executive following in the footsteps of Helene Britton, who became president of the St. Louis Cardinals in 1916. Her daughter Dorothy remained treasurer of the White Sox.

At that point in time, women in high places in organized ball were scarce. The most notable woman in the Major Leagues in 1941 was Mrs. Florence W. Dreyfuss, who had been serving as chairman of the board of the Pittsburgh Pirates since her husband, legendary owner Barney Dreyfuss, died in 1932. While Mrs. Dreyfuss appointed her son-in-law William E. Benswanger to succeed her husband as president of the Pirates, she was known to occasionally put the final approval on trades.

Also, Mrs. Gerry Nugent, wife of the Philadelphia Phillies president, was a vice president of the club and drew an annual salary of $5,000. Lastly, the New York Yankees were owned by a trio of women (Helen Winthrope Weyant, Mrs. J. Basil McGuire, and Mrs. Joseph Holloran), who inherited the ball club from Jacob Ruppert. But they had no say in the running of the ball club, which placed in the hands of trustees.

The immediate ownership of the White Sox had been settled by the court. But the vague intention of J. Louis Comiskey in his will that eventual administration of the team be passed on to his son Chuck was still undetermined and no time table for his ascension had been planned or proposed. Grace Comiskey had stated, "Both my husband and his father Charles A. Comiskey, who had started the club in 1900, had planned for the team to be passed on to my son, Charles II. The boy knows nothing but baseball. He plans his life around it, and has never known anything else."[9]

It was a fact that young Charles A. II, aka Chuck, had been appearing on the practice field at Comiskey Park in uniform since he was two years old. Now in his teens, he often worked out with the regular players and knew many of the star players in the game personally, such as Boston Red Sox slugger Jimmy Foxx.

The remarks of his mother and those published in the press such as "She (Mrs. Comiskey) will serve a six-year term—until young Charles comes of age and can assume control,"[10] often implied that Chuck was preordained to be the president of the White Sox. While everything seemed warm and fuzzy for the Comiskeys at the present time after regaining control of the team, fifteen-year-old Charles A. Comiskey II was starting to believe that being president of the Chicago White Sox was his birthright, and that meant future crises looming on the horizon of the south side of Chicago.

The 1941 American League season will be forever known as the year that Joe DiMaggio hit safely in fifty-six consecutive games and Ted Williams won the batting title by hitting .406. But in Chicago, it was the first year of Grace Comiskey's tenure as president of the White Sox, and she was attempting to legitimize herself in the role.

On July 5 the White Sox were in fourth place and playing the Cleveland Indians at Comiskey Park when manager Jimmy Dykes was ejected from the game by umpire Steve Basil. The fray got Dykes a suspension from American League president Will Harridge. Immediately, Grace Comiskey came to the defense of her manager and let it be known that she intended to back him to the limit. In fact, Grace put her check book where her mouth was and signed Dykes to a new three year contract calling for a salary of $27,500 a year. Dykes enjoyed the free reign that he had in trading, buying, and selling players as he saw fit since being named manager of the White Sox in May 1934.

The White Sox finished in fourth place in 1941 with a record of 77-77, twenty-four games behind the New York Yankees.

Jimmy Dykes managed the White Sox through the period of World War Two, never finishing higher in the standings than in fourth place (1943). Then in the spring of 1946, Dykes was hospitalized and had stomach surgery. He didn't join the team until the beginning of May. By that time, the White Sox had already dug themselves in a hole in the pennant race. By May 25 the White Sox had a record of 10-20. When Dykes attempted to negotiate a contract extension with Grace Comiskey, this time he was turned down. So after managing the White Sox for twelve years and thirteen days, he resigned and was replaced by Ted Lyons.

A fan favorite, Ted Lyons had pitched for the White Sox for twenty-one years and won 260 games since being signed off the Baylor University campus in 1923 by Charles Comiskey. Lyons was rejoining the team after a stint as a captain in the U.S. Marine Corp in World War Two. Under Lyons, the White Sox finished the 1946 season in fifth place, thirty games behind the pennant winning Boston Red Sox.

On November 18, 1946, Charles A. Comiskey II turned twenty-one years old. However, young Chuck was not installed as president of the White Sox. His mother Grace had just been re-elected as president of the club for 1947. Furthermore, Chuck had just started college as a freshman at St. Thomas College in St. Paul, Minnesota and Grace wanted her son to finish his education before embarking on a baseball career. So it looked like it would be at least four more years before Charles II could ascend to the throne of the White Sox front office.

Nonetheless, Charles's public remarks would be a harbinger of an internal conflict among the Comiskeys to come. At a luncheon at the Quarterback Club in Chicago he stated, "I'll be with the team all summer, at home and on the road, to learn all I can about the business. I hope I'll be ready to take over after I've finished college. Being president of a Major League club is no job for a woman, even my mother."[11]

To provide Chuck Comiskey with some seasoning, his mother appointed him as vice president of the White Sox Waterloo, Iowa farm team in the Three-I League.

The Chicago White Sox, under Ted Lyons, stumbled through the 1947 and 1948 seasons, finishing in the American League cellar in 1948 loosing 101 games.

On October 4, 1948, Charles A. Comiskey II was promoted to vice president and secretary of the Chicago White Sox. On November 1, Frank Lane, then president of the American Association, who was Chuck Comiskey's personal choice, was hired as general manager of the White Sox under a five-year contract. Then sixty-year-old Jack Onslow, who had managed at Memphis in 1948, was hired as manager with a two-year contract.

All through the 1949 season Jack Onslow feuded with Frank Lane. Onslow and Lane were at odds at how the team should be handled on the field with Onslow calling Lane a second guesser. The only reason that Onslow was not fired was because Grace Comiskey intervened and stood by him. However, after a poor start in the 1950 season, Onslow was replaced by one of his coaches, Red Corriden, who guided the White Sox to a sixth place finish.

On November 25, 1944 MLB's first baseball commissioner, Judge Kenesaw Mountain Landis, died in a Chicago hospital. On April 24, 1945 the baseball moguls elected A. B. "Happy" Chandler as the new commissioner. At the time, Chandler was a U.S. Senator from Kentucky.

Happy Chandler had been very proactive in his tenure. He gave the green light to Branch Rickey's plan for integration of Major League Baseball in 1947 with Jackie Robinson joining the Brooklyn Dodgers. He also protected the purity of the game from unsavory characters like those who had nearly destroyed it in the cloud left by the scandal of the 1919 World Series, prior to the 1947 season he had suspended Dodgers manager Leo Durocher for associating with gamblers. In addition, Chandler had infiltrated a player's movement in 1946 to form a union with spies. In a complete turn-around on the matter of labor relations, the following year, Chandler would sell the radio broadcasting rights to the World Series for $475,000 and use the money to start a player's pension fund.

But when Chandler asked the owners for an extension of his contract in 1950, he was turned down. In December 1950 at a hastily called and closely guarded meeting in St. Petersburg, Florida, the Major League owners voted nine for and seven against to not extend Chandler's contract beyond May 1, 1952. Chandler needed twelve yes votes to keep his job. Representing the Chicago White Sox at the meeting and casting one of the no votes against Chandler was Chuck Comiskey.

One of the leaders of the coup to unseat Happy Chandler was Yankees co-owner Dan Topping, who, with his partner Del Webb, had become upset with him when he vetoed a trade that would have sent Dick Wakefield to the Chicago White Sox for cash. Topping was hopeful that Chandler might resign in a huff after the negative vote on his receiving a new contract.

Grace Comiskey was personally supportive of Happy Chandler and very angry that Chuck had cast the White Sox vote against him. Furthermore, she claimed that she had no advance notice or knowledge of the way the matter was going to be handled. "I did not approve of it from the moment I heard of what had taken place," said Grace. "I hadn't been consulted so didn't even know that such a move was afoot. I believe that it should have been taken up with me and I will have a nice talk with Chuck when he returns and Frank Lane."[12]

Vowing to take her son to task over the negative vote on Chandler, Grace Comiskey reached into the family's heritage in the game pointing out that Charles A. Comiskey had been among the pioneers that set up the office of the commissioner and strongly believed that he would not want that form of government torn down.

Joining Grace Comiskey in support of Happy Chandler were American and National League heavyweights Connie Mack of the Philadelphia Athletics, Tom Yawkey of the Boston Red Sox, Clark Griffith of the Washington Nationals, P. K. Wrigley of the Chicago Cubs, Horace Stoneham of the New York Giants, and Warren Giles, representing Powell Crosley, Jr. and the Cincinnati Reds.

On March 12, 1951 the Major League moguls voted again on the matter of whether or not to retain Happy

Chandler as commissioner, and the results were the same, nine votes for and seven against.

On July 15, 1951 A. B. "Happy" Chandler resigned as commissioner of baseball. He was succeeded by Ford Frick. Chandler maintained that his support of allowing Jackie Robinson to break the color line in Major League Baseball was a key factor in his not being rehired by the owners.

However, following World War Two, Major League Baseball was starting to change. Integration was but one factor of change. Soon it would be a coast-to-coast enterprise and there would be huge challenges to its conservative practices in labor relations. So there is also the argument that Happy Chandler, after serving six years as commissioner, convinced a lot of the team owners, who saw broad sweeping change to the game on the horizon, to come to the conclusion that the office of commissioner could be better served by someone steeped in the long-established conservative tradition of the game.

The 1951 season got off to a slow start for Grace Comiskey. In late April 1951 she had been taken to Mercy Hospital in Chicago, suffering from influenza, and spent a good deal of the spring recovering. But for the White Sox, it would be a year in which it appeared the team was finally becoming competitive.

Following the 1950 season, Luke Appling retired after being the star of the Chicago White Sox for twenty years. Entering the post-Appling era in 1951, the White Sox were under the direction of a new manager, Paul Richards. Meanwhile, General Manager Frank Lane was working hand-in-glove with Chuck Comiskey and started to make trades that would define the team for a decade. Lane arranged separate deals with the Philadelphia Athletics to acquire future Hall of Fame second baseman Nellie Fox (who would become one of Grace Comiskey's favorite White Sox, along with Ted Lyons, Red Faber, and Ray Schalk) and Cuban outfielder Minnie Minoso. Then he signed a slick-fielding Venezuelan shortstop by the name of Chico Carrasequel. A year earlier he had made a trade for left hander Billy Pierce from Detroit.

Later, Bill Veeck was to remark, "Grace let Frank Lane do most of the talking. She allowed Frank to make the player trades. But when money was involved, Grace always told him how much he could spend."[13]

Nonetheless, with these key players in place and under the direction of Paul Richards, the White Sox were an improved ball team and finished the 1951 season in fourth place while drawing 1,328,234 fans into Comiskey Park and netted a profit of $600,000. It was the financial peak of the club's long history in the game and both Frank Lane and Chuck Comiskey deserved credit.

While the fortunes of the Chicago White Sox seemed to be on the rise, a family feud was about to breakout between the Comiskeys. In mid-January 1952 Chuck Comiskey, now twenty-seven years old, abruptly resigned as vice president and secretary of the team. The seeds of young Comiskey's dissatisfaction were sewed in the issues of his inadequate salary and lack of office tenure that had been extended to other officials of the team that were not family members—mainly Frank Lane and Paul Richards. Chuck's salary was reported to be $27,000 a year with expenses and incidentals being extra. Many analysts at that time saw the young Comiskey's move as an attempt to take over as president of the team and remove himself from the authority of his mother in critical decision making matters. But according to Chuck, he had been waging this fight for over a year.

When questioned by the press, Grace Comiskey stated that Chuck's resignation came as a complete surprise. "I don't know what the youngster has in mind," she said, "but I have called a meeting for Friday (January 18) and I hope at that time we can sit down and work everything out satisfactorily."[14]

The board consisted of Grace Comiskey, her daughter Dorothy (Comiskey) Rigney, Thomas J. Sheehan and Roy Egan (both attorneys), and Charles (Chuck) A. Comiskey II. Another daughter, Grace Lou Comiskey, was an owner but not a board member. The meeting was held at the S. La Salle Street law offices of Sheehan and Egan.

Chuck Comiskey, along with his attorney Bryon M. Getzoff, arrived late, although the board had not yet gone into formal session. But when Thomas Sheehan objected to Getzoff's attendance in the meeting, despite the pleas of his mother and sister to remain, Chuck Comiskey hastily departed.

While Chuck Comiskey's resignation was accepted, overall, the meeting was conciliatory with the other board members stating that the door is always open for Chuck. To that end, the vice president's position he had occupied was kept open by the insistence of Grace Comiskey, and the title of secretary was conferred upon Dorothy Rigney, who was already serving as treasurer. "If he had just sat down and told us what he wanted," said Grace after the meeting, "everything would have worked out all right."[15]

From his attorney's office, Chuck Comiskey called a news conference and blamed Sheehan and Egan, the two attorneys on the board, for his troubles. He stated that since there were two attorneys on the board he felt that he was entitled to representation at the meeting. "If anyone is ill-advised," he said, "I personally believe it is the board of directors. The board lawyers all the way along, in refusing to negotiate, are creating the artificial barrier between my mother and myself. It seems to me that the lawyers, by their arbitrary action, are trying to humiliate me and meanwhile are creating adverse publicity for the White Sox."[16]

In blaming the attorneys for blocking him from advancing his personal agenda, Chuck Comiskey was bucking a strong allegiance that his mother had to Sheehan and Egan. It had been they who had been Grace's legal advisors when she squared off against the First National Bank of Chicago for control of the White Sox; she trusted their advice to the fullest extent without any reservations.

However, Chuck offered the White Sox an olive branch when he told a reporter that he would be open to speaking with his mother privately. Nonetheless, Chuck Comiskey still owned outright 484 shares of White Sox stock, and when he reached the age of thirty-five he would come into possession of further stock giving him one third of two-thirds of all the stock. Lastly, he was still a member of the board, and it would take majority vote to unseat him.

Chuck Comiskey then accepted a job with Liberty Broadcasting Company in Dallas, Texas. When the company went out of business in June, Chuck returned to Chicago and to his old job with the White Sox. His mother Grace made the following statement: "Mr. Comiskey returns under the same circumstances and conditions as existed at the time of his resignation."[17]

On June 15, 1952 the Comiskey family shared a tragic loss when Grace Lou Comiskey, youngest daughter of Grace Comiskey, died at Mercy Hospital of a heart attack complicated by pneumonia. She was just thirty-one years old. A semi-invalid, Grace Lou, like her father J. Louis Comiskey, had been overweight and suffered from a weak heart.

Frank Lane kept making trades, including acquiring veteran pitcher Virgil Trucks from the St. Louis Browns on June 13, 1953, who then won fifteen games and lost six the remainder of the season as the White Sox remained competitive finishing in third place in both 1952 and 1953.

At the end of the 1953 season the St. Louis Browns were sold to a syndicate headed by Clarence W. Miles, and the franchise received approval to move to Baltimore for the 1954 season. Miles then attempted to lure Frank Lane away from Chicago by offering him the chance to acquire stock in the Orioles. Lane, who was under contract with the White Sox through the 1955 season, asked out of his contract.

Once again, the Comiskeys were at odds over an issue with Chuck supporting Lane's departure and Grace's displeasure with Miles's attempt to lure him away from the White Sox. Grace Comiskey liked continuity in management, and just as she had trusted Jimmy Dykes, she also felt secure with Frank Lane. The matter was resolved when Chuck once again acquiesced to the wishes of his mother, and on November 5, 1953 signed Frank Lane to a five-year contract extension through the 1960 season. The contract called for a base pay of $35,000 to $40,000 and a percentage agreement of five cents on each home paid admission in excess of 900,000, thereby making the estimated contract to be worth $50,000 annually.

In 1954, for the third straight year, the White Sox finished in third place. In late September, Paul Richards was fired and Marty Marion was hired as the new White Sox manager.

By 1955 Frank Lane had built a pennant contender in Chicago, and the White Sox battled the Cleveland Indians and New York Yankees all summer long for first place in the American League. In late August, the White Sox were leading the league by one-half game when trouble in the front office began.

On Tuesday August 30 the White Sox were at home playing the Boston Red Sox when Frank Lane stormed out of the press box at Comiskey Park and descended upon the box occupied by American League president Will Harridge and Cal Hubbard, supervisor of the league's umpires. Lane went into a profanity-laced tirade protesting the action of home plate umpire Larry Napp after he ejected White Sox catcher Sherman Lollar from the game for heckling Napp from the dugout after he called Dixie Walker out on strikes in the sixth inning. Lane felt that Red Sox Jim Piersall should have been equally tossed out of the game for his antics earlier when he was jumping up and down protesting Napp's calling Sammy White out at the plate.

The commissioner of baseball, Ford Frick, summoned Lane to New York the following day and fined him $500 for the incident and ordered him to apologize to the Chicago fans. Then Chuck Comiskey blasted Lane while upholding the action of Frick. According to Chuck, Lane's language was improper even for the men's room. "That type of language is inexcusable, especially when women are present."[18] Chuck said he had been in the vicinity of the president's box and saw and heard everything that went on.

When Frank Lane was informed of Chuck's comments, he stated, "I appreciate the keen sense of loyalty of Mr. Charles Comiskey."[19] Lane was defiant in stating that he had no intention of apologizing to the Chicago fans. However, he was sorry for his outburst toward Will Harridge, his tirade had only been for the ears of Cal Hubbard.

The fact was that Frank Lane and Chuck Comiskey had been feuding. So Lane called Grace Comiskey. He said that

Grace told him "to simmer down, that 'you're my general manager, go to Cleveland and let's win the pennant.'"[20]

As the White Sox arrived in Cleveland on September 2 to begin a four game series, they were in first place with a one-half game lead over the Indians and Yankees. But the White Sox lost three out of the four games to the Indians and fell out of first place.

After splitting a doubleheader on September 11 with the Red Sox in Boston, the White Sox were three and a half games out of first place and never recovered, compiling a 12-12 record in September. Still, it had been an exciting season for White Sox fans and 1,175,684 of them went through the turnstiles of Comiskey Park. Under manager Marty Marion, the White Sox finished the 1955 season in third place with a record of 91-63, five games behind the New York Yankees.

According to utility infielder Bob Kennedy, the White Sox lost the pennant by eight inches, the length of surgical scar from pitcher Dick Donovan's mid-season appendectomy. Before the operation, Donovan had won thirteen games, but post-operative won only two from July 30 until the end of the season.

Frank Lane saw the collapse of the White Sox differently, telling the press that the team just didn't have the horses.

The collapse of the 1955 White Sox was a huge disappointment to Grace Comiskey. She had been making World Series plans and was telling friends that so much excitement about the White Sox had not occurred since they last won the American League pennant in 1919.

Nonetheless, the tension in the White Sox front office had been building all summer. Frank Lane was uncertain as to his future with the White Sox. As the White Sox were going into a September swoon in the final days of the season, rumors were surfacing that Frank Lane might be going to St. Louis even though he was legally under contract to the White Sox until 1960. While Lane was guarded on the rumor, he let it be known that he had no intentions of continuing to work with Chuck Comiskey under the existing conditions. "I have no intention of doing anything about my personal affairs until after I have seen Mrs. (Grace) Comiskey."[21]

He stated that Chuck Comiskey had taken every opportunity to ridicule him, and he was fed up with it. "Did it occur to anyone that I might get tired of Chuck's tactics?"[22] Lane asked. He said that he didn't want to be in a position of coming between a mother and her son, because he knew he would lose. But it was a matter of pride and peace of mind. He had to know where he stood.

Lane was particularly upset with a recent interview that Chuck had given to a reporter from the Waterloo, Iowa *Courier* in which he stated, "Frank Lane is one of our capable executives. But there can be only one person whose orders are final in any business, and in the case of the White Sox, I am in charge. Mother wants an explanation at some things I do once in a while, but I make the final decisions."[23]

The key to Frank Lane's future with the Chicago White Sox was Grace Comiskey. But according to Grace, she had no recollection of Lane making or asking for an appointment with her today, tomorrow, or any other day.

Grace told the press, "If Frank wants a date to talk matters over with me, then why doesn't he call me? He seems to be getting himself a lot of quotes in the newspapers, but he hasn't bothered to contact me. I think the man is on the verge of a nervous breakdown. Right now, I don't wish to express myself. Mr. Lane seems to be doing all the expressing. I've been in baseball for 43 years and I know how to run my business, so when the right time comes, I'll do some expressing."[24]

On September 22, 1955 Frank Lane sent a letter of resignation to Grace Comiskey asking that he be let out of his contract on October 15, or earlier if she preferred. Grace Comiskey immediately accepted his resignation. Lane then became general manager of the St. Louis Cardinals.

Grace Comiskey had once said her son knew nothing but baseball. She also had said he "couldn't run a peanut stand."[25] She knew that her son's showdown with Frank Lane, a highly skilled and shrewd baseball executive, was an attempt to become the recognized spokesman of the

White Sox—so now the success of the team going forward was at his direction.

Chuck Comiskey had now turned thirty years old, and according to terms of his father's will had received another chunk of White Sox stock. With Frank Lane departed, his plan for success of the White Sox seemed to be to fall back on the family heritage in the game. To that end, he started giving newspaper interviews in which he connected himself to his legendary grandfather Charles A. Comiskey.

On November 17 Grace Comiskey appointed her son-in-law Johnny Rigney, former Major League pitcher, to jointly run the White Sox as co-general manager along with Chuck for the 1956 season.

Together, Chuck and Rigney, in the spirit of Frank Lane, made some key player deals trading Jim Busby and Chico Carrasquel to the Cleveland Indians for Larry Doby and picking up relief pitcher Gerry Staley from the New York Yankees on waivers.

While shortstop Louis Aparicio was named rookie of the year, it turned out that the Chicago White Sox didn't have the horses in the 1956 season either. The team was competitive until suffering a disastrous July when they won only nine games while losing twenty-one. The White Sox finished the season in third place with a record of 85-69, twelve games behind the New York Yankees. Chuck Comiskey and Johnny Rigney, working in harmony, fired Marty Marion and replaced him with Al Lopez.

All throughout the 1956 season Grace Comiskey had been experiencing failing health. She had not been to many games, and following a night game at Comiskey Park, she told Roy Egan that she couldn't go through the ordeal of attending a night game anymore.

On the morning of December 10, 1956 Rosemary Allen, the maid for Grace Comiskey, arrived for work at her apartment at 3240 Lake Shore Drive. She went to the back door and opened it as far as the chain would permit. There she saw Grace Comiskey lying on the floor. The building engineer, Albert Neuser, was summoned and gained entrance into the apartment. Dr. William H. Gehl was making a house call in the building and was summoned. He pronounced Grace dead. She had apparently just poured herself a cup of coffee while reading a newspaper, and was suddenly stricken with a massive coronary.

Grace Comiskey was sixty-two years old and had been in poor health for the past few years. At the time, other members of her family were preparing for the Major League winter meetings in downtown Chicago.

Although well hidden from the public, Grace Comiskey had developed a drinking problem and there has been speculation that her addiction to alcohol could have hindered her judgment in her final years.

Four hundred people attended last rites for Grace Comiskey at a requiem high mass in Our Lady of Mount Carmel Church in Evanston, Illinois. Those in attendance included the Mayor of Chicago, Richard J. Daley, one of the White Sox most ardent fans. Representatives from Major League Baseball included Will Harridge, President of the American League, and Spike Briggs of Detroit. Interment took place in Calvary Cemetery in Evanston.

Dorothy Rigney succeeded her mother as the White Sox principal owner as a result of a specific bequest in Grace's will of 500 shares of White Sox stock. When Chuck left the White Sox in a huff after the 1952 season, Grace Comiskey had come to the decision that upon her death, Dorothy should be given majority control of the team.

The fact was that Dorothy holding a degree in economics from Northwestern University had long been interested in the family business, having approached her late father in 1937 about a job with the team while still attending classes. While the White Sox had not won a pennant since 1919, Dorothy working as treasurer and vice president along with her mother had kept the franchise solvent during some difficult years.

With the special bequest, it would leave Dorothy with 3,975 shares and her brother Chuck, thirty-one years old, with 3,475 after he received the 500 shares still do to him from his father's will upon reaching the age of thirty-five. The balance of Grace Comiskey's estate was divided equally between Dorothy and Chuck.

Dorothy and Chuck agreed to leave the office of president of the team open for a year in respect for their mother. But peace among the Comiskey heirs would be short lived.

A year and a day after his mother died, Chuck Comiskey began a court battle to gain control of the White Sox through board member selections. Chuck filed a petition to compel Dorothy Rigney to immediately turn over 1,781 shares of White Sox stock to him in time to vote them at the annual meeting. By gaining control of the stock, Chuck would be able to ensure that the board was increased from three members to four, giving him equal power in decision and policy making. As things stood, Dorothy as executrix of the estate had the legal right to vote the full member shares until the estate was distributed. To that end, Chuck asked for the court to give a proxy vote.

Dorothy's attorney, Roy Egan, was concerned that if distribution of Grace Comiskey's estate was done before its value was determined, it could result in it becoming insolvent because of unknown tax obligations. Therefore, as executrix, Dorothy would be stuck.

Some observers saw Chuck's action as another self-aggrandizing attempt to gain the presidency of the White Sox. Even if he was granted the stock and appointed a fourth board member, he would not be able to gain control of the team if Dorothy opposed him.

Sports Illustrated offered a sibling rivalry analysis of the latest Comiskey family flap stating:

> If Chuck Comiskey and John Rigney work so smoothly together, what is the fight all about? Principally this: there is no close relationship between Dorothy and Chuck. They don't really know each other, and they don't know how to handle each other. Dorothy, eight years older does not want Chuck in a position where he can do what he wants with the club without her ultimate supervision. Chuck, mature, married, the father of two children, feels that he has both the traditional right and the native ability to run the club as he sees fit without being subjected to what was maternal and is now sisterly discipline.[26]

Chuck Comiskey won the first battle of the new Comiskey family feud on December 19, 1957 when a probate judge ordered that 4,062 shares left by Grace Comiskey not be voted at the shareholders meeting scheduled for the same day. As the ruling prevented a majority of the shares being represented at the meeting, Dorothy Rigney cancelled it.

The legal battle dragged on into late April 1958 before a probate judge ordered distribution of the White Sox stock in Grace Comiskey's estate. The court order insured Chuck Comiskey that his sister could not maneuver his ouster from the team's hierarchy as she would only be permitted to elect two board members, the same as her brother.

Meanwhile, potential buyers for the team were making inquiries, including former Cleveland Indians and St. Louis Browns owner Bill Veeck, Jr., representing a syndicate and Chicago insurance broker Charles O. Finley, who was going to handle the entire sale price himself.

In early January 1959 Dorothy Rigney announced that her majority stock in the Chicago White Sox had been sold to a syndicate headed by Bill Veeck that included former Detroit Tigers slugger Hank Greenberg, Jerry Hoffberger, a Baltimore brewer, and others. Furthermore, Dorothy stated if the Veeck syndicate failed to go through with the transaction, then she had a contract with Charles O. Finley to sell him the stock.

During the court battles the White Sox financial records were made public for 1957, which showed that the team had netted $396,036 and had a payroll for coaches and players of $609,343. Dorothy Rigney's stock was valued at $2,700,000.

However, the sale still faced some obstacles. For one, Chuck Comiskey was attempting to buy his sister's stock and filed a petition for a court hearing. "The White Sox always have been in the Comiskey family and I hope to keep them there. I will not be squeezed,"[27] said Chuck. But Dorothy Rigney, smitten with the arrogance of her brother in the battle over their mother's estate, was of no mind to sell her stock to him.

On March 2, 1959 Probate Judge Robert Jerome Dunne dismissed both of the petitions filed by Chuck Comiskey. The first had sought to block the sale of Dorothy Rigney's stock to Bill Veeck and asked that she be removed as executrix of Grace Comiskey's estate. The second asked that Dorothy be given her share of the residuary estate in cash, rather than stock and that the remaining 1,041 shares go to him (Chuck), who would then hold a majority of the White Sox stock.

The court had clearly grown weary of the Comiskeys' legal shenanigans prompting Judge Dunne to scold Dorothy and Chuck. Judge Dunne said, "The litigants here are merely enjoying the fruits of their parents' and grandparents' industry, who thru their efforts and hard work built up a considerable fortune. In the interest of family unity and solidarity, it is regrettable that the litigants here could not have seen fit to settle their dispute between themselves without any attendant publicity."[28]

The philosophical directive of Judge Dunne did nothing to stop the unrelenting quest of Chuck Comiskey, and he fought another unsuccessful round in court to gain control of the team.

Finally, on May 1, 1959 Bill Veeck, Jr. gained control of the Chicago White Sox. He was elected to the club's board of directors after a plea for an injunction filed by Chuck Comiskey to stop the election was denied. After purchasing Dorothy's stock Veeck now controlled 54 percent of the White Sox stock and had a 3-1 majority on the board that besides him included, Dorothy Comiskey Rigney, Roy Egan, and Chuck Comiskey.

On September 22, 1959 the Chicago White Sox clinched the American League pennant. It was the White Sox first league championship in forty years since the days of their founding father, Charles A. Comiskey. In celebration, Mayor Richard J. Daley had all the civil defense sirens in the city activated.

After leaving baseball, Dorothy Comiskey Rigney and her husband John turned their interest toward thorough bred horse racing. One of their horses, Fast Hilarious, captured the 1969 American Derby at Arlington.

Dorothy Comiskey Rigney died on January 1, 1971 in Oak Park, Illinois.

Chuck Comiskey never became President of Chicago White Sox. In 1962 he sold his stock in the White Sox to a group headed by insurance executive William Bartholomay, thereby ending a sixty-two year Comiskey family involvement with the team.

On August 27, 2007 Charles A. Comiskey II died at the age of eighty-one years old in Hinsdale, Illinois.

4

JOAN W. PAYSON

NEW YORK METS

Joan Whitney was born on February 5, 1903 in New York City. She was born into a family of considerable financial wealth and one that was rich in its legacy of American history. Listed in the Social Register and a proud member of the DAR, in her early twenties, Joan would become the heiress to a family fortune and go on to establish herself as a notable sportswoman, philanthropist, and patron of the arts.

Joan was the daughter of Helen Hay Whitney whose father, John Hay, had been a personal secretary to President Abraham Lincoln.

Following the months after his election to the presidency in November 1860 and his inauguration in March 1861, Abraham Lincoln was overwhelmed while attempting to answer the baskets of mail that arrived each day at his law office in Springfield, Illinois. To expedite the matter, Lincoln's personal secretary John G. Nicolay hired John Hay, a recent graduate of Brown University to assist him. For Hay, it would be the beginning of a most distinguished public service career that would see him serve President Lincoln as an aide throughout the Civil

War. In 1890 Hay, in collaboration with Nicolay, would author a ten-volume biography of Lincoln titled *Abraham Lincoln: The Observations of John G. Nicolay and John Hay.*

Later, John Hay would help negotiate the Treaty of Paris, which ended the Spanish-American War and serve as Secretary of State in the cabinets of Presidents William McKinley and Theodore Roosevelt.

William C. Whitney, Joan's grandfather on her father's side of the family, had been secretary of the Navy. The Whitney's American experience had begun arriving on the *Arbella* ten years after the *Mayflower.*

Joan's father, Payne Whitney, was one of the richest men in America having made a fortune in lumber, banking, and real estate. Included in his holdings were 600 acres in Manhasset, Long Island on which stood the Whitney home, described as one of the grandest in America. In 1924 Payne Whitney paid $2,041,951 in income taxes. That year, only Henry Ford and John D. Rockefeller paid more income tax.

Occasionally, Joan would go with her father on the family yacht to New Haven to watch the Yale Crew workout. It was on one of those visits that Joan met Charles Shipman Payson whose lineage was from an old line family in Portland, Maine.

In 1924 at Christ Episcopal Church in Manhasset, twenty-one-year-old Joan Whitney, a graduate of Columbia University's Barnard College, married Charles Shipman Payson, a Yale graduate. The couple would have five children, two boys and three girls.

Three years following Joan's marriage to Charles Payson in 1927, her father died leaving an estate valued at $239,301,017, the largest ever recorded in the United States at the time. It was said that Joan inherited both the spirit for her lifestyle and the money to sustain it.

Joan had two siblings. Her sister Barbara was a beautiful woman who married William Paley, chairman of the board of CBS.

Joan Payson also had a brother, John Hay (Jock) Whitney, born on August 27, 1904. He would become Joan's lifelong friend and for a time, horse breeding rival. Like Joan, Jock would go on to distinguish himself in several areas. Educated at Oxford and Yale, Jock would become a noted thoroughbred horse breeder and serve as a lieutenant colonel in the Army Air Force in World War Two. After his sister Joan donated $65,000 to the Republican National Committee in 1956, Jock would be named Ambassador to the United Kingdom (1957-1961) by President Eisenhower. In 1961 Jock Whitney would acquire the New York Herald Tribune and serve as the newspaper's last publisher (1961-1966).

In the 1930s Joan Payson and brother Jock Whitney became interested in the entertainment business. They read vigorously and had a keen sense for picking popular scripts. Subsequently, they would become backers of some extremely successful movies and shows including, *A Streetcar Named Desire*, *Kind Lady*, *A Star Is Born*, and *Rebecca*, which all handsomely added to the family fortune.

Also, Jock was the financial backer for the 1939 Academy Award winning film *Gone With The Wind*. In 1938 he was on board a plane from New York bound for California. He had with him a copy of the melodramatic novel of the Civil War written by Margaret Mitchell. The book, although a best seller, had already been turned down by Samuel Goldwyn who considered it just another run-of-the-mill Civil War story. Jock began reading the book, and when the plane stopped for refueling in St. Louis, he got off and telephoned his office and told someone to send $50,000 to that girl Mitchell to hold the dramatic rights to the book. In the end, Jock Whitney actually put up half of the money. *Gone With The Wind*, produced by David O. Selznick and his International Pictures company, went on to become one of the most successful movies of all time. Jock and his sister Joan attended the premier of the film in Atlanta and mingled among the stars Clark Gable and Vivien Leigh.

Joan Payson would spend her life dividing her time between ballparks, race tracks, and board rooms in support of her charities and socializing in the drawing rooms of the super-rich. In the late 1960s and early 1970s, it was not uncommon for Joan to start her afternoon off at the Belmont track and then be driven in her green Bentley bearing license plate "MET 1" by her chauffer Arthur

Desmond down to Shea Stadium to catch the late innings of a Mets game.

Nonetheless, Joan's style in the ballpark resembled that of bleachers fans, and her demeanor at the track was characteristic of bettors at the $2 window; she was a cordial lady, who appeared somewhat embarrassed by her wealth and not snobbish. One of Joan's race track associates described her as "a simple, generous person with no swank."[1]

When children swarmed around her box during batting practice seeking an autograph, she cheerfully accommodated them. She dressed simple and wore little makeup. She was even superstitious. No hats were allowed on the bed, and she had a habit of crossing her fingers. If she was eating chocolate or ice cream when her team was rallying, she continued eating them until they cooled off. If you entered her box when the Mets were ahead, you became a captive and were not permitted to leave until the score changed.

Joan had become a baseball fan by the age of six. As a child, in the summer she played first base in a blue and white middy with a sash for Bunny Wood's camp on the outskirts of Boston. It was also about that time that she started attending New York Giants games at the Polo Grounds with her mother Helen. Her mother would even take her to Brooklyn when the Giants were playing there. "Mother used to take me to the ballpark all the time," recalled Joan. She was the greatest fan around. Once she wanted to vote for Joe DiMaggio in a box top contest. I didn't know about it, but she told the cook to feed our children "Wheaties" and save the box tops for her."[2]

Helen Hay Whitney was a Giants fanatic. According to Joan, "When the team went out of town and mother turned on the radio to listen to the games no one dared come into the room."[3] One year Joan took her mother to the World Series and she got in such a heated argument with another fan they nearly came to blows. Helen had a sports philosophy: "Win as you enjoyed winning, lose as though you were prepared for it."[4]

Her mother often invited ball players to their home. Once, she invited Babe Ruth to lunch. Joan recalled that as they all sat down at a big long table, "As usual we started off with hard-boiled eggs. Mother pitched them to each of us. Babe caught his neatly, but I'll never forget the look on his face. I knew that he wouldn't believe that mother did that every day. She always threw strikes."[5]

One of the first players that made an impression on Joan was Casey Stengel. The Whitney's box at the Polo Grounds was located directly behind first base, and Joan was mostly interested in Giants six foot four inch first baseman George "Highpockets" Kelly. Later, it would be Giants first baseman Bill Terry who would stand out the strongest in Joan's memory.

Helen Hay Whitney was also a huge racing fan. So Joan split her summer days between attending Giants games at Polo Grounds and accompanying her mother to the track at Saratoga where she was permitted to bet 25 cents on each race. Her father had established Greentree Stable in Red Bank, New Jersey in 1925 soon after Greentree Farms was started in Lexington, Kentucky as a breeding farm. Joan's mother, who took over the operation of Greentree Stable and Farms after the death of her husband, had been called the "first lady of the turf" and had adapted the Greentree colors of pink and black from one of her favorite tea gowns. During the years the Whitney family owned Greentree Farms it would produce three Kentucky Derby winners, one Preakness winner, and four Belmont Stakes winners.

Joan and brother Jock had maintained separate stables. While Joan was a huge racing fan, she didn't know as much about racing as her brother. So when their mother Helen Hay Whitney died, they began to pool everything.

According to Ruth Arcaro, wife of famed jockey Eddie Arcaro, when Eddie was set down for an entire year from riding, he attempted to make a go of it by exercising Greentree Stable horses. Ruth said that every once in a while she would get a note from Joan Payson asking how the baby was doing, and included would be a nice little check. Joan understood their hardship.

A patron of the arts, Joan Payson would become a trustee of the Museum of Modern Art and Metropolitan

Museum of Art. While serving in 1971 as a member on the Committee on Preservation of the White House, Joan donated a $25,000 American Chippendale library table for the new Map Room.

Joan Payson owned Palm Beach Gallery and Country Life Gallery in Locus Valley, Long Island. She filled her home with masterpieces by Goya, Matisse, Cezane, El Greco, Toulouse-Lautrec, and Corot.

In 1947 Joan bought Van Gogh's masterpiece "Irises" for $87,000. Van Gogh had painted it in 1889 during his first week at the asylum at St. Remy. Upon her death, Joan bequeathed the painting to her son John Whitney Payson. At auction by Sotheby's in New York in November 1987, "Irises" was sold for $53.9 million. At the time, it was the highest price ever paid for an artwork at auction. John Payson said that when his mother had been told forty years ago what the price of the paining would be, she said, "I'm not going to spend that much for a painting." Then the art dealer told her, "Now don't be stingy." John also commented saying, "Thank heaven she gave in."[6]

But Joan Payson wasn't just all about stuffy art auctions and lazy green grassy summer days at Saratoga. During the Great Depression Joan gave $50,000 to the Emergency Unemployment Relief Fund.

On September 24, 1944 Joan's mother Helen Hay Whitney died. She left an estate valued at $6,128,304 to Joan and her brother Jock that included interest in Greentree Stables and Farms, real estate holdings in Manhassett, and her home at 972 5th Avenue in Manhattan. She also left one of her Kentucky Derby cups (Twenty Grand, winner 1931 & Shut Out, winner 1942) to Joan and Jock.

The Helen Hay Whitney Foundation had been started by Joan's mother to help in medical research. Following her death, Joan Payson would continue to run the organization. Also with her brother Jock, they would start North Shore Hospital in Manhassett and become involved with the United Hospital Fund.

Joan's first born child, John Carroll Payson, had enlisted in the U.S. Army in 1944 at the age of eighteen and became an infantryman. On her forty-first birthday in

February 1945, Joan received the news via telegram that her son had been killed in action in the Battle of the Bulge. In retrospect, Joan asked, "Would anyone be interested in that? People forget such things. Parents don't."[7]

By the middle of the 1950s Bobby Thompson's dramatic ninth inning home run off the Dodgers Ralph Branca to give the New York Giants the pennant in 1951 ("The Shot Heard Round the World") had disappeared in the rear view mirror of owner Horace Stoneham and apparently the Giants fans too. Attendance at Polo Grounds began to decrease dramatically as the Giants fan base began moving out of Manhattan and the Bronx to new post-war suburbs on Long Island and Northern New Jersey. Also, inadequate parking facilities existed around the Polo Grounds and more games were being televised. Furthermore, it appeared that Robert Moses, New York City's non-elected czar of urban planning and construction, was attempting to force the Giants out of the city.

In November 1953 Robert Moses invited New York Giants president Horace Stoneham and other club officials to meet with him at his office on Randall's Island. At the meeting, Moses told Stoneham that the Polo Grounds and its parking lot was situated on one of the last large open spaces in Manhattan, and he wanted to build public housing on the site.

Moses suggested to Stoneham that he seek a lease with the New York Yankees to use Yankee Stadium for his home games. Moses stated, "I have no direct knowledge about the matter, but it would seem to me that the owners of the New York Yankees would welcome the idea of having another club in a different league use their park as has been done successfully in other places. To an outsider, it would appear that it would certainly save money for both clubs."[8] Horace Stoneham was against the idea and told Moses that such doubling-up was not customary in Major League Baseball.

Then in 1955 after Horace Stoneham had leased a small parking lot on the north side of 155th Street, the city condemned the site and put a school there. For Stoneham, it was evident that the writing was on the wall, he was being forced out of Manhattan by Moses.

In 1956, after the Giants had tanked in attendance with only 630,000 entering the Polo Grounds, Horace Stoneham began looking for a site to relocate the team. At first, it appeared that the Giants would move to Minneapolis. In fact, steel girders had already been placed in the ground to build a new stadium. Then Brooklyn Dodgers owner Walter O'Malley got National League approval to move to Los Angeles if another team relocated to the west coast as well, thereby making road trips for the other teams in the league cost-effective. So O'Malley convinced Stoneham to abandon Harlem and the Giants' glorious seventy-four-year history in New York City and move to San Francisco.

On August 19, 1957 the New York Giants board of directors approved the move to San Francisco by a vote of 8-1. The lone dissenting vote was cast by M. Donald Grant representing minority stockholder Joan Whitney Payson, who had bought one share of her beloved Giants.

Horace Stoneham was asked at a press conference, "How do you feel about taking the Giants from the kids in New York?" He answered, "I feel bad about the kids but I haven't seen many of their fathers lately."[9]

In an attempt to keep the Giants in New York, Joan Payson had actually made a last ditch attempt to buy the team from Stoneham. But after all was said and done, Joan, although heart broken by the relocation of the Giants, flew to San Francisco and attended the team's opening day game in 1958. She had also become a huge fan of Willie Mays, and with the Giants departure for the west coast Joan would now occasionally travel to see him play in Philadelphia.

With the Giants and Dodgers relocated from New York to California, in 1958 it left the largest media center in the country without a National League team. New York mayor Robert Wagner asked attorney William Shea to form a committee dedicated to bringing a National League team back to the city.

At first, it looked like Powell Crosley, Jr., who was having troubles with the City of Cincinnati over adequate parking facilities at his ballpark, might move the Cincinnati Reds to New York, but the rumors quickly faded. Then there were rumors that the Pittsburgh Pirates or Philadelphia Phillies might relocate. Once again, those rumors faded. Still, growth in post-World War Two America had changed the urban landscape, and the public in more and more cities were pushing for Major League Baseball. There was considerable political pressure, and expansion was inevitable.

William Shea then turned his attention on Major League Baseball's anti-trust exemption. He felt that if he could convince powerful friends in Washington that Major League Baseball held an unfair advantage in the form of a monopoly, he could bring a team back to New York. Then on July 27, 1959, William Shea along with seventy-eight-year-old Branch Rickey announced the formation of a third Major League—the Continental League. Teams in the league were planned for New York, Atlanta, Houston, Dallas, Denver, Minneapolis-St. Paul, Buffalo, and Toronto.

The owners of the American and National League teams did not want a repeat of the war with the Federal League that occurred in 1914-1915, or to have a challenge to baseball's anti-trust exemption. So on August 2, 1960 they agreed to expand both leagues from eight teams to ten teams. The American League would expand first in 1961 by placing a franchise in Los Angeles. Then Calvin Griffith, owner of the Washington Senators, decided to move his Senators to Bloomington, Minnesota and a new American League franchise would be granted for Washington. Then the National League would expand in 1962 by placing teams in New York and Houston.

Dwight F. "Pete" Davis was a wealthy sportsman that had created the international Davis Cup competition in tennis and was also the Long Island summer neighbor of Joan Payson. On Davis's suggestion, William Shea approached Joan Whitney Payson about becoming one of the owners of a Continental League franchise for New York. However, Joan, still grieving over the loss of the Giants and still holding her one share of stock in that franchise, informed Shea that she did not want to be part of a second-rate baseball team. But after Branch Rickey flew down to Florida and assured Joan that he and Shea were only using the Continental League to pressure Major League Baseball into granting a new National League franchise for New York, she agreed to join them.

Initially, the plan called for Joan Payson to own one-third of the new team being joined as a co-owner of the new franchise by Dwight F. "Pete" Davis and Dorothy Killiam, a wealthy sportswoman and die hard Brooklyn Dodgers fan. But when Dorothy Killiam made it clear that she wanted to run the franchise, Joan Payson and Pete Davis bought her out. Then Joan bought out Pete Davis. Suddenly, Joan Payson owned 80 percent of the forthcoming franchise. Joan Payson became the first lady in Major League history to buy a team with her own finances. Her investment totaled between $3.75 and $5 million. The other 20 percent was held by Joan's stockbroker, M. Donald Grant, whose father was enshrined in the National Hockey League Hall of Fame, and Herbert Walker, Jr., a friend of Joan's husband, who was future president George H. W. Bush's uncle.

With the American League and National League expanding to ten teams, Joan Payson now had her New York National League franchise. Still, she was reluctant to part with her one share of San Francisco Giants stock and asked baseball Commissioner Ford Frick that she be permitted to keep it for sentimental reasons. Of course, it constituted a conflict of interest, and the request was denied. So Joan Payson donated her Giants stock to New York Hospital.

The Meadowlarks, a reference to the rolling meadows where a stadium was being planned for the team, was the name first suggested by Joan Payson for the new National League club in New York. But ultimately, the team would become the Mets, referencing their official league status as The New York Metropolitan Baseball Club. The team's colors of blue and orange were selected to reflect the city's loss of the Brooklyn Dodgers (blue) and New York Giants (orange). Until a new ballpark could be constructed in Flushing Meadows, the Mets would have to play in the dilapidated Polo Grounds.

William Shea suggested that eighty-year-old Branch Rickey be named the general manager of the Mets. Joan Payson was initially receptive to hiring Rickey until he named his terms. He wanted a $5 million budget and complete control of the team. So Joan decided to pass on Rickey and instead named her stockbroker M. Donald Grant as president, and at the suggestion of Branch Rickey, hired his nephew Charles Hurth as general manager. However, Hurth's tenure was to be very short.

On October 17, 1960, the day after the National League awarded the expansion New York franchise to Joan Payson, the New York Yankees shocked the baseball world in the wake of losing the World Series to the Pittsburgh Pirates by firing both manager Casey Stengel and general manager George Weiss. Joan quickly offered the Mets general manager job to Weiss, and he accepted. Charles Hurth was out of the job before he had found his way to the executive washroom.

But George Weiss was an excellent choice for the job; he was a career baseball man, had produced Yankees teams that won ten pennants in twelve years and had for years run the Yankees fruitful farm system.

Casey Stengel, who had managed those successful Yankees teams, was named the manager of the Mets. Originally, Stengel said no to the job. But after Joan Payson and George Weiss kept calling him, he changed his mind.

Then the team that Stengel would manage was stocked with a roster of players in the 1961 National League expansion draft that the other Major League teams did not want or were either marginal in ability or at the end of their careers: Richie Ashburn, Elio Chacon, Jay Hook, Charlie Neal, Roger Craig, Bob Miller, Frank Thomas, Marv Throneberry, Gene Woodling, Felix Mantilla, and others; a lot of cast offs that cost Joan Payson a tidy sum of $1.8 million.

When aging Brooklyn/Los Angeles Dodgers first baseman Gil Hodges joined the Mets for the 1962 season, Joan Payson remarked, "It's wonderful to be rooting for him after having hated him for so many years. I haven't many dislikes, although I used to dislike the Dodgers."[10]

Joan did offer $1,000,000 to the San Francisco Giants to bring her favorite player Willie Mays back to New York. But Horace Stoneham, without blinking an eye, turned the deal down.

To hype the New York Mets it would require a powerful TV and radio broadcasting team to compete with the New York Yankees trio of established broadcasters Mel Allen, Red Barber, and Phil Rizzuto. So George Weiss hired Ralph Kiner, who had been broadcasting the Chicago White Sox games, and Lindsey Nelson, who was familiar to sports fans across America from his national broadcasts of baseball games on NBC as well as doing the play-by-play for Notre Dame Football, NBA games, golf, and tennis. To team up with Kiner and Nelson, Joan Payson insisted that George Weiss hire Baltimore Orioles broadcaster Bob Murphy. Joan liked the way that Murphy had called Roger Maris's sixtieth home run in 1961.

While Nelson would leave the Mets in the late 1970s for the San Francisco Giants, Murphy would call Mets games from 1962 until 2003, and Kiner would continue to do part time broadcasting for the Mets even longer.

A few days after the Mets's opening game in 1962, Joan, along with her daughter and son-in-law, left for the Greek Islands. While away, she wanted to be informed of the Mets's game results by telegrams. So the telegrams started to reach her mentioning one Mets loss after another. Joan became so frustrated that she wired back "PLEASE TELL US ONLY WHEN METS WIN."[11] According to Joan, that was the last word she received from America during the summer of 1962.

In their inaugural season of 1962, the New York Mets proceeded to finish in tenth place with a season record of 40-120.

Still, they had an amazing season attendance of 922,530. However, approximately 40 percent (369,013) of that attendance figure was for crowds attending fifteen home dates with the Los Angeles Dodgers and San Francisco Giants. When the Dodgers played a Memorial Day doubleheader against the Mets at the Polo Grounds on May 30, there were 55,704 in attendance. Two days later when the Giants returned to the Polo Grounds for the first time since relocating to San Francisco, there was a highly emotionally charged crowd of 43,742 in attendance. Prior to the game, Willie Mays shook hands with his New York fans in the stands. Then, to the delight of the many Willie Mays fans in attendance, he hit his seventeenth home run of the season as the Giants beat the Mets 9-6.

Through all the trials and tribulations of the Mets inaugural season, Joan Payson stuck by the team and looked forward to the future. She even referred to their close loses such as 3-2, 4-3, etc. as "moral victories."

In 1963 columnist Jimmy Breslin asked Joan, "If you had it to do all over again, would you go in with all that money to buy the team again?" "Of course," she said. "How else in the world could we have gotten Marvelous Marv into New York? I think the whole thing was just wonderful."[12] (Note: Marv "Marvelous Marv" Throneberry would historically be regarded as an iconic, bumbling first baseman for the New York Mets in 1962-1963, who fielded like he had a cement glove.)

Some New York sports commentators such as Howard Cosell where relentless in their stinging criticism of how the New York Mets were being run. In particular, Cosell targeted the hiring of seventy-one-year-old Casey Stengel as manager, whom he professed was not hired to lead the team, but rather as a mascot and pitchman.

During spring training in 1963, to show her players that they were appreciated despite their dismal performance in the 1962 season, Joan Payson invited the entire team, club officials, and the press to a posh dinner party at Nando's Miramar, a swank bistro in West Palm Beach. During the shindig, Joan was introduced to Ed Kranepool, a young bonus player that the Mets had shelled out $90,000 to the previous summer. When Joan's son-in-law Vincent de Roulet was introduced to the players, he got the biggest howl of the evening when he blurted out loud, "Mr. Kranepool, I want you to know I cost less than you do."[13]

While her husband had been and remained a Boston Red Sox fan, Joan Payson would become one of the New York Mets premier cheerleaders. In February she would have her personal Pullman car, *Adios II*, hooked to the rear of the Florida East Coast Champion and accompanied by two or three dachshunds to head to spring training in Florida. She became a fixture seated in her box, first at the Polo Grounds then at Shea Stadium, to right of the Mets dugout wearing a floppy hat or a blue and orange Mets cap. She kept score using her own personalized code while sometimes chewing nervously on her pencil.

The Mets would have a hapless encore season in 1963 finishing in tenth place again with a slightly improved record of 51-111 and an attendance figure of 1,080,108. But there was a bright spot in the Mets lineup that gave reason toward looking to the future—rookie second baseman Ron Hunt. While Pete Rose won the 1963 National League Rookie of the Year award, Ron Hunt's statistics were close to those of the Reds second baseman (Hunt: BA .272, Hits 145, HR 10, RBIs 42) (Rose: BA .273, Hits 170, HR 6, RBIs 41).

The following season, Ron Hunt would become the first New York Mets player voted to start an All-Star Game, receiving 172 votes from his fellow National League players for the starting second base position as opposed to the Pirates Bill Mazeroski, who received fifty-two votes.

Ron Hunt would become one of Joan Payson's favorite players on the Mets in the early years of the franchise. After Hunt got a key hit against the Milwaukee Braves at the Polo Grounds in 1963, Joan sent Hunt and his wife a dozen roses. Then following the 1964 season when George Weiss and Casey Stengel attempted to trade Hunt to the Minnesota Twins in a deal that would have brought catcher Earle Battey to New York, Joan Payson vetoed the deal. Nonetheless, following the 1966 season Hunt was traded to the Los Angeles Dodgers.

Finally, in the 1964 season the Mets abandoned the dilapidated Polo Grounds and moved into the team's new facility in Flushing Meadows—Shea Stadium. At the time the stadium opened, the 1964 World's Fair was taking place just a few blocks away, and Queens seemed like the center of the universe. Shea Stadium had its inaugural game on Friday April 17, 1964 with the Pittsburgh Pirates defeating the Mets 4-3 with 50,000 plus fans on hand.

Shea Stadium experienced its first no-hitter in 1964 when Jim Bunning tossed a perfect game against the Mets on Father's Day. Then on July 7 the 35th All-Star Game was played at Shea. While season attendance at Shea Stadium in 1964 was 1,732,547, the Mets continued to occupy the National League cellar finishing with a record of 53-109.

In early August 1964 it was reported by the Associated Press that Joan Payson and M. Donald Grant were going to fire Casey Stengel when the season concluded. The general feeling in the Mets front office was that Casey Stengel had served his purpose in publicizing the Mets as they were organized and began playing. But now it was time for the team to start developing on the field and that a younger manager would serve that purpose better. But Stengel was not ready to leave and fought for his job and did return in 1965, but then in August after ninety-five games, he broke his hip and was replaced by Coach Wes Westrum.

In 1965 Bing Devine, after having engineered the 1964 World Series champions the St. Louis Cardinals, accepted the job as the Mets general manager. With the arrival of Devine, George Weiss could concentrate on being the Mets president. Still, the Mets continued their loosing ways in 1965 and continued to put established players at the end of their careers in the lineup like Roy McMillan, Warren Spahn, Jack Fisher, Tom Sturdivant and others.

In February 1966 Tom Seaver, a young college pitcher from the University of Southern California, signed a contract for $40,000 with the Atlanta Braves. However, baseball commissioner William D. Eckert declared the contract void, because Seaver's college team had already played two games that year, although Seaver had not played in either.

So Tom Seaver decided to finish college, but the NCAA ruled him ineligible, because he had signed with the Braves. When his father threatened Major League Baseball with a law suit, William Eckert announced that any team willing to match the Braves' $40,000 offer could sign Seaver. Three teams were interested: the Cleveland Indians, Philadelphia Phillies, and New York Mets. So

Eckert announced that a lottery would take place on April 2, 1966 with the winning team being pulled out of a hat.

George Weiss had passed up drafting Reggie Jackson in the 1966 season for the Mets and instead took catcher Steve Chilcott; now he did not want to participate in the lottery for Seaver. But Bing Devine convinced him to do so, and the Mets won the rights to Tom Seaver.

In his first season with the New York Mets in 1967, Tom Seaver had a record of 16-13 and was named National League Rookie of the Year. Early in his second season with the Mets in 1968, Seaver was first introduced to Joan Payson while standing near her box to the right of the Mets dugout at Shea Stadium. Joan told Seaver that she knew all about him. Then she asked Seaver for an autographed picture of himself for her grandchildren

At the end of the 1966 season, George Weiss retired. Then, after the 1967 season, Bing Devine left to return to St. Louis thereby leaving both the Mets positions of president and general manager vacant. Bing Devine went to see Joan Payson personally with his decision to leave the Mets. Later, Devine was to say that he never had any interference from either Joan Payson or M. Donald Grant while he was general manager. He just needed to inform them of his intent to trade certain players so there were no surprises. He also said that Joan Payson was about as nice an owner you could meet.

Prior to the 1968 season, still waiting for her team to climb out of the basement, sixty-four-year-old Joan Payson agreed to accept the appointment by the board as Mets president on one condition—she didn't have to make any speeches. Then board member John Murphy was named general manager.

In the 1968 season Gil Hodges would become manager, and the New York Mets would show promise; led by the strong pitching of Tom Seaver (16-12) and Jerry Koosman (19-12), for the second time in the team's brief history they finished out of last place, winding-up in ninth place in the National League ten team race.

In June 1968 Stage Door Johnny, a three-year-old horse bred at Greentree Farms and owned by Joan Payson and her brother Jock Whitney, won the 100th Belmont

Stakes with twenty-seven-year-old jockey Heliodoro Gustines by a length and quarter over Kentucky Derby and Preakness winner Forward Pass, thereby preventing the horse from becoming racing's first triple crown winner since 1943. Stage Door Johnny had gone off at 4-1 as opposed to even odds for Forward Pass. The winning purse for Joan and her brother was $117,000.

Prior to the Belmont, Joan had a transistor radio plugged into her ear listening to the Mets game. As Stage Door Johnny crossed the finish line, Jock Whitney turned to his sister Joan and said, "Since your Mets lost today, we had to win something."[14] It was the fourth time that one of the Greentree Farms horses had won the Belmont following Twenty Grand (1931), Shut Out (1942), and Capot (1949), which was also named Horse of the Year.

Twenty-eight days later, Stage Door Johnny would win the Saranca Handicap. But he would be retired by the end of the season with a bowed tendon after having compiled winnings of $221,765, winning five victories in six starts.

In 1969 Major League Baseball, celebrating its 100th anniversary, expanded for the second time in the decade adding four more new teams. In the American League, new teams were added in Kansas City and Seattle. The National League added teams in San Diego and Montreal. Then each league was split into two divisions of east and west.

The New York Mets entered the 1969 season as 100-1 shots at winning the National League Pennant and World Series, having finished in ninth place in the ten team race in 1968.

The Mets began the 1969 campaign by losing their opening day game to the expansion Montreal Expos 11-10. But as the season progressed, manager Gil Hodges implemented a lineup that had Tommy Agee, Cleon Jones, and Bud Harrelson playing every day while platooning at all the other positions. At the same time, the Mets were getting strong starting pitching performances from Tom Seaver, Jerry Koosman, Gary Gentry, and Tug McGraw in relief.

In early July as the Mets started to pick up momentum, Joan was enrolled at an Elizabeth Arden Health Farm in Maine and could not be in New York for a crucial series with the Cubs. So she arranged to have the games televised by a station that normally did not broadcast them.

In mid-July Joan Payson flew to London to visit her daughter and son-in-law, George and Lady Weidenfield. Her daughter's husband, a London publisher, had just turned fifty years old and had been knighted. So there was a full calendar of social events to attend throughout the remainder of the summer.

Meanwhile, the Mets lost seven out of eleven and by mid-August were nine and a half games behind the Cubs. But the Mets never threw in the towel and kept fighting back. By early September they had a ten game winning streak and had won twenty-four out of the past thirty-one games.

On September 8 the Mets pulled within two and a half games of the East Division leading Chicago Cubs. That day, the swooning Cubs arrived at Shea Stadium and promptly dropped a two game series to the Mets. On September 10 the Mets reached first place for the first time in their history. From that point, the momentum the Mets had been building continued to drive them on until they had won 100 games and the National League East Division Championship.

When the Mets clinched the National League East Division Championship on September 24 with a 6-0 win over the St. Louis Cardinals, Joan Payton was sick in bed in London with a case of bronchitis. She sent her congratulations by cable, and her husband Charles stood in for her during the wild champagne spraying celebration that ensued in the Mets locker room. By telephone, Joan asked if Charles would go with her to the playoffs. "Goddamit," said Charles, "I certainly won't go if they are in California. Atlanta maybe."[15] Joan finally arrived back in the United States on September 29.

The first game of the 1969 National League Championship Series took place in Atlanta on October 4. Joan Payson flew into the city in the morning and arrived at Atlanta Fulton County Stadium fifteen minutes before the game began. It was the first time Joan had been back to Atlanta since 1938 when she attended the premier of *Gone With The Wind* with brother Jock. The Mets won game one 9-5, scoring five runs in the eighth inning of Phil Niekro.

Prior to game two of the series, Joan Payson sitting in her box told reporters, "This year, I didn't think they'd turn around and win so in April I made plans to be in Europe visiting my daughter in September. Then when they did get into first place, I was too superstitious to change my plans and stay home."[16]

The following day in game three at Shea Stadium behind seven strong innings of relief pitching by Nolan Ryan, the New York Mets completed a sweep of the Atlanta Braves in the series, three games to zero, to advance to the 1969 World Series.

The New York Mets entered the 1969 World Series 5-8 long shots. But after losing the first game in the series, the Mets would win the next four in a row and defeat the powerful Baltimore Orioles.

Throughout the series, Joan Payson's superstitious nature held her captive. In game two in Baltimore she couldn't watch Mets pitcher Ron Taylor's final pitch in the bottom of the ninth inning to Brooks Robinson with two out and two on and the Mets leading 2-1. So she placed a scarf over her eyes and didn't see Robison ground out to Ed Charles.

She showed up for game four at Shea Stadium wearing a new coat. Joan said that she brought the coat because of the change in the weather, but was concerned that it could be a hex on her Mets. She told reporters, "It's the first time I've worn it and I'm worried because I can't stick with my lucky clothes."[17]

With Tom Seaver pitching for the Mets, the Orioles entered the ninth inning down 1-0, then they scored a run sending the game into extra innings. In the bottom of the tenth, Jerry Grote led off with a double, then scored when Pete Richert's throw on J. C. Martin's bunt hit his wrist and went wide of first to give the Mets a 2-1 victory.

Joan Payson was ecstatic! Almost out of breath, she said, "I simply can't stand it, it's just too much. What a beautiful bunt, and that beautiful run coming across the plate."[18]

The following day in game five, the Mets defeated the Orioles 5-3 to win the 1969 World Series, four games to one.

Following the final out, third baseman Ed Charles went into a victory dance and pitcher Jerry Koosman jumped into the arms of catcher Jerry Grote as thousands of the 57,397 delirious fans in attendance poured onto the field. They ripped up the turf, one stole home plate, and another threw an usher off the roof of the Mets dugout sending him to the hospital, while another fan attempted to scale the twenty-five-foot scoreboard before falling off and being sent to the hospital. In the spirit of the "peace and love" movement of the late 1960s, some reporters wrote about the incident calling it an urban Woodstock in Flushing. But it was hardly a love fest, it was a riot. Nonetheless, for posterity the team would be forever known as the "amazin' Mets."

As the players whooped it up in the Mets clubhouse with the obligatory Champaign showers, Joan Payson modestly hugged manager Gil Hodges. She preferred to stay in the background and let the focus of the media be on the players. Joan was accustomed to winning; only a week ago as Nolan Ryan was wrapping up the National League pennant for the Mets, one of her Greentree Stable horses, The University, ridden by Angel Cordero, was crossing the finish line at Belmont ahead of the field in the Long Island Handicap to earn $14,917.

Sandy Koufax was working for NBC and he pulled Tom Seaver aside for an interview. Koufax asked, "Tom, is God a Met?" Seaver replied, "No. But he's got an apartment in New York."[19]

The magic of 1969 for the "amazin' Mets" did not crossover into the beginning of the 1970s. For the next three seasons the Mets could do no better than third place as the Pittsburgh Pirates dominated the National League East Division.

Near the end of spring training on April 2, 1972 with a players strike beginning, Mets manager Gil Hodges suddenly died of a heart attack.

A few days later, a funeral mass for Hodges was held at his church, Our Lady Help of Christians in Brooklyn. The streets around the church were lined with thousands of mourners. Joan Payson, dressed in a black hat and purple coat, was helped up the steps of the church as New York mayor John Lindsay and scores of baseball players past and present arrived. Attendees included Tom Seaver, Jerry Koosman, Yogi Berra, Pee Wee Reese, Jackie Robinson, and Don Newcombe.

Inside the church as everyone rose to their feet, the organ began to boom out a stirring march. Joan Payson turned to M. Donald Grant and said, "What is that song?" "The Battle Hymn of the Republic," answered Grant. "I like that," she said. "Please see that it is played at my funeral."[20]

Less than four hours after Hodges's burial, Yogi Berra, still dressed in his blue funeral suit, was informed that he would become the Mets' new manager.

While Joan Payson stayed in the background during the labor dispute, Mets board chairman M. Donald Grant, along with a few other hardliners such as August Busch of the Cardinals, Calvin Griffith of the Twins, and Dan Galbreath of the Pirates representing his father John, had made it clear that they were out to brake the player's union. But the strike was costing the owners a huge loss of revenue due to cancelled games. According to Los Angeles Dodgers owner Walter O'Malley, his club was losing $1 million each weekend the strike continued. Finally, the owners agreed to add $500,000 for health care benefits and agreed to a cost of living increase in retirement benefits. The players strike lasted for thirteen days, but by April 15, the call "play ball" was once again heard throughout the Major Leagues.

On May 11, 1972 Joan Payson finally got her long heartfelt wish to bring Willie Mays back to New York. Mays, clearly at the end of his brilliant career, had been benched in favor of a younger player by manager Charlie Fox and was becoming a financial liability to cash-strapped San Francisco Giants. So owner Horace Stoneham agreed to trade the player that Joan Payson had once offered one million for to the New York Mets for just $50,000 and Minor League pitcher Charlie Williams.

At the time, Mays was in the second year of a two year contract at $165,000 a year. Recently he had asked the Giants for a ten year retainer at $75,000 a year in some capacity. Horace Stoneham just couldn't afford it and began to look for a team to trade Mays to. Stoneham told the press, "The Mets are the only club that could take care of him. Don (Grant) and Mrs. Payson are as much in love with Willie as I am."[21]

For Willie Mays, it was a baseball player's equivalent of a corporate golden parachute. Terms of his contract with the Mets called for a salary of $175,000 a year (presumably for two years), and after he retired, the Mets agreed to keep him as a coach for three years at $75,000 a year.

Other than sentimentality, the presence of the aging superstar in a New York Mets uniform had little impact on the team's finish in the 1972 pennant race. The Mets finished in third place in the National League East with Willie Mays hitting .267 with eight home runs in 195 at bats.

Politically speaking, 1972 was a great year for Joan Payson. Keeping in line with her family's long Republican Party heritage, Joan had contributed $80,000 to President Richard M. Nixon's reelection campaign that saw him win by a landslide over Democrat Senator George McGovern.

In 1973 the New York Mets won their second National League pennant. They won the National League's East Division title by coming out on top of one of the most mediocre Major League pennant races in history. On August 17, the Mets had been seven and a half games behind the division leading St. Louis Cardinals. But by September, every team in the division was still in the race, and by September 27 the Mets were in first place. The Mets won the division with a record of 82-79 and a winning percentage of .509, the lowest winning percentage of any pennant winner in Major League history.

The Mets entered the National League Championship Series against the heavily favored Big Red Machine of Cincinnati. Although they lost the first game at Cincinnati, the Mets prevailed to win the series three games to two.

The series was marred by a bench clearing brawl in the third game at Shea Stadium following a hard slide by Pete

Rose into Bud Harrelson in the fifth inning. When order was restored, both Rose and Harrelson remained in the game. In the bottom of the fifth with Rose playing in left field, a fan seated in the upper tier of the Shea Stadium grandstand hurled a whiskey bottle at Rose just missing his head. Then a beer can was thrown that hit Reds' Garry Nolan in the bullpen. Rose called time and began walking toward the dugout.

With the booing and trash throwing increasing by the 53,967 fans, Reds manager Sparky Anderson pulled his players off the field fearing for their safety. Then National League president Chub Feeney left his box, walked on the field and began to confer with the six-man umpiring crew. Feeney went over to the Mets dugout and warned them that the game was in jeopardy of being forfeited unless the unruly crowd in left field was brought under control. He then asked Willie Mays to be the peacemaker, go out to left field and attempt to pacify the fans.

Mets manager Yogi Berra thought it would be better if several of the Mets went, so he quickly put a peace delegation together consisting of himself, Tom Seaver, Willie Mays, Cleon Jones and Rusty Staub. The five walked out to left field and personally appealed to unruly fans to cease fire. As a calm returned to Shea Stadium, Rose once again took up his position after NYPD officers were positioned in the left field grandstand to control the heavily alcohol laced Mets fans.

As the mayhem ensued in the stadium, a stoic Bowie Kuhn, commissioner of baseball, sat in his box seat next to the Mets dugout with a NYPD officer crouched down alongside of him, taking no action. New York mayor John Lindsay, who was seated nearby also, took no action. This was the same mayor who only a few years earlier had walked through the streets of Harlem to cool a riot. Also, there was no appeal from Joan Payson or M. Donald Grant. It appeared that the commissioner, the mayor, and the owners of the Mets were not concerned that both Major League Baseball and New York City were being embarrassed on national television.

The next day in game five the Mets defeated the Reds 7-2 as pitchers Tom Seaver and Tug McGraw held the Reds to seven hits to win the 1973 National League pennant.

After the Mets had broken a 2-2 tie by scoring four runs in the fifth inning, several thousand of the 50,232 in attendance, mostly youngsters and teenagers, began working their way down to the box seat area. They filled the aisles straining to get to a position where they could run onto the field after the last out. Following the final out, over five thousand fans poured onto the field and began to tear up more than 1,200 square feet of sod. Fights broke out among the fans as they ripped up home plate and the pitcher's mound and made off with all the bases. One fan even attempted to mug Willie Mays!

When the mob had finally been cleared, the field looked like the surface of the moon. Tom Seaver remarked, "The sad part is that those fans would have done this to the field even if we had lost. I think a lot of them didn't care whether we won or not. They just wanted to rip up the field."[22]

Now the Mets were about to square off in the 1973 World Series against the defending World Champion Oakland A's. Still there was no public statement from either Joan Payson or M. Donald Grant. They left the matter of stadium safety and security to club vice president James Thompson, who assured everyone that the Mets would not be fooling around with security at Shea Stadium. For the World Series there would be 325 stadium guards and 400 NYPD officers on duty, and any acts of violence or rowdiness would be prosecuted.

In the end, all the security precautions weren't necessary as the A's defeated the Mets in seven games with the final game being played in Oakland.

By the early 1970s Joan Payson had become a heavy woman with greying blond hair but she still maintained an expressive face. With her health failing and circulatory problems, the past few years of her life she was confined to a wheelchair. However, her condition did not keep her away from games at Shea Stadium or attending Mets board of directors meetings—she just attended fewer of both.

On June 19, 1975 Joan suffered a stroke and was taken to New York Hospital. She died at 6:35 a.m. on

October 4, 1975. She was seventy-two years old. That day at Belmont Park the flag in the infield was flown at half-staff in her memory, and a Greentree Stable entry was scratched. Funeral services were held at Christ Church in Manhasset, New York prior to her interment in Maine where the family had a summer home.

In a twist of fate, Joan had become the third New York baseball figure to die within a week following the deaths of Casey Stengel and former Yankees co-owner Larry McPhail.

Less than two years after Joan's death, her seventy-nine-year-old husband Charles married again. The bride was forty-seven-year-old Virginia Kraft, associate editor of *Sports Illustrated*.

Joan Whitey Payson's will called for her 78 percent majority stock in the Mets to be divided up evenly among her husband and children. But somehow Joan's husband, Charles Payson, retained 47 percent of the stock and divided up the remaining shares among his three daughters and one son.

But only one daughter was interested in running the team—Lorinda de Roulet. At forty-five years old, Lorinda, a former Wellesley student and the mother of three children, following in her mother's footsteps, was named the Mets president. Her recently deceased husband, Vincent, had been the U. S. Ambassador to Jamaica.

But following Joan's death, the chemistry of the team's ownership had been drastically altered and the New York Mets lurched toward self-destruction under the leadership of her daughter Lorinda, her husband Charles, and M. Donald Grant.

The Mets struggled to remain competitive in 1975 and 1976, then in 1977, M. Donald Grant did the unthinkable; refusing to meet his contract demands—he traded Tom Seaver, a.k.a. "The Franchise," to the Cincinnati Reds.

Yankees owner George Steinbrenner had just given Reggie Jackson a contract calling for $2.7 million for four years. Tom Seaver, who was then making $225,000 a year felt underpaid and underappreciated. M. Donald Grant would not agree to renegotiate Seaver's contract, even calling him "an ingrate."[23]

Jack Lang, a reporter for the *Daily News*, advised Tom Seaver to take the matter to Joan Payson's daughter

Lorinda de Roulet. As the inheritor of the ball club, she was Grant's boss. So Seaver approached Lorinda, who was well aware of what he meant to the Mets and their fans. She agreed to amend Seaver's contract calling for $300,000 in 1978 and $400,000 in 1979.

But the deal fell apart after Dick Young of *The Daily News* wrote a column accusing Seaver's wife Nancy of being jealous of Nolan Ryan's wife Ruth, because Nolan was making more money than her husband Tom. When Young was questioned about the source of his information, he stated that he got the information from M. Donald Grant.

It was the last straw for Tom Seaver; he was livid that Grant had made an attack on his family and demanded to be traded. Oddly enough, when the trade of Tom Seaver to the Cincinnati Reds was announced on June 15, 1977, Dick Young endorsed it in his column.

However, M. Donald Grant was just starting to disassemble the Mets. The same day that Tom Seaver had been traded to the Reds, Dave Kingman was traded to the San Diego Padres. Two months later on August 31, Jerry Grote was traded to the Los Angeles Dodgers. Then on December 8, 1977 pitcher Jon Matlack was traded to the Texas Rangers. Then Felix Millan voluntarily left to sign with the Yokohama Whales in Japan. Others would soon go on the block including Bud Harrelsson.

Rumors were starting to fly that the Mets were for sale. At spring training in 1978 Charles Payson assured manager Joe Torre and the thirty-seven players in camp that the franchise was not up for sale. Sitting in his front row box prior to an exhibition game with St. Louis in St. Petersburg with M. Donald Grant, who was roundly booed, Charles stated in regard to his meeting with the Mets players, "I didn't say it would never be sold. I told them I wouldn't sell the team. But after I die my children can do what they want with it."[24]

With the Mets last championship team thoroughly dismantled by Grant, the team finished in last place in the National League East division in both 1977 and 1978. On November 8, 1978 Lorinda de Roulet announced that she had forced M. Donald Grant to resign as Mets board chairman after seventeen years, and that she was personally taking over. Her father Charles Payson blamed the performance of the team on Grant. It was no secret that Charles had resented Grant for years, feeling that he had too much influence over his wife Joan.

Immediately, Lorinda attempted to turn the fortunes of the Mets franchise around. She spoke at the annual black-tie New York baseball writer's dinner and received a standing ovation from the 1,400 men in attendance. Also, she led the Mets delegation to the owner's winter meeting in Orlando.

Then Lorinda attempted to sign free agent Pete Rose. She explained that the Mets were still against multiple year contracts and big numbers. "We still think the best way to help the team is through the farm system. But we do need something extra too, and that's why we made such a serious effort to sign Pete Rose."[25]

The common belief in Rose turning down Lorinda's offer has been that he wanted to be on a winning ball club more than he wanted a mega contract, so he signed with the Philadelphia Phillies who had won the National League East Division the past three years. However, what Rose may or may not have been told about the Mets front office by Reds teammate Tom Seaver could have certainly played a big part in his decision to avoid the Mets. Rose was leaving Cincinnati, where for several years he had battled an indifferent front office with general managers Bob Howsam and Dick Wagner. So he may have been leery that somewhere in the decision making process in New York, M. Donald Grant might be lurking, and consequently, he might be just jumping out of the frying pan into the fire.

When Willie Mays was elected to the Hall of Fame in January 1979, Lorida de Roulet spoke on behalf of her deceased mother at the press conference. "Mother loved him, talked about him at home. She would have loved to be here. I rather think she is watching and smiling."[26]

For several years in the 1970s as the Yankees struggled, the amazin' Mets had been the hot ticket in New York baseball. But now with the Yankees reenergized under the new ownership of George Steinbrenner and manager Billy Martin and winning pennants in the Bronx, the Mets were once again the doormat of New York baseball and the brunt of jokes. It was 1962 all over again. Both in 1977 and 1978 when the Yankees had won American League pennants, they had out drawn the Mets by over a million fans (1977: NYY 2,335,871, NYM 1,066,825) (1978: NYY 2,103,092, NYM 1,007,328).

After two cellar-dwelling seasons, Charles Payson's bank account was a lot lighter. Reportedly, the Mets had lost $1 million each of the past two years. So Charles was forcing the front office to pinch pennies in order to have operating funds. Furthermore, Charles refused to invest any more family money in the team. When daughter Lorinda de Roulet had to borrow $3 million to keep the team going, Charles refused to co-sign the bank loan.

As spring training in 1979 was coming to an end, Charles was stating that if the losses continued in the coming season, it was likely he would sell the Mets. The Mets pitching staff was weak and Charles refused to permit any free agent pitchers such as Nelson Briles to be signed, so general manager Joe McDonald was forced to add three rookies to the staff.

In 1979, for the third consecutive year, the New York Mets finished in last place in the National League East division. Only 788,905 fans went through the turnstiles of Shea Stadium and the financial losses were considerable. On November 8, 1979 Lorinda de Roulet announced that the Mets were for sale.

On January 24, 1980 controlling interest in the New York Mets was sold to Nelson Doubleday and Doubleday & Company, Inc., along with Fred Wilpon, chairman of the board for Sterling Equities, Inc. and City Investing Company, for $21 million, a record purchase price at that time for a Major League team.

In 1981 the team's new ownership announced that a New York Mets Hall of Fame would be started at Shea Stadium. A committee of broadcasters and sportswriters were asked to vote. The first two inductees into the Mets Hall of Fame were Joan Whitney Payson and Casey Stengel.

Helene Britton and National League Owners
National Baseball Hall of Fame Library, Cooperstown, NY

Roger Bresnahan. Author's Collection.

Effa Manley
National Baseball Hall of Fame Library, Cooperstown, NY

Satchel Paige. Sports Story Reprints.

Jackie Robinson. Sports Story Reprints.

Grace Comiskey
National Baseball Hall of Fame Library, Cooperstown, NY

Joan Whitney Payson
National Baseball Hall of Fame Library, Cooperstown, NY

Tom Seaver, Yogi Berra, and Jon Matlack. Sports Story Reprints.

Marge Schott, Pete Rose, and Schotzie
iamsportsimages - Steve Light

Tom & Jean Yawkey
National Baseball Hall of Fame Library, Cooperstown, NY

Linda Alvarado. Courtesy of Alvarado Construction.

Florence Dreyfuss. Courtesy of Pittsburgh Pirates.

5

JEAN R. YAWKEY

BOSTON RED SOX

Jean Remington Hollander was born on January 24, 1909 in Brooklyn, New York and grew up in the village of Freeport, Long Island. Jean never spoke about her parents. Some believe their names were Gabriel and Maybelle Hollander, and were in the parquet tile business. She had an older brother, George, a strapping 6'2" football player at Freeport High School known by the nickname "Blub."

Jean graduated from Freeport High School in 1926. She was tall, pretty, and well liked. She was the editor of the school paper, *The Student*. Jean also participated in science, drama, French, athletics, and public speaking clubs. In 1926 Jean, along with classmate James Staros, won the school's annual public speaking contest and a prize of $10 each. These extravert personality traits demonstrated by young Jean stand in stark contrast to the reserved, shy, and highly personal individual she would become in later years.

Jean's first marriage to Charlie Hiller, a star basketball player at Freeport High, was brief and ended in divorce. From the early 1930s until the 1940s, going by the name of Jean R. Hiller, she worked as a New York fashion model and sales clerk at Jay Thorpe, a fashionable women's store on West 57th Street in Manhattan. It was there that Jean first met Tom Yawkey, owner of the Boston Red Sox, when he visited the store with his first wife Elsie.

On Christmas Eve 1944 a thirty-five-year-old Jean Hiller would marry forty-one-year-old Tom Yawkey in Georgetown, South Carolina at the home of Leila and Ralph Ford. The Fords owned the general store in Georgetown and were simple folks. The couple had been hunting that day on the vast Yawkey estate, and they were married in their hunting clothes.

Following their marriage, Tom and Jean turned over the Yawkey mansion to a caretaker and moved into a small cabin they called the clubhouse. When the clubhouse burned down, they moved into a trailer. The couple had a penchant for the outdoors, and Jean drove a Jeep around the vast property. Together they hiked through the woods, hunted, and fished. Enjoying this serene life, Tom wore old clothes and had his hair cut at the local barbershop. Townsfolk would say that if you met Tom Yawkey on the street, you would never guess that he was a millionaire.

Upon the death of her husband in 1976, Jean Yawkey would succeed Tom as majority owner and president of the Boston Red Sox and become the most powerful woman in Major League Baseball history. Not only would Jean Yawkey own one of the most profitable sports franchises in the world, but also became the first woman director of The National Baseball Hall of Fame & Museum. Until her death in 1992, the Boston Red Sox would remain in the Yawkey family for fifty-nine years. While Tom Yawkey used to refer to Jean as mother, or Hiller (her name from her first marriage), to all of Boston, sportswriters, players, fans, politicians, bankers, bakers, and candlestick makers, she was known as Mrs. Yawkey, not Jean, she had no nickname.

Thomas Austin Yawkey was born in Detroit on February 21, 1903. His father, Thomas J. Austin, died when he was quite young and then his mother Augusta L. (Yawkey) Austin died in 1917. After his mother died he was taken into the home of his uncle William Hoover Yawkey, adopted and given the last name of Yawkey.

Tom Yawkey's grandfather, William Clyman Yawkey, had cultivated a huge lumber and iron ore empire. He was about to buy the Detroit Tigers but died before the deal could be consummated. So Tom Yawkey's uncle Bill bought the team. As a result, Tom Yawkey would have fond childhood memories of playing catch with Ty Cobb and having friendships with other baseball stars such as Hughie Jennings, Sam Crawford, Don Bush, and Bobby Veach.

Tom Yawkey, who was known as T.A. to his friends and the press, was raised and educated in New York City and Connecticut. He prepared for college at Yale by attending the Irving School in Tarrytown, New York.

One of the school's most famous alumni was Philadelphia Athletics and Chicago White Sox future Hall of Famer second baseman Eddie Collins. Each year the school awarded an Eddie Collins medal to the student who achieved the highest standards in academics and athletics. In both his junior and senior years Tom Yawkey was edged out of the award finishing second.

During Yawkey's junior year at the Irving School in 1919, his uncle Bill died. The estate of William Hoover Yawkey left $40 million to Tom Yawkey. But a clause in the will stated that Tom could not take possession of the money until he had reached his thirtieth birthday.

Tom Yawkey graduated from Yale's Sheffield Scientific Institute with a B.S. degree in 1925. Yawkey also played baseball at Yale. During summers while attending Yale, Yawkey worked in the family timber and mineral business working in the field with lumberjacks and miners. The experience provided Yawkey with respect for strong work ethics, and throughout his life he carried with him deep empathy for the plight of the working man.

Also in 1925, Tom Yawkey married Elsie Sparrow in grand style with a ceremony at the Ritz in New York City. Elsie was a former Miss Birmingham, a typical southern belle, charming, bubbly, and very social. She loved parties, fine silver, and linens. Tom and Elsie would live part of the year in Georgetown, South Carolina, where they would have huge parties in the Yawkey mansion on South Island. The land had been an old rice plantation just off the coast.

Then they would reside part of the year in the Pierre Hotel in New York City, where Yawkey maintained offices for his inherited timber and mining interests. But the marriage failed, and following a three year separation, the couple divorced in November 1944 at Reno, Nevada.

On December 2, 1944 Elsie remarried to a businessman by the name of Harry Dorsey Watts. A little less than a month later, Tom Yawkey would marry Jean Hiller.

Since his childhood, Tom Yawkey had a love for the game of baseball. Supposedly, Ty Cobb encouraged Yawkey to buy a Major League team with his inheritance. So on February 25, 1933, four days after his thirtieth birthday, with his inheritance legally in hand, Tom Yawkey bought the Boston Red Sox for $1.2 million.

It was the middle of the Great Depression and both the Red Sox franchise and their ballpark were in shambles, haunted by the curse of the Bambino. The Red Sox had been decimated by the incompetent operation and shabby player trades of owner and Broadway producer Harry Frazee, who ran the franchise from 1917 to 1923. It was Frazee who sold Babe Ruth to the New York Yankees in 1920 for $125,000 and a $300,000 loan from Yankee owner Jacob Ruppert using Fenway Park as collateral. As a result of Frazee's blatant neglect, the Boston Red Sox would become the doormat of the American League for a decade following his departure at the end of the 1923 season when he sold the franchise to J. A. Robert Quinn.

Between 1924 and 1932 the Red Sox would finish last in the American League seven times with a record of 477 wins and 897 loses. In five of those seasons the club would lose more than 100 games. In 1932, the year before Tom Yawkey bought the franchise, the Red Sox had finished last with a record of 43-111, and attendance had dwindled to less than 200,000.

At the time Yawkey bought the Red Sox, Fenway Park was the smallest ballpark in the Major Leagues and crumbling from neglect. In the fall of 1933 Yawkey proceeded to spend another $1.5 million refurbishing Fenway leaving little more than structural steel in the grandstand as the project began. When fire destroyed the half-finished new construction in January 1934, including the new centerfield bleachers, Yawkey rebuilt it again.

But Tom Yawkey wanted to win. He hired his hero Eddie Collins as general manager and spent $250,000 to bring Joe Cronin from Washington to manage the team. He also spent $25,000 in a trade with Cleveland for Wes Ferrell, $125,000 for Lefty Grove, and another $150,000 to acquire Jimmy Foxx, both from the Philadelphia Athletics. Almost immediately, Yawkey's spending spree started to pay dividends for the club and fans. In 1934 the Boston Red Sox finished in fourth place in the American League. It was the first season that the team had finished in the first division since winning the American League pennant in 1918.

Again in 1935, the Red Sox finished in fourth place and had two twenty game winners on their pitching staff: Wes Ferrell 25-14 and Lefty Grove 20-12. In 1938 the Red Sox finished in second place behind the pennant winning New York Yankees. Jimmy Fox won the American League batting crown with an average of .349 while hitting fifty home runs, second in the league to Hank Greenberg, who hit fifty-eight.

Meanwhile, the Red Sox began spending money to cultivate some great talent in their farm system. Second baseman Bobby Doerr would join the team in 1937 and go on to play for fourteen years in Boston, retiring after the 1951 season with 2,042 hits. In 1939 the Boston Red Sox brought up a prize rookie, Ted Williams, who hit for an average of .327 with thirty-one home runs. The following season Dom DiMaggio would be brought up joining Ted Williams and Doc Cramer to give the Boston Red Sox one of the finest outfields in the Major Leagues in the 1940 season.

Despite a great season by Ted Williams in 1941 that saw him finish with a batting average of .406, lead the league with thirty-seven home runs, but fall short of the triple crown by five RBIs (Ted Williams 120, Joe DiMaggio 125), the Red Sox finished in second place, seventeen games behind the New York Yankees as Joe DiMaggio's monumental fifty-six game hitting streak fueled a rousing Yankee comeback to take the pennant.

Tom Yawkey became a quintessential Red Sox fan, and one of the grounds crew put his initials on the scoreboard at Fenway Park in Morse code. Yawkey kept a locker in the clubhouse, and sometimes when the Red Sox were on the road, he would picnic with his first wife Elsie on the outfield grass at Fenway. He also reserved uniform number 44 for himself, and when the team was traveling he would don his Red Sox uniform play pepper and take batting practice with the grounds crew, having the clubhouse men pitch to him. It was the perfect baseball fantasy that any fan would have relished.

When Tom Yawkey married Jean, he discovered that she too had a huge passion for baseball. She became the perfect mate for such a fanatic. Charlie Wagner, who served as a longtime member of the Red Sox organization as both a pitcher (1938-1942, 1946) and scout, stated, "Mr. Yawkey and Mrs. Yawkey were both out of the same clip. The heart of the man and the heart of the woman were the same."[1] Jean Yawkey had even played a little ball. On August 17, 1942 Jean played in the 2nd Annual Ladies Baseball Game at the Madstone Club at East Hampton, Long Island.

Although Tom and first wife Elsie had adopted a daughter Julia in 1936, he and Jean had no children. The Red Sox became Tom and Jean Yawkey's family.

Almost until the day she died, Jean Yawkey attended all the Red Sox home games at Fenway Park. She could be found seated in her rooftop box situated slightly on the third base side and kept score of every game in a set of custom-bound score cards, while chain smoking and sipping martinis.

While Tom attended all the games too, the Yawkey's maintained his and hers rooftop boxes. Tom Yawkey had a keen sense of humor, and he liked to sit at games with his cronies, drinking, cussing, and carousing. Tom had his own private bar in Fenway Park, and it was rumored that he drank a bottle of whiskey per day. But the more refined Jean preferred to sit in her box alone or with close friends or the wives of Tom's buddies. In the late 1940s when Major League Baseball teams still traveled by train, Jean

Yawkey would take at least one western trip with the team each season.

Both Tom and Jean Yawkey were considered very good people to work for. Every year, every worker got a bonus and two weeks off at Christmas in addition to their regular earned vacation pay. Jean Yawkey would adopt the management style of her husband and continue his legacy following his death. She, like Tom, was visible around the Red Sox office; she cared about the personal lives of her employees. Although she was somewhat shy, Jean Yawkey knew everyone's name in the front office and knew what they did.

Owning the Boston Red Sox was more like a hobby for Tom Yawkey than a business. In the 1970s he told a reporter that over the years he had pumped more than $10 million of his own money into the Red Sox in order to keep them going. In the early years that Tom Yawkey owned the team he would invite many of his players to visit him in South Carolina in the off-season to hunt and fish on his vast plantation. Star-struck, Tom Yawkey had a habit of doting on his most talented players; in the 1940s and 50s it was Ted Williams, and Carl Yastrzemski in the 1960s and 70s. They, like all his star players, were paid well, and he rarely, if ever, cut their salaries following sub-par season performances. In fact, in 1947 Ted Williams signed a contract calling for $75,000. At the time, it was said to be the second highest contract in Major League history to Babe Ruth's $80,000.

In return for all his generosity, Tom Yawkey's players would only win three pennants for him and no World Series title in forty-four years of ownership. Yawkey's Red Sox lost the World Series to the St. Louis Cardinals in 1946 and 1967, and lost the 1975 World Series to the Cincinnati Reds. Also in 1948, the Red Sox lost a league championship playoff game to the Cleveland Indians. Then in 1949 the Red Sox came into Yankee Stadium with a one game lead with two games to go and lost the American League pennant on the final day of the season to the Yankees.

Although Tom Yawkey was a charitable man who gave money to worthy causes without announcements and was a generous employer, there was a dark side to his personality when it came to race. Following World War Two, Major League Baseball cautiously began to move away from its edict of white players only as Major League owners like Branch Rickey and Bill Veeck, Jr. made overtures that they would like to integrate Major League Baseball by signing Negro Leagues players. In 1945 Tom Yawkey turned down a chance to sign Jackie Robinson. In April Boston City councilor Isadore Muchnick threatened to take away the Red Sox permit to play Sunday games if they didn't take a look at a few black players. So one afternoon, Jackie Robinson, Marvin Williams, and Sam Jethroe, players signed by Negro Leagues teams, were given tryouts at Fenway Park. The story has it that Tom Yawkey and general manager Eddie Collins were both standing in the back of the park watching the players when Yawkey allegedly said, "All right get those niggers out of the ballpark."[2] For years Jackie Robinson branded Yawkey as a racist.

In 1946 Tom Yawkey, along with Larry MacPhail of the New York Yankees, Sam Breadon of the St. Louis Cardinals, and Phil Wrigley of the Chicago Cubs, was a member of Major League Baseball's steering committee and charged with presenting a report to owners on the key issues facing the game. Aware of the fact that Branch Rickey of the Dodgers had signed Jackie Robinson and was planning to bring him up to the majors as early as the following season; the committee addressed the integration issue by issuing a negative report on the possible benefits. According to the committee report, the integration of Major League Baseball would possibly lessen the value of every Major League franchise. It was the opinion of the committee that the supply of qualified black players was small and that most of the players in the Negro Leagues didn't receive adequate training in the game's fundamentals. Furthermore, signing black players would harm the Negro Leagues owners by putting hundreds of black players out of work and take money from white team owners who rented their ballparks to Negro Leagues teams.

Even though circuits in the Deep South, such as the Texas League, began to sign black players in 1952, it wasn't until 1959, thirteen years after Jackie Robinson broke the color line in Major League Baseball, that the Boston Red Sox became the last team in the Majors to integrate its Major League roster.

Although Tom Yawkey had some very talented players in the 1940s, 50s, and early 60s, part of the reason that he could not mount a serious challenge to the New York Yankees dynasty of the era is that, instead of surrounding himself with a circle of knowledgeable sportsman with deep baseball knowledge and a keen business sense to run his team, Tom Yawkey surrounded himself with cronies and drinking buddies, men he felt more comfortable in the presence of. His choices of confidants and friends ultimately affected the Red Sox's ability to win.

The charitable side of Tom Yawkey and his wife Jean was considerable. In the South, Yawkey carried out extensive development work to provide feeding and resting ground for migratory birds and other wild life. He also provided the funding for a hospital wing to Georgetown Memorial Hospital and built a church and gave extensive support to Tara Hall—a home for boys. Yawkey was good to the people around Georgetown; he gave them jobs and helped them through tough times. At Christmas time, he and Jean would load a truck with toys on Christmas morning and distribute them playing Santa Claus.

In the 1930s Tom Yawkey even financed a bordello for Georgetown, setting up the Sunset Lounge, which became internationally famous. According to one resident, "Go to Europe and say "Sunset Lounge" and the person you'd be talking to would say Georgetown, South Carolina."[3] Ms. Hazel Weiss was the madam of the Sunset. She was said to have ran the establishment with an iron hand and had tight control over her girls. She never allowed them to go into town in shorts and didn't allow drunks or rough characters in her house. She always paid her bills on time. Some townsfolk remember that the Boston Red Sox would visit the Sunset Lounge each spring on their way to spring training in Florida. The Sunset Lounge was closed by the sheriff in 1969.

It is not known what Elsie Yawkey thought about the Sunset Lounge. However, supposedly, Tom Yawkey drove

Jean there one time and she was furious. Nonetheless, Jean Yawkey was known to support whatever her husband did.

But both Tom and Jean Yawkey are best remembered for their support of the Jimmy Fund. The mission of the Jimmy Fund is that it supports Boston's Dana-Farber Cancer Institute, raising funds for adult and pediatric cancer care and research to improve the chances of survival for cancer patients around the world.

It was actually the Boston Braves that helped launch the charity in 1948 in a national radio broadcast. Then Lou Perini, the Braves owner, kept the team involved for the next few years with player appearances and radio appeals during games. The money raised during this time helped finance the building in 1952 of a state-of-the-art facility for research and patient care. But in 1953, with declining attendance, the Braves franchise relocated to Milwaukee. Before leaving Boston, Lou Perini asked Red Sox owner Tom Yawkey to continue the work with the charity.

On April 10, 1953 Tom Yawkey announced that the Red Sox would adopt the Jimmy Fund as the team's official charity. Quietly over the next forty years, both Tom and Jean Yawkey, through their commitment, made the Jimmy Fund a household name in New England. Tom Yawkey served as the fund's president and board chairman, and encouraged his players to visit the children being treated in the Jimmy Fund Clinic and to attend fund raisers, golf tournaments, and other events. He also brought in teams to play exhibition games with the Red Sox and then gave the proceeds to the charity. Although Tom Yawkey had banned advertising in Fenway Park starting in the 1950s, he made an exception for the Jimmy Fund, allowing a huge Jimmy Fund sign to be installed on the right field roof above the club's retired numbers.

Upon the death of her husband in 1976, Jean Yawkey continued the Red Sox longtime association with the Jimmy Fund-Dana Farber Cancer Institute, serving as a trustee and chairman of the board. The relationship between the Jimmy Fund and the Boston Red Sox continues to exist to the present day and represents one of the most remarkable partnerships between a team and a charity in the history of professional sports. Over the years, Tom and Jean Yawkey raised and donated millions of dollars to support the fund.

By the late 1960s Tom Yawkey had become reclusive and was rarely seen in public. When the season began, he would not arrive in Boston until June, checking-in unceremoniously into his suite on the sixteenth floor at the Ritz-Carlton, overlooking the Charles. Tom and Jean didn't socialize much. Following games accompanied by players, they would return to the Ritz and order from room service. Tom didn't like putting on a tie and going out to a restaurant.

Now at Fenway Park, Tom Yawkey would often sit by himself in his private box watching the game, sometimes simultaneously listening to a game in another city. Still on occasion in the afternoon before a night game, he would go out on the field accompanied by the clubhouse attendants and the bat boy, and they would all take batting practice.

Some people wondered why Tom Yawkey didn't hire Ted Williams as manager when he retired following the 1960 season. The reason was simple—while Tom and Ted were great friends, Williams didn't fit into Yawkey's idea of a nightly drinking buddy. They were just too different away from the ballpark.

In 1966 the Red Sox finished in ninth place, twenty-six games behind the pennant winning Baltimore Orioles. Going into the 1967 season they were considered to have a 100-to-1 shot to win the American League pennant. However, there was a sudden resurgence in the Red Sox fueled by Jim Lonborg, who led American League pitchers with a record of 22-9, and Carl Yastrzemski, who won a Triple Crown with a batting average of .326, 44 home runs and 121 RBIs.

Going into the final week of the season, Boston was in the thick of a tight four team race for the pennant with the Chicago White Sox, Detroit Tigers, and Minnesota Twins. All four teams had been unable to gain control of the race. The Red Sox won the 1967 pennant on the final day of the season by one game when Jim Lonborg defeated Dean Chance of the Twins before a capacity crowd at Fenway

Park, while the Tigers split a doubleheader with the California Angels.

At the advice of his doctor, Tom Yawkey quit drinking in 1966, but still by 1967 his health started to rapidly degenerate. He would live on for nine more years and see his Red Sox lose a dramatic seven game World Series to Cincinnati's Big Red Machine in 1975. But by then Yawkey was suffering from leukemia and about a year later at 4:20 p.m. on July 9, 1976, he died at New England Baptist Hospital.

The death of her husband was absolutely devastating to Jean Yawkey. She experienced sleepless nights and alternating emotional bouts of anger and despair. The only person she would permit to console her was Red Sox general manager Haywood Sullivan. Night after night, Sullivan went to the Ritz and sat with Jean all night long. One unnamed source stated that, "Sully was the fair haired boy. He was like their son."[4]

Haywood Sullivan was a backup catcher for the Boston Red Sox and Kansas City Athletics from 1955 to 1963 playing in 312 games with a lifetime batting average of . 226. In the 1960s, Sullivan nurtured a sort of father-son relationship with Tom Yawkey over many dinners that eventually resulted in him being named director of player operations.

On August 21, 1976 Mrs. Jean Yawkey was named as Tom Yawkey's successor as president of the Boston Red Sox. At the time, Jean Yawkey, overwhelmed with grief, didn't think that she could continue her involvement with the Red Sox other than in a very minor capacity. Her initial inclination was to turn the franchise over to those who could run the team best. For three decades her role had been that of the woman behind the man. Now she was suddenly cast into the limelight and expected to make all the executive decisions. It was a task she was unsure about. So on July 9, 1977 in New York City, the Board of Executors for the Yawkey estate, without Jean being in attendance, decided to divest the estate's interest in the Boston Red Sox.

But with the franchise in turmoil, Jean Yawkey had second thoughts. She had a sudden awareness of the

Yawkey/Red Sox legacy that she was part of and decided that she wanted to be a limited partner with no voting power.

A local group, which included Haywood Sullivan and Edward G. (Buddy) LeRoux, a former Red Sox and Boston Celtics trainer and for several years manager of the New England Rehabilitation Hospital in Woburn, made a bid of $15 million for the franchise. Including Jean Yawkey, the group also had seven limited partners. Although there were higher bids, the Yawkey trust accepted the Sullivan-LeRoux bid.

In actuality, Sullivan and LeRoux were attempting to acquire 52 percent of the franchise without any substantial assets or collateral. While Buddy LeRoux submitted a net worth statement to the bank of $4.7 million including $4 million in real estate ownership, Haywood Sullivan had no major holdings and could only pledge his Canton home to the bank.

Both Sullivan and LeRoux were only investing $100,000 each of their own money, while the limited partners invested $500,000 per unit for the thirty shares with Jean Yawkey putting up $3 million for six shares. Most of the money being used to purchase the franchise, $8 million, was being borrowed from the State Street Bank & Trust Company and that came with stipulations.

For one, the bank mandated that the player payroll could not increase more than 10 percent in any one year and some player contracts would be subject to bank approval. This clause got the attention of the Major League Baseball Players Association head Marvin Miller, who announced that he would challenge the clause if the sale went through. Also, the bank laid claim to the franchise media revenue and Fenway Park as collateral. If the new owners went into default, the team would be run by the bank prompting some observers to refer to the team as the State Street Red Sox.

There were even questions being raised about the legality of Jean Yawkey's dual role in the sale of the Red Sox as a seller on one side and limited partner on the other side. A lot of probate lawyers were of the opinion that for an executrix to buy one of her own assets would require court approval.

The purchase of the Red Sox required approval from ten of the thirteen other American League team owners. Some owners were worried that the Sullivan-LeRoux group, having to pay back $1.3 million a year for the next seven years to the bank, lacked proper working capital and might not be able to keep the team going in hard financial times. Tom Yawkey had the club free and clear and the franchise was free of financial burden. Furthermore, the fact that Sullivan and LeRoux were investing $100,000 of their own money raised the eyebrows of some owners. The American League owners met on November 3, 1977 and declined to approve the sale coming to the decision that the price was too low.

So the potential buyers regrouped. This time Jean Yawkey came to the rescue and entered the deal as a general partner with voting power along with Haywood Sullivan and Buddy LeRoux. She brought the Fenway Park real estate into the deal with her that had a value of $5.5 million. The general partners, including Jean Yawkey, put up $1 million more each and the limited partners that included concession company mogul H. M. Stevens, former Boston Celtics star Frank Ramsey, Rodgers Badgett (a Kentucky coal mining executive), Arthur R. Pappas (the new team physician), Albert F. Curran (the Red Sox legal counsel), Harold Alfond (president of Dexter Shoe Company of Boston), Thomas Di Benedetto (an investment broker), and Ernest Dade (a retired Winchester businessman), added more money thereby increasing the purchase price to $20.5 million. The restructured bid offset the previous high bid of $18,750,000 submitted by the A-T-O Corporation of Ohio. This time the American League approved the deal.

However, from the start, the partnership between the major shareholders, Yawkey, Sullivan, and LeRoux, would be filled with dissension. Haywood Sullivan had borrowed his additional $1 million from Jean Yawkey to buy his shares of the Red Sox. The loan was troublesome to Buddy LeRoux as he felt that it made Sullivan too beholden to Jean Yawkey.

By 1977 Major League Baseball had changed dramatically and the free agent era had begun. Jean Yawkey and Haywood Sullivan were content to run the ball club like Tom Yawkey had by not being overly concerned if they lost money. However, Buddy LeRoux had promised some of the limited partners a return on their investment. LeRoux and Sullivan battled frequently on policy, while LeRoux was regularly out-voted 2-1 with Jean Yawkey siding with Sullivan.

In order to make money on his Red Sox investment, Buddy LeRoux advanced the management philosophy of fielding a team of young players making the Major League minimum salary. When the ability to declare themselves as free agents arrived the year before, LeRoux wanted to trade them and reset the free agent clock with a group of new young players. LeRoux also wanted to demolish Fenway Park and build a 70,000 seat stadium in Foxboro. He was keenly aware of new ballparks built in National League cities in the past few years, such as in Cincinnati, Pittsburgh, and Philadelphia, attracting record attendance each season.

Although Jean Yawkey felt uncomfortable in the spotlight, she was appalled by LeRoux's cheesy cost-cutting plan. She was truly passionate about her love for the Boston Red Sox and was not going to allow the club to become a later day version of the St. Louis Browns or Philadelphia Athletics. It was Jean Yawkey's philosophy as had been her husbands, that owning a Major League team was about winning and counting the cost of winning later.

Circumstances evolved in the Red Sox organization that made it so it was Jean Yawkey who approved major decisions. It was she who approved the firing of general manager Dick O'Connell in 1977. On October 24, 1977, ten days before approval of the sale of the team was scheduled, in order to pave the way for Sullivan and LeRoux, Jean Yawkey and another executor of the Yawkey Will, Joseph LeCour, a lawyer and accountant from New York, fired general manager Dick O'Connell and two of his assistants, John Claiborne and Gene Kirby.

O'Connell had been general manager under Tom Yawkey and had been selected as *The Sporting News*

Executive of the Year in 1967 and 1975. In all, he had served for thirty-one years in the Red Sox organization. When he was fired, O'Connell was handed an envelope with a message inside telling him to clean out his desk. Under Tom Yawkey, O'Connell had acted as the club's chief executive. However, he and Jean Yawkey had never had a very cordial relationship.

The firing of O'Connell and his assistants was controversial with the fans and press. In the past eleven years with O'Connell directing operations, the Red Sox had averaged attendance of 1.72 million fans a year. It had been his assistant general manager John Claiborne that had made the Red Sox competitive, beating down agents and signing such players as Rick Burleson, Carlton Fisk, and Fred Lynn to long-term contracts at less than an exorbitant price. Furthermore, Gene Kirby had arguably negotiated the best media contract for the Boston Red Sox in the Major Leagues.

Mike Barnicle of the *Boston Globe* had been quite critical of the sale of the Red Sox, stating that the financial arrangements were about the same as those involved in putting together a forty-eight-month car loan. In regard to the firing of Dick O'Connell, Barnicle wrote, "Jean Yawkey owning the ball club and Joe LaCour, being her principal messenger, are entitled to do anything they want. Except treating the fans arrogantly, taking us for granted. On Monday, the two of them did a poor imitation of the oil lobby and the big insurance companies. LaCour and the widow Yawkey told us in effect, we do not care what you fans think, what you, fans feel or how much you care. Tough Bananas."[5]

Jean Yawkey never blinked at the public criticism of her decisions. Dick O'Connell was replaced by Haywood Sullivan, who now held the title of executive vice president/general manager. Haywood Sullivan would remain general manager until 1984 when he appointed Lou Gorman.

Haywood Sullivan's first year as GM in 1978 was controversial. The Red Sox held a fourteen-game lead over the New York Yankees on July 17. But they let their lead dwindle away and ultimately found themselves in a one game playoff with the New York Yankees for the American League pennant, which was decided by Bucky Dent's three-run home run in the seventh inning.

More controversy would surround the tenure of Sullivan as the Red Sox general manager. One of the more notable events was when he used a second round choice to pick his son in the annual Major League draft. Catcher Marc Sullivan became a career .186 hitter playing in parts of five seasons with the Red Sox (1982, 1984-1987).

It isn't clear if it was Jean Yawkey or Haywood Sullivan, or both, who finally approved the Red Sox to part ways with former rookie of the year Fred Lynn and future Hall of Fame catcher Carlton Fisk following the 1980 season. It all seemed like a fiasco—unbelievable.

Carlton Fisk's five-year contract had expired. All season long Fisk and Sullivan had been at odds on a new contract. Under the basic agreement that existed with the Major League Baseball Players Association, the Red Sox had to offer a renewal of the contract on or before December 20 for the following year. If that did not occur, Fisk would become a free agent. The story is that someone in the Red Sox front office forgot to mail contracts to both Fisk and Fred Lynn missing the deadline by one day. The fact is, no contracts were ever mailed.

Consequently, the Player's Association filed for free agency for both players. In late January 1981 an arbitration hearing was held for Fisk, and the Red Sox had no case to present. Fisk was subsequently granted free agency and signed a multi-million dollar contract with the Chicago White Sox. During the 1981 season when the White Sox played the Red Sox, Fisk wore a tee shirt that read, "HAYWOOD AND BUDDY SUCK."[6]

In the matter of Fred Lynn, the California Angels were offering him a five-year, guaranteed contract. Lynn was a former University of Southern California star and was eager to return home. So Lynn's agent Jerry Kapstein talked to the Red Sox, and they were eager to cut him loose. So Lynn was traded to the Angels for three players, Frank Tanana, Jim Dorsey, and Joe Rudi, and the arbitrator had one less case to handle.

By 1980 Jean Yawkey and Buddy LeRoux could not stand the sight of each other. There were reports that Jean would not get out of the car at Fenway Park if she knew Buddy was in the facility.

On the afternoon of June 6, 1983 Buddy LeRoux, backed by limited partners Al Curran and Rodgers Badgett, arrived at Fenway Pak and announced to reporters that the limited partners had voted to make him the man in charge of the Red Sox. In short, LeRoux was declaring that the partnership had been amended by virtue of Curran, Badgett, and himself having majority control of limited shares. LeRoux asserted that he was now the sole managing general partner, and he was taking control of the team. Furthermore, he was bringing back Dick O'Connell to replace Haywood Sullivan as general manager.

Haywood Sullivan was at that session; he and John Harrington, representing Jean Yawkey, spoke to the press: "Mrs. Yawkey and I feel that it is illegal, invalid and above all not effective," said Sullivan of LeRoux's action. "I'm still in charge. The partnership has not been changed. We don't recognize Buddy's action."[7] It was apparent that legal action was eminent.

Buddy LeRoux seemed smarmy with greed from the recent denial of his attempt to sell his 42 percent of the team. It had been reported that LeRoux had been offered $20 million for his forty-two shares by Boston television executive David Mugar and former Red Sox slugger Carl Yastrzemski. The offer was withdrawn after Jean Yawkey and Haywood Sullivan blocked the bid by a 2-1 vote.

Jean Yawkey had stopped talking to Buddy LeRoux in the fall of 1982 when he authorized an eleven-page memo critical of her. Following the release of the memo to the limited partners, the general partners met and Jean jumped all over LeRoux. In regard to the memo, Jean Yawkey remarked, "It was insulting. I have lost a great deal of respect for him (LeRoux) over the past couple of years."[8]

The timing of Buddy LeRoux's attempted coup was controversial and ill-advised—June 6 was "Tony C. Night" at Fenway Park. The event had been organized by the ball club with members of the 1967 Red Sox to honor fallen star and teammate Tony Conigliaro. LeRoux's actions went over like a lead balloon with the press and fans, who viewed his timing in the matter as bush league in turning a night to remember a Red Sox hero into a three ring circus.

Tony Conigliaro came up to the Boston Red Sox in 1964 and had an outstanding rookie season hitting for an average of .290 with twenty-four home runs. The following season in 1965 he led the American League with thirty-two home runs. On August 8, 1967 as the Red Sox were marching toward the American League pennant, California Angels pitcher Jack Hamilton beaned Conigliaro. He missed the rest of the season and the next suffering from blurred vision. He returned to the Red Sox in 1969, and while virtually seeing out of one eye, hit twenty home runs. Following an outstanding season in 1970 when he hit a career high of thirty-six home runs; he was traded to the Angels. Once again suffering a vision disability, he lasted only seventy-four games and retired. In 1975 Conigliaro attempted to make a comeback with the Red Sox, but after twenty-one games was hitting just .123. In 1980 he had a heart attack, entered into a coma, and emerged brain damaged. He died in 1990 at the age of forty-five from pneumonia and kidney failure.

Jean Yawkey boldly stood up to Buddy LeRoux. She allied herself with Haywood Sullivan, went to Superior Court, and won control of the team. The judge in the case, James P. Lynch, Jr., permanently enjoined LeRoux from any future attempt to take control of the team as managing general partner. On camera, a Boston TV sportscaster asked Jean if she was happy with the court's decision. The quintessential lady of low public profile replied with a two-word answer, "I am."[9]

In 1987 Jean bought-out Buddy LeRoux's partnership for $7 million giving her two of three general partner votes. Jean Yawkey and Haywood Sullivan formed the JRY Corporation to run the Red Sox, and John Harrington was appointed president.

Buddy LeRoux had never cared for John Harrington, didn't like working with him, and once blocked an attempt by Jean Yawkey to donate a limited partner share to him. According to Harrington, LeRoux had once called him a "Johnny Come Lately."[10]

John Harrington was the son of a Jamaica Plain MBTA mechanic. When the Red Sox won the 1967 American League pennant, Harrington was not even able to buy a ticket to the deciding game in the World Series. Instead, he and his family circled Fenway Park in their car listening to the game on the radio.

When Joe Cronin (one of four Red Sox to have their number retired) became president of the American League in 1970, he moved the league office from New York to Boston and hired Harrington as an accountant. He was a former accounting professor at Boston College. When Cronin retired in 1973, the league office was moved back to New York, and Harrington was out of a job. But Cronin got Haywood Sullivan to hire him as an assistant treasurer.

In the late 1970s Harrington went to work for Massachusetts governor Edward F. King in the office of administration and finance. When King lost the re-election, Harrington was out of work again. This time, Jean Yawkey came to his rescue. She had moved all of her business and foundation offices to Boston, and she hired Harrington as an assistant to Joseph LeCour, who ran the business. When LeCour died a year later, Harrington became the top man in the business.

Harrington and his wife Maureen had become close companions of Jean Yawkey. Instead of taking her sandwich and martini up to her box, Jean now ate with Harrington in the press dining room at Fenway Park. Thanks to Jean's generosity, Harrington now had limited partnership interest in the team valued at $5 million without ever putting up a dime of his own money.

In the structure of the JRY Corporation, Jean owned two of the three general partner shares of the Red Sox, thereby providing her with a 2-1 voting edge over partner Sullivan on any important decisions. There were still seven limited partners who would share in the team's profits but not have voting power. When Haywood Sullivan demanded an equal voice in team operations, it angered Jean so much that she refused to be in the same room with him. Suddenly, the tight friendship between the two was alienated.

Since the attempt by Buddy LeRoux to take over the Red Sox, Jean Yawkey was evolving as an executive. Although she listened to advice and did a lot of delegating, she was not afraid to make decisions. She had become a lot stronger than when she inherited the team. Some said that her management style was somewhere between feisty and vindictive. According to a man who knew her well in Georgetown, South Carolina, "If you displease her, you never get a second chance."[11]

In 1984 Jean Yawkey was named as a director to the National Baseball Hall of Fame & Museum. She became the first female elected to the board. Since the time Jean was named to the Hall of Fame board, Jane Forbes Clark was appointed in 1992 and was named Chairman of the Board of Directors in 2000.

Jean Yawkey would become a major contributor of the museum by donating two wings to the building and commissioning an elegant basswood, life-size statue of Ted Williams by Armand LaMontagne. A year earlier LaMontague had done a similar statue of Babe Ruth, and it was the opinion of Jean that Ted Williams was also deserving of such a likeness. Williams was present at the unveiling in 1985 and was delighted.

In 1989 Jean's favorite Red Sox player, Carl Yastrzemski, was inducted into the Hall of Fame, so she traveled to Cooperstown for the ceremony. Sitting on the veranda of the Otsega Hotel in a rocking chair, she opened up in a rare public display of her feelings and told how she felt about Yaz as a ball player. "You know what I wish young people would remember when they think of Carl? He never had the natural talent Ted (Williams) had, and wasn't as graceful. But oh how he worked to make himself a good hitter, to make himself a good fielder, a good runner, a good thrower. He worked to make himself as good as he was, and then you know what? He kept working, even after he had achieved all his goals. On the last day of his career he was still trying as hard as he could!"[12]

In the 1986 World Series the Boston Red Sox came within a pitch of winning that long elusive World Championship—twice. The Red Sox won the first two games of the series at Shea Stadium, and then the New

York Mets won the next two at Fenway Park. In game five Bruce Hurst scattered ten hits to beat the Mets for the second time and give the Red Sox a three games to two lead in the series.

Game six saw the Red Sox and Mets battle to a 3-3 tie through nine innings. Then in the top of the tenth inning the Red Sox scored two runs to take a 5-3 lead and put the Mets on the brink of elimination. As the Mets came to bat in the bottom of the tenth, baseball commissioner Peter Ueberroth escorted Jean Yawkey from her seat in the stands into the Boston locker room feeling pretty confident that he would be presenting the championship trophy to the Red Sox.

According to Bob Costas of NBC, who had gone to the locker room for the anticipated celebration, "A TV platform had been set up in the middle of the Sox locker room. The championship trophy was covered with some kind of plastic and sitting on a table on the platform. The players' lockers were all covered with plastic and taped shut."[13]

The first two Mets went down to start the bottom of the tenth inning. Now the Boston Red Sox were just one out away from their first World Championship since 1918. Jean Yawkey, Peter Ueberroth, Bob Costas, and everyone were watching the game on the monitor in the Boston locker room. Then all at once, Gary Carter, Kevin Mitchell, and Ray Knight hit successive singles off Red Sox reliever Calvin Schiraldi to score a run. Twice the Mets had been one strike away from going down. Bob Stanley relieved Schiraldi and proceeded to uncork a wild pitch allowing the tying run to score. Then Mookie Wilson followed with a slow roller down the first base line that went through the legs of first baseman Bill Buckner allowing a run to score giving the Mets a 6-5 victory.

All during the Mets's comeback Jean Yawkey, standing with Peter Ueberroth, never said a word; she just looked up at the ceiling as the ball went through Buckner's legs. Immediately, workers started packing up the championship trophy and pulling down the plastic on the players' lockers. Jean Yawkey never uttered a complaint. Ueberroth extended his arm to her and they both walked out.

It's not really known what Jean would have said that evening had she been fortunate to have been presented the championship trophy, but it is fairly safe to assume that she would have said this if for my late husband.

The following evening at Shea Stadium the Mets overcame a 3-0 deficit through five and a half innings to beat the Red Sox 8-5 and capture the 1986 World Series title. It was the fourth time that Jean Yawkey had seen her team lose the World Series in seven games (1946, 1967, 1975, and 1986). For Jean, like all of the other Red Sox fans, it was once again a case of wait until next year.

Troubles for Haywood Sullivan with Jean Yawkey began following the 1980 season when he sided with Buddy LeRoux to fire manager Don Zimmer against her wishes. Sullivan publicly stated, "That decision cost me."[14] Then, for some reason, the loss to the New York Mets in the 1986 World Series further strained the relationship between Jean Yawkey and Sullivan. The two hardly spoke for the final few years of her life. Now Jean and Sullivan constantly clashed over the hiring and firing of managers, free agent signings, and other matters. Jean began to view Sullivan's dissention as disloyalty. The feud even filtered down to the Fenway Park groundskeepers and clubhouse workers, who were forced to choose in their loyalty to either Jean Yawkey or Haywood Sullivan. In 1989 Sullivan's title was changed from "chief executive officer and chief operating officer" to simply "owner and general partner."

In 1988 Jean Yawkey unabashedly approved the firing of the 1986 American League manager of the year, John McNamara, three days after the All-Star break. It was July 14 when McNamara received the news that he had been canned. At that time he was dressing in his office for a game against the Kansas City Royals at Fenway Park. At that point in the season, McNamara had piloted the Red Sox to a 43-42 record. Haywood Sullivan publically opposed the firing and was appalled at the timing. John McNamara was more philosophical about it stating upon his dismissal, "You know baseball's Golden Rule. Whoever has the gold, rules."[15]

McNamara was replaced by Coach Joe Morgan, and the Red Sox got hot following the break winning their first twelve games. Also, between June 24 and August 14, led by Roger Clemens, Bruce Hurst, Wade Boggs, Mike Greenwell, and Dwight Evans, the Red Sox won twenty-four straight home games. At the end of the 1988 season the Red Sox had squeaked by Detroit by one game to win the 1988 American League East division title. The press was stating that Joe Morgan was a great story, but Mrs. Yawkey would decide if it was going to be a short story.

As Jean Yawkey started to advance in age, John Harrington's influence in the Red Sox organization was increasing, and he wanted more than ever for the Red Sox to win their first World Championship since 1918. Harrington convinced Jean to spend bundles of money to acquire marginal free agents to go along with the team's established stars such as Roger Clemens, Wade Boggs and Mike Greenwell, a plan that didn't go over well with Haywood Sullivan, who was attempting to cut team expenses, including payroll.

At the end of the 1990 season, which saw the Red Sox win the America League East Division, both Haywood Sullivan and Manager Joe Morgan wanted to release long-time fan favorite Dwight Evans. Evans, who the fans called "Dewey," had been one of the premier right fielders in the Major Leagues for two decades. He had played for the Red Sox for nineteen years, hit 379 career home runs, had 2446 hits, and won eight gold gloves. But by 1990 age and a back injury had slowed him down and Evans hit for an average of .249. Manager Morgan was also concerned that Evans was becoming a discipline problem in addition to his declining statistics. During the 1990 season Evans had bolted a team flight and booked a private flight with Roger Clemens and had also missed an important charity event appearance. Rather than sign Evans as a DH (designated hitter) for the 1991 season at $1.5 million, Sullivan and Morgan got Jean Yawkey's approval to buy him out for $200,000.

Sullivan was pleased, believing that he had cut his payroll, but much to his displeasure, in December 1990 with Jean's approval, Harrington signed three free agents to multi-million dollar contracts: Jack Clark (2 years, $2,900,000 per year), Danny Darwin (4 years, $2,975,000 average per year), and Matt Young (2 years, $2,266,667 per year).

By early August 1991 the Red Sox had fallen into fourth place, eleven games behind the Toronto Blue Jays in the American League East. It appeared that the Red Sox had tanked and WBCN held a mock on-the-air funeral for the team. Then the Red Sox started to rally and moved into third place, five and a half games back. But, in the end, the Red Sox finished a disappointing second place, seven games behind Toronto.

Those costly free agents didn't help the Red Sox much in the 1991 season. Jack Clark hit twenty-eight home runs, but only hit for an average of .249. Danny Darwin finished with a record of 3-6 with a 5.16 ERA, and Matt Young, whom the press declared was psychologically incapable of throwing the ball to first base, earned his $2.4 million by finishing with a record of 3-7 with an ERA of 5.18. Nonetheless, Jean Yawkey's solution to the Red Sox 1991 dilemma was to fire manager Joe Morgan.

During the final five years of her life, Jean Yawkey made Boston her full-time home; she sold the last acreage of the magnificent Yawkey plantation in South Carolina and moved year round into the Four Seasons Hotel next to the public garden. She was eating out now a lot more than when she was married to Tom. She was also taking long solitary walks from the Four Seasons up Newbuy Street and, on nice days, along the river.

Recognition was finally coming her way. On Sunday May 15, 1988, the Boston Pops celebrated Jean Yawkey with "Night at the Pops." Two thousand people were in attendance, including all the Red Sox managers, administrators, and all the players and their wives. Curt Gowdy read "Casey at the Bat," and everyone sang "Take Me Out to the Ball Game." Jean was presented with the first Jean R. Yawkey Award established to honor a woman each year who embodies outstanding leadership qualities and significantly contributes to New England's health and community spirit. All the proceeds from the evening were donated to charities.

The following year, the second award was presented to Kitty Dukakis, wife of former Massachusetts Governor and 1988 Democratic presidential candidate Michael Dukakis.

For a person with such a high public profile, Jean Yawkey never gave interviews and only on occasion spoke with the press. From the time she became a co-owner and general partner in the ball club with Haywood Sullivan and Buddy LeRoux in 1978, she never held a formal press conference, nor granted any interviews. When her husband Tom was inducted posthumously into the Baseball Hall of Fame in 1980, she had no public comment.

As Jean approached her 80s, she developed a slight hearing problem in one ear. The condition reinforced her reluctance to appear in public. According to Dick Bresciani, the Red Sox vice president of public relations for more than twenty years in the 1970s into the 1990s, Jean Yawkey "never wanted to give the impression that she didn't know what was going on."[16]

In her early 80s she considered writing a book, but then abandoned the idea for personal reasons. "If I did it, I'd want to tell the truth. And if I did that, I would hurt some feelings and it might be upsetting to the organization, and I didn't want that to happen,"[17] she explained.

On February 20, 1992 a security guard at the Four Seasons Hotel noticed that Jean had not picked up the morning newspaper. Suspicious, he entered her condominium and found her unconscious. She had a massive stroke, and at 5:36 p.m. was admitted to Massachusetts General Hospital. Slipping further and further from consciousness, she died six days later on February 26. Jean Yawkey was eighty-three years old.

At the time of her death Jean Yawkey was one of three women who owned Major League baseball teams along with Marge Schott in Cincinnati and Joan Kroc in San Diego. When Schott was informed of Jean Yawkey's passing, she stated, "She was a very nice lady. I met her at the World Series in 1986, and she's not someone you forget."[18]

John Marzano was a back-up catcher for the Red Sox for six years (1987-1992). When informed of Jean Yawkey's passing he stated, "We used to sit in the bullpen and look up and seer her in her booth with her binoculars. She never forgot a thing. She knew everything we were doing. She knew every player, every stat. That's what everybody in the bullpen talked about. Everybody on the ballclub is going to miss seeing her in that box."[19]

It was forty-six days until opening day when fifty-nine years of the Yawkey family ownership of the Boston Red Sox came to an end. At the Red Sox spring training camp in Winter Haven, Florida the flag in centerfield was lowered to half-staff. To honor Jean Yawkey in the 1992 season the Red Sox players wore the initials "JRY" on their uniforms, and at the opening game the Star-Spangled Banner was sung by Arthur Rawding, Jean's favorite concierge at the Four Seasons Hotel.

When Tom Yawkey died most Boston Red Sox fans would have been quite content if Jean Yawkey had just kept the status quo in the Red Sox organization, but she was much more than a widow who inherited a Major League team, she was a true sportswoman and proceeded to put her own mark on the ball club. Jean Yawkey's money and love for baseball brought stabilization to the Boston Red Sox franchise, and at the time of her passing, the team and property including Fenway Park and its parking lot were valued at $200 million.

On November 1, 1995 Jean R. Yawkey was inducted into the Boston Red Sox Hall of Fame.

6

MARGE SCHOTT

CINCINNATI REDS

In 1973 majority control of the Cincinnati Reds was purchased by Louis Nippert, an heir of James Gamble, one of the founders of Procter & Gamble. Nippert's management style was to leave baseball matters in the hands of his capable general manager Bob Howsam.

Bob Howsam, along with his brother Earl and his father Lee, had founded the Denver Broncos—one of the eight charter members of the American Football League (AFL). Howsam also served three years (1964-1966) as general manager of the St. Louis Cardinals, and had built the club's pitching staff that won the 1968 National League pennant.

Coming to Cincinnati as general manager in 1967, Howsam was partly responsible for building the Big Red Machine along with his predecessor Bill DeWitt, Sr. Under Bob Howsam, the Cincinnati Reds of the 1970s, a.k.a. "The Big Red Machine," became arguably one of Major League Baseball's greatest teams ever. Led by manager Sparky Anderson, and an All-Star line-up that included, Johnny Bench, Joe Morgan, Tony Perez, Pete Rose, Dave Concepcion, Ken Griffey, Sr., and George Foster, during the 1970s, the Reds won six National League Western Division Conference Championships, four National League Pennants, and back-to-back World Series championships in 1975 and 1976.

Following the 1977 season, Bob Howsam retired as Reds general manager. Dick Wagner was selected to replace him. Then in 1980, Louis Nippert sold his controlling interest in the team to brothers William J. Williams and James R. Williams. The Williams brothers then formed a limited partnership. One of the fifteen shares was sold to Cincinnati auto dealer Marge Schott, who the Williams had known for years.

But by 1982, due to the conservative approach of Dick Wagner in dealing with free agency, his firing of manager Sparky Anderson and the aging of the star players on the Reds that were hold-overs from the 1970s, such as Johnny Bench, Dave Concepcion, Dan Dreissen, and Tom Seaver, the once proud and powerful Big Red Machine ran out of gas, finishing both the 1982 and 1983 seasons in last place in a division that they had dominated for over a decade.

Marge Schott was a huge Reds fan. She enjoyed joining in "the wave" with other fans from her box seat and would talk with people about the team on the streets and in restaurants. It was during this period of the slumping Reds that in 1983 Marge rented a plane to fly over Riverfront Stadium with a banner pulled on its tail that read "Pete (Rose), Joe (Morgan) & Tony (Perez), We Need Your Help."[1] That day all three were playing against the Reds as teammates on the Philadelphia Phillies. Rose and Morgan had left the Reds in free agency signings, and Perez had been traded to Montreal following the 1976 season.

By 1983, with a roster made up of over half its players having barely more than a little experience at the AAA level, the Reds franchise was in shambles and had lost an estimated $25 million since the Williams brothers took control. It was clearly time for new ownership and front office administration in Cincinnati.

In July 1983 Dick Wagner was fired as general manager. When the announcement was heard on the radio and TV, people in Cincinnati took to the streets and began honking their car horns and setting off firecrackers. Former general manager Bob Howsam returned on an interim basis to rebuild the team. On December 6 he reacquired fan favorite Tony Perez from the Phillies. Then the next day Howsam took his first major step in rebuilding the Reds when he signed free agent Dave Parker to a $970,000 a year contract.

Parker, raised in Cincinnati, had been a star with the Pittsburgh Pirates in the late 1970s, winning two National League batting championships (1977 and 1978), was the 1978 National League MVP, and the Major League All-Star Game MVP in 1979. However, due to his cocaine use and his sinking statistics, the fans in Pittsburgh had subjected Parker to some rather questionable and harsh treatment. Parker was tired of the booing, threats, and criticism in the Steel City and wanted out. Also in the 1984 season, talented rookie Eric Davis would make his Major League debut with the Reds.

On August 16, 1984 Bob Howsam fired manager Vern Rapp. Then the same day, he brought forty-three-year-old Pete Rose back to the Reds as player/manager in a trade with the Montreal Expos for Tom Lawless. On April 13 Rose had got the four thousandth hit in his career and was beginning to close in on Ty Cobb's all-time Major League hits record of 4,191. Howsam was sure that having Rose once again in a Cincinnati uniform would fill a lot of seats in Riverfront Stadium as he closed in on Cobb's record.

On Friday morning of August 17, 1984 the Cincinnati newspapers proclaimed in huge bold headlines not seen since the end of World War Two—PETE'S BACK! That evening Rose made his debut as player/manager when the Reds met the Chicago Cubs in a Friday night game at Riverfront Stadium before a crowd of 35,056 fans. To the delight of his fans, Rose pounded out two hits, a single (career hit 4,063) and a double (career hit 4,064), as the Reds pulled out a 6-4 victory.

The Reds finished the 1984 season in fifth place with a record of 70-92. Under Rose, the Reds had been 19-23. Rose had played in twenty-six games for the Reds and hit .365. He now had 4,097 career hits and was just ninety-four hits behind Ty Cobb. Dave Parker, in his first season with Cincinnati in 1984, was named the Reds MVP. Eric Davis had ten home runs playing in just fifty-seven games.

Nonetheless, Bob Howsam wanted to return to semi-retirement as a consultant. He approached the Williams brothers about letting him out of his contract by July 1985 and asked them to authorize him to hire a successor. The Williams brothers agreed. So Howsam hired Bill Bergesch away from the New York Yankees to be his heir apparent as general manager.

The Williams brothers also wanted out and began to look for a buyer for the Reds. At first, it looked like one of the limited partners, local insurance magnate and Chiquita banana tycoon, Carl H. Lindner might buy the team. But talks broke down. There were several other interested parties from outside Cincinnati who were willing to put up as much as $25 million for the Reds, including a group from Louisville. But the Williams brothers, fearing transfer of the team to another city or even across the Ohio River to Northern Kentucky, were really looking for a local buyer and reserved the right to reject all outside bids if a local buyer surfaced and matched their bid.

At that time, Marge Schott was a limited partner and owned one of the fifteen shares valued at $1.6 million. So she needed to come up with an additional $22.4 million to buy the team. To that end, Marge approached the Fifth Third Bank and obtained a loan of $10 million. That amount would give her nine and a half shares and controlling interest in the Reds if the other limited partners stayed, and she could find a few additional buyers.

So Marge, as she was commonly known around Cincinnati, began to wheel and deal, selling and buying shares of the Reds. She sold one of her shares to Frisch's Restaurants, Inc. and another to William Riek, Jr. Then she purchased the shares of limited partners J. Barrett Buse and Lloyd I. Miller and also acquired a half share from Priscilla Gamble. By the time she was done, Marge had put together a very shrewd business deal that saw her gain majority control of the ball club's fifteen shares for less than $9 million.

On December 21, 1984 fifty-six-year-old Marge Schott called a press conference and accompanied by her behemoth 170 pound St. Bernard dog "Schottzie," sporting a Reds cap, announced that she had purchased the Cincinnati Reds. Marge called her purchase of the Reds a Christmas gift to the people of Cincinnati. She said the reason she stepped up to the plate was because, "This is the city of bratwurst, beer and baseball, and I couldn't stand the thought of the Reds moving somewhere else."[2] Then she became tearful.

It was estimated that the Cincinnati Reds had lost $4 million in 1984. As for Marge's business plan in operating the Reds, Marge announced that she planned to bring back Ladies Day, keep a close watch on expenses, a controversial move that would define her ownership and get down into the stands and talk with fans.

Player/manager Pete Rose was present at the press conference and stated, "I think Marge and I are pretty much alike—in a baseball sense—except she's got long hair and shaves her legs. She knows the game as well as anybody. I don't think she'll step on anybody's shoes."[3]

On February 7, 1985 Marge Schott would be approved by Major League Baseball as owner of the Cincinnati Reds. Marge Schott was only the second woman in Major League history (Joan Payson was first) to buy a team rather than inherit one. At the time Marge purchased controlling interest in the Cincinnati Reds, it was a watershed event for women in Major League Baseball. With Marge Schott gaining control of the Cincinnati Reds, it brought the number of women to three who owned Major League teams at that time. The others were Jean Yawkey of the Boston Red Sox and Joan Kroc of the San Diego Padres, both of whom had inherited the teams from their husbands.

Unlike her contemporary Jean Yawkey, who spent more time giving away tickets to nuns than making executive decisions, Marge immediately let it be known that she would take an active role in the management of her team. Within a couple of days of taking control of the Reds, she said in an interview that George Steinbrenner, owner of the New York Yankees, was "ruining baseball." Steinbrenner replied that "he wouldn't buy a car from her."[4] However, soon Marge and George would become good friends and she would rely on his advice.

Marge Schott wanted it known that she was not a feminist. "I can't stand Ms.," she said. "Every time somebody addresses me as Ms. on a letter, I throw it away. I bought the Cincinnati team as a Cincinnatian, not as a woman. The women I admire most are the women who are wives and mothers. They don't get enough credit."[5]

Around Cincinnati, Marge Schott was known to the general population for personal flamboyance and for her colorful car dealership commercials. But entering into baseball, Marge would become one of the most complex persons to ever own a Major League team.

Marge Schott seemed to live in a psychologically-gated mind-set, in which she believed her abundance of wealth gave her the right to speak as she pleased without thinking about the consequences of her words. She had a very strong business acumen, and if it had not been for her racial insensitivity, Marge Schott may have been remembered more as a role model for business women, instead of the popular legacy that was to befall upon her as a chain-smoking, loud-mouth that constantly made stupid statements in public about Adolf Hitler and hateful expressions of prejudicial feelings toward every race, creed, and color of people on the planet Earth.

Born Marge Unnewehr in Cincinnati, Ohio on August 18, 1928, she was part of the sixth generation of her family in the city and the second of five daughters born to Edward and Charlotte Unnewehr. Her father made a fortune in the lumber business. According to Marge, "my father was Achtung-German. He used to ring a bell when he wanted my mother. When I was 21 and went to vote, he told me who to vote for. I said, 'Yes Daddy.'"[6]

Her father called her Butch for her love of sports. He taught her to always be tough—never soft. At school, the kids would make fun of her last name, calling her "Un-aware" and "Underware." Marge graduated from Scared Heart Academy and then attended the University of Cincinnati for a couple of years. She described her educational experience at Sacred Heart as "white gloves, 12 years of French and curtsy."[7]

In 1952 Marge Unnewehr married Charles Schott, a member of a very wealthy and influential Cincinnati family.

Charles Schott owned and operated a highly successful Buick dealership in the Cincinnati satellite town of Norwood. In addition, Charles had business interest in insurance, brick manufacturing, concrete products, and landfills. Marge became notable for the parties she held for friends, charities, and the Cincinnati Zoo at her forty-room mansion located on seventy acres in the affluent Cincinnati suburb of Indian Hill.

However, due to Charles's alcoholism and infidelity, the marriage was on the brink of divorce when he died of a heart attack in 1968. Charles had tried to battle his addiction to alcohol by going to A.A. meetings, going to church, and quitting cold turkey. Nothing seemed to work, and he would disappear on binges for several days.

According to Joe Schott, nephew of Charles's father, during a business and drinking trip to Florida in the early-1960s, Charles and his uncle Harold Schott, another big drinker, had made a couple of good deals in Palm Beach and were celebrating. "They went to the Rolls Royce dealer and took a Rolls Royce for a demo ride—only they never came back," said Joe. "They sent the man a check."[8]

Marge Schott continued to keep that car in her garage well into the 1990s. Although, for personal use she drove a black Buick Century with a customized Ohio license plate with "MARGE" emblazoned on it.

At the time of Charles's death, Marge Schott was forty years old and had been doing volunteer work and raising St. Bernards. Executives at General Motors, informed Marge that they would make arrangements to have someone run the Schott auto dealership. Marge quickly informed G.M. that she had someone to run the business—herself. It took Marge two and a half years to convince General Motors to make her the first U.S. woman to be awarded a metropolitan area G.M. dealership, even after sales had risen by 40 percent. When G.M. finally relented, they told her to come to Detroit and sign a contract. She refused and told G.M. to come to Cincinnati. They did. Marge had always alleged that G.M. just didn't want to give the dealership to a woman.

Marge continued to not only run the auto dealership successfully but expand her financial interests into such areas as a land fill company, an insurance company, and real estate. She also became the first woman ever named to the board of trustees of the Cincinnati Chamber of Commerce and was inducted into Ohio Women's Hall of Fame in 1985. In addition, she served on the advisory boards of Xavier University and the Cincinnati Zoo. In December 1986 Marge was among eighty-five other women entrepreneurs from all over the country honored by President Reagan at the White House.

Marge and Charles didn't have any children. Marge openly admitted that not having had any children was a terrible heartache. She had even visited a doctor who had treated the Shah of Iran's wife. She considered adoption out of the question. "When you don't have kids and you're in a Catholic family—one of my sisters had 10 children in 11 years—she's part rabbit—you feel kind of guilty about that. So I want to do things for other people's children."[9]

So dogs, other people's children, the zoo, and the Cincinnati Reds became Marge's passion. She donated $25,000 to the Warren County Humane Association's facility. She donated $6 million for a new elephant facility at the Cincinnati Zoo. For forty-one years, she annually held a Reds rally at her posh home that was a combination "meet and greet" with the Red players and an auction. The events raised more than $1 million for the association that aids heart research at Cincinnati's Children's Hospital. When asked about her generous donations, Marge simply replied, "It's only money honey."[10]

Alone and a widow, Marge espoused a sense of humor about her circumstances. She retreated into the old refrain that all the good men were gone. She joked that her employees wanted to get her together with Lee Iacocca just to get rid of her. When she didn't have a date for a dance at the exclusive Queen City Club in Cincinnati, she took a live dancing bear as her escort. In the end, Marge's love for her Saint Bernard Schottzie would fill the companionship void in her life.

On July 1, 1985 Bob Howsam returned to retirement and Bill Bergesch, his handpicked successor, took over as general manager. Then, on July 8, Marge Schott became

President and Chief Executive Officer of the Cincinnati Reds and her tumultuous fifteen-year reign began.

Bob Howsam was glad to be leaving the Cincinnati Reds front office. Almost from the day that Marge took control of the team, he had been in conflict with her. They fought over press releases, whether or not the Reds had made a profit in 1984, even the guest list for the Reds Opening Day party. Marge didn't want to invite former Reds great Johnny Bench and didn't want to invite the Williams brothers either, from whom she had just bought the team. While Bench received a snub from the festivities, Howsam invited the Williams brothers on his own. Howsam was also tired of the late night phone calls from Marge when she had been drinking and didn't make any sense.

Pete Rose advised Howsam not to talk to Marge after 10:00 p.m. In the evenings, alone in her mansion, Marge liked to chain smoke Carlton 120 cigarettes and drink copious amounts of Kamchatak vodka and water—an inexpensive brand. Then before getting into bed she would get on her knees and pray to the two most important men she had in her life, her late husband and late father.

Going into the 1985 season, Dave Parker was now employed by Marge Schott. Almost immediately, Schott started to refer to Parker in the presence of members of the Cincinnati Reds front office, including general manager Bill Bergesch, as "my million dollar nigger."

Roger Blaermie, who was at the time serving in the Reds front office as vice president of business operations, states that Schott would refer to Parker that way commonly. "When she talked about the 'million dollar nigger,' she was referring to Dave Parker. And she always referred to Eric Davis as the "trouble making nigger,"[11] said Blaemire. Later, Reds Hall of Fame second baseman turned broadcaster, Joe Morgan, was dubbed the "little nigger" by Marge.

But Marge was also known to use insulting terms when referring to Jews, even ones that worked for her were not exempt from her insults. She once referred to her marketing director Cal Levy as a "beady eyed Jew."[12]

Eric Davis said that he first heard that Marge Schott referred to him using the "N" word during his rookie season in 1984, before she was the majority partner. Speaking in regard to Schott's insult, Davis remarked, "To have my owner call me her 'million dollar nigger;' it didn't really sit good with me. I got calls from the NAACP and the Reverend Jessie Jackson, but as a 22-year old, what was I going to do? I put that under my hat and used that as my motivation, that if I'm going to be a million dollar ..., then she's going to have to keep paying me well over $1 million, because I'm going to prove my worth to her."[13]

Regardless of all the slurs that Marge used in referring to Davis, she also attempted to please him by giving him the contract that he wanted and yielding to the demands of his agent Eric Goldschmidt. She even threw in a Corvette one year at Davis's insistence.

In 1984 the FBI, on a tip, began to investigate drug dealing among the Pittsburgh Pirates. The FBI decided to build their case against the dealers rather than the users. Several Major League players were called before a Grand Jury in Pittsburgh and all were given immunity in exchange for their testimony, including Dave Parker.

With the seven dealers indicted, in September 1985, Dave Parker was called to testify in the Pittsburgh Drug Trials. At that time, the Cincinnati Reds were fighting for the National League Western Division Championship, and player/manager Pete Rose was closing in on Ty Cobb's all-time career hit record. Dave Parker had regained his All-Star status in Cincinnati and was having his best season since 1979, leading the league in doubles and RBIs while once again hitting over thirty home runs.

The logistics of getting Parker back and forth to Pittsburgh for his testimony during the pennant race became an unsettling issue with Marge Schott. Parker's agent Tom Reich was sensitive to the fact that the Reds were paying him a lot of money and that it was necessary to have Parker in the lineup during the stretch run. To that end, Reich informed Reds general manager Bill Bergesch that Parker would pick up the cost of flying back and forth in a charter plane for a few days. But when Bergesch attempted to explain the arrangements to Marge, she couldn't comprehend the details and said that she didn't want to do that for Parker. "I guess that was one of the times she referred to him as a 'million dollar nigger,'"[14] said Bergesch.

During testimony in the Pittsburgh drug trials in the United States District Court for the Western District of Pennsylvania in September 1985, Dave Parker openly admitted that he had used cocaine while playing for the Pirates and had shared cocaine with, or arranged to have the drug supplied to several other Major Leaguers.[15]

Dave Parker became one of seven players suspended for one year by Commissioner Peter Ueberroth. However, Uberroth permitted the players with a one-year suspension to play in return for donating 10 percent of their base salaries for the 1986 season to drug-related community service programs, submitting to random drug testing, and contributing 100 hours of drug related community service. So Dave Parker's donation amounted to about $100,000. It was surprising that Marge Schott made no public statement on the matter.

As the 1985 season got underway, the countdown for Pete Rose to break Ty Cobb's all-time hits mark began. While Rose was obsessed about breaking the record, Marge Schott was hoping that Rose's quest for the all-time hits record would result in a bonanza at the Reds ticket booths. By the end of April, Rose needed seventy-nine hits to catch Cobb. In mid-August Rose got five hits in two days against the Huston Astros to reduce his magic number to the number he wore on his uniform jersey—14.

On September 6 the Reds arrived in Chicago for a three game weekend series at Wrigley Field with Rose just four hits behind Ty Cobb's record, and the drama really began to build. Both Rose and Marge wanted him to break the coveted mark of 4,191 hits in front of the hometown fans in Cincinnati, where the Reds were scheduled to return immediately following the Chicago series. Nonetheless, Rose played on Friday September 6 and got two hits including his second home run of the season. Now he was just two hits from tying Cobb's record and three hits away from breaking it.

Rose wasn't going to play on Sunday September 8, and the huge press corps that had been following him day-to-day had begun to leave Chicago for Cincinnati where the

Reds would open a three-game series with the San Diego Padres on Monday, sure that Rose would tie and break Cobb's record there.

Steve Trout, a left-hander, was supposed to be the Cubs starting pitcher on Sunday. But he fell off a bicycle while playing with his daughter, hurt his elbow and shoulder, and had to be scratched from the lineup. So the Cubs started rookie Reggie Patterson, a right-hander that Rose had got hit number 4,189 off in Friday's game. So impulsively, Rose decided to pencil his name into the lineup.

Batting second in the lineup behind leadoff hitter Eddie Milner, Rose swung at the first pitch he saw from Patterson and drove it into right-center field for a single and hit number 4,190. Then in the fifth inning with the count full, Rose lined a single over the head of Cubs second baseman Ryne Sandberg off Patterson for hit number 4,191. He had just equaled Ty Cobb's all-time hit mark. The electronic scoreboard attached to the old permanent score board in Wrigley Field began flashing a message—"Ty Cobb 4,191" on one line and beneath it "Pete Rose, 4,191." The entire crowd of 28,269 fans in Wrigley Field was on their feet applauding Pete as were the spectators on the roof tops of the apartment buildings across the street behind the outfield fences on Waveland and Sheffield Avenues. Pete stood on first base tipping his batting helmet to the crowd.

Back in Cincinnati, Marge Schott didn't know that Pete Rose had been in the lineup for the Sunday game. When Rose got the hit that tied Cobb's record, she received a call from Roger Blaemire, the Reds vice-president of business operations and marketing. Marge was keenly aware of the box office windfall that she had going for her with the possibility of Rose getting his historic hit at home in Riverfront Stadium. So she was understandably upset. "If that son of a bitch gets that base hit, I'm gonna kill him," said Marge. "If he gets that base hit in Chicago, he doesn't even need to come back to Cincinnati."[16]

Marge, feeling confident that Rose would wait to get his historic hit at home, had gone to the Cincinnati Bengals game that day. "I'm hysterical," she said. "I've never spent a day like this in my life. No one bothered to inform me that Pete was going to play. I went to the Bengal game, and I was a little late. I no more than walk in when someone tells me Pete is playing. I almost died. I'm really upset that someone in the Reds organization couldn't call me and let me know."[17] Chicago time is an hour behind Cincinnati; Marge had a private plane waiting for her at Cincinnati's Lunken Airport and could have arrived at Wrigley Field in plenty of time to be with Rose on the historic occasion.

The Reds-Cubs game was delayed on several occasions by rain and drizzle, still Rose kept himself in the lineup and went to bat two more times, grounding out and striking out. The Cubs failed to score in the bottom of the ninth, then the rain returned, and with no lights in Wrigley Field at that time, the game had to be called because of darkness. The National League office said that that game counted and was a tie. It would only be replayed if it had a bearing on the outcome of the division race for either team, so for now, Rose's hits counted.

In the Reds clubhouse, Rose told *Cincinnati Enquirer* sports reporter Tim Sullivan that he didn't know what to do about putting himself in the lineup that day, "I was real confused. I didn't know what to do. I was in sort of a situation where I didn't want to disappoint everybody. I had 30,000 yelling here and one lady back in Cincinnati, every time I got a hit, kicking her dog."[18] (A reference to Marge Schott's pet Saint Bernard, Schottzie.)

As the Reds prepared to open the three game series with San Diego at Riverfront Stadium and with Rose on the brink of breaking Cobb's record, they announced that there were 15,000 tickets still available for the first game, 16,000 for Tuesday's game, and 24,000 for Wednesday's game. Dave Dravecky, a lefthander, was going to be the starting pitcher for San Diego in the first game of the series, so Rose announced that he would not play.

But on Tuesday September 10 Rose was in the lineup as 51,045 enthusiastic fans jammed the stands at Riverfront Stadium. Every time Rose came to bat, they stood up cheering and chanting his name, "Pete, Pete, Pete!" In the red seats high up in centerfield, children unfurled rolls of toilet paper that drifted like confetti down on to the outfield. Even the granddaughter of Ty Cobb,

Peggy Cobb Schug, was in the stands having come from Charlotte, North Carolina to attend the game. In the seventh inning Ms. Schug visited with Marge Schott in her box and reminisced about her grandfather and said he was undeserving of his villainous reputation. However, the fans went home disappointed as Rose went 0 for 4 at the plate and the Padres beat the Reds 3-2.

Baseball Commissioner Peter Uberroth was a guest in Marge Schott's box at Riverfront Stadium that night. Uberroth experienced an unwanted surprise while viewing the game when Schottzie urinated on his shoe.

According to Marge Schott, Schottzie means "sweetheart" in German. Schottzie had been a source of controversy ever since Marge took over the Reds. Schottzie appeared at the press conference when she took over controlling interest of the team. Immediately, the dog was inserted into the Reds media guide with a photo of her sporting a Reds cap and a twelve-line profile that read in part: "Schottzie joined the Reds in December, 1984, when her mistress became general partner, and made an immediate impact at the press conference by sitting on the foot of Manager Pete Rose ..."[19] The dog also appeared annually in the Reds yearbook.

Pete Rose attempted to tolerate the dog in public by just chalking it up to showing loyalty to his employer. Still, privately he complained, "I was at Marge's house one day trying to explain why we needed more pitching, and how we might get it without busting our salary frame, and the dog comes over and puts it big head on my lap and starts drooling through these enormous teeth, onto my crotch. The feeling wasn't great."[20]

With Marge Schott, it was simply a case of love me, love my dog. She permitted Schottzie to go on to the artificial turf in Riverfront Stadium and often the dog relieved itself —to the surprise and consternation of some visiting players. Years later, Marge would rub dog hair on manager Lou Pinella's chest and demanded that St. Louis Cardinals slugger Mark McGwire, who was allergic to dog hair, pet Schottzie.

The 3-2 loss to the San Diego Padres on September 10 all but eliminated the Cincinnati Reds from the 1985

National League West Division race as the Los Angeles Dodgers swept a doubleheader from the Atlanta Braves leaving the Reds nine and a half games behind. But with Pete Rose going hitless and the fans craving the chance to see history made, immediately following the game, long lines formed at the Riverfront Stadium ticket office and 10,000 tickets were sold for the next night's game.

On Wednesday night of September 11 47,237 fans jammed into Riverfront Stadium and at 7:49 p.m., Pete Rose came up to bat against the Padres Eric Show. At 8:01 p.m., with the count two balls and one strike, Rose stroked a clean single into left field for the record breaking hit number 4,192.

Immediately, all hell broke loose in Riverfront Stadium! The Reds radio network team of Marty Brennaman and Joe Nuxhall were drowning out each other's voices as they broadcast the call on the hit. The Goodyear blimp hovered over Riverfront Stadium flashing the news. More than 300 journalists and photographers were on hand and flashes on cameras began to explode like rifle fire at The Battle of Gettysburg. High above Riverfront Stadium in center field, fireworks exploded from the scoreboard and the huge crowd was standing and cheering continuously, letting out all the emotion that had been building up in them since opening day.

As Pete Rose stood on first base, tears began to stream down his cheeks. Rose was to say later in a melodramatic remembrance that as he looked up into the lights above the stadium, he saw images of Ty Cobb and his father, Harry Rose, looking down upon him. Rose grabbed his former teammate and friend, first base coach Tommy Helms, and began to cry. Helms then motioned toward the dugout for Rose's oldest son Pete, Jr. (Petey), and he ran out on to the field and embraced his dad as the tears continued to flow. The Reds dugout had emptied and teammates Tony Perez and Davy Concepcion arrived at first base and hoisted Rose on their shoulders. Padres pitcher Eric Show just sat down on the mound to wait out the pandemonium, then he got up and came over to first shake Rose's hand.

Soon after Marge Schott strolled out to first base and embraced Pete in a tight bear hug, a red Corvette that she had arranged for G.M. to give him was wheeled through a gate in the outfield wall and delivered to Pete at first base. The car was bearing the license plate number "Ohio PR 4192." The celebration went on for seven minutes before play was resumed.

In the seventh inning Rose would get hit number 4,193 when he tripled down the left field line. Then he would score the Reds' second run of the game on a sacrifice by Nick Esasky. When it was over, the Reds had defeated the Padres 2-0, and Rose had scored both runs.

There was a post-game ceremony and President Reagan called to congratulate Pete Rose. Then Marge Schott and Reds' radio broadcaster Marty Brennaman presented Rose with an engraved silver punch bowl. The bowl was equipped with a ladle and twelve cups that were each engraved with a highlight from Rose's career: April 13, 1963, his first game in the majors and hits numbers: 1,000; 1,500; 2,000; 3,000; 3,500; 3,631; 3,772; 4,000; and 4,192. Marge Schott explained that she wanted to give Pete something lasting, just not another loving cup—something that he could use. Still Marge could not resist memorializing "Schottzie" in the ceremony; to that end, the handle of the ladle was engraved to Pete reading, "Woofs and licks, Schottize."[21]

Pete Rose finished the 1985 season with 4,204 career hits. He had batted .264 with 107 hits in 119 games. The Reds, under his first full year as manager, finished second in the National League West Division with a record of 89-72, five and a half games behind the Los Angeles Dodgers. Rose's pursuit of Ty Cobb's hit record had lured 1.8 million fans into Riverfront Stadium, making the year a huge success in ticket sales for Marge Schott and the other partners.

In 1986, under Pete Rose, the Reds again finished in second place in the National League West Division, this time ten games behind the Houston Astros. For a while, Rose now forty-five years old, had attempted to play, even though it was clear to everyone that his bat speed had slowed down considerably and he was having trouble hitting the ball out of the infield.

Pete's former teammate Johnny Bench once suggested that, when it came time for Rose to retire, they would have to cut the uniform off him. But who was going to do that to Charlie Hustle, not Marge Schott, not his teammates, not the press, not his fans. In the end, it was Rose who spared all of them the agony as he cut the uniform off himself.

On August 17, 1986 Rose struck out against Goose Gossage of the San Diego Padres. It was his last at bat in the Major Leagues and he never played again. There was no grand farewell tour around the league for Pete Rose, no hoopla, no special tributes in the media, one day he just decided to stop playing.

One would have thought that Marge Schott might have retired Pete Rose's number. However, Marge thought that kind of ceremony was expensive and counterproductive to her cost-cutting management philosophy. But in all fairness to Marge on this issue, at that time, she was following a precedent set by decades of past Reds owners, Garry Herrmann, Powell Crosley, Jr., Bill DeWitt, Sr., Francis Dale, the Williams brothers, etc., all who seemed to lack any feelings of nostalgia for player memories. In fact, at that time in the long history of the Cincinnati Reds, only two numbers had been retired: manager Fred Hutchinson (1) and Johnny Bench (5).

By 1987 Dave Parker had been through a drug rehabilitation program and was giving out tee shirts that stated, "Dave Parker: Say no to drugs."[22] Parker had resurrected his career in Cincinnati and was an All-Star. With his veteran leadership, along with several talented young players, such as Eric Davis and Kal Daniels and an outstanding bullpen, the Reds were pre-season favorites to win the National League West Division Championship in 1987. However, the Reds faltered and finished in second place, six games behind the San Francisco Giants.

Manager Pete Rose wanted to blame the loss of the division title on the lack of leadership by Dave Parker. Right or wrong, Rose's dilemma with Parker was solved on December 8, 1987 when, without any objection from Marge

Schott, Parker was traded by the Cincinnati Reds to the Oakland Athletics for Jose Rijo and Tim Birtsas.

During the tenure of Pete Rose as manager and Bill Bergesch as general manager, the Reds became a competitive team again with a roster that included such talented young players as Eric Davis, Paul O'Neill, Jose Rijo, Tom Browning, Kal Daniels, and future Hall of Fame shortstop Barry Larkin. Still in 1988, for the fourth straight year, the Reds finished second in the National League West Division. But both Pete Rose and Marge Schott were hopeful that 1989 would finally be the season the Reds would reach the top of the standings.

For Marge Schott, other than the Reds disappointing finish in 1988, it had been a banner year for her personally. Among the highlights of the year for Marge was a visit to the Vatican, where she presented Pope John Paul II with a Reds jacket. Also, she was featured in an interview on the highly regarded CBS Sunday evening program *60 Minutes*. Finally, she was honored by *Savvy Magazine* as the operator of one the top forty largest businesses in the country to be headed by a woman.

Spring training began in 1989 with outfielder Kal Daniels walking out of camp in a dispute over the contract the Reds had offered him for the coming season. Daniels wanted $325,000, but the Reds were offering him $300,000. So Marge Schott suggested they flip a coin to determine the amount of his contract. Daniels agreed, the coin was tossed and Marge called heads—the coin came up tails. Daniels signed his contract.

However, as far as gambling, the Daniels contract resolution coin toss would be paled in comparison to a larger gambling story about to encompass the Cincinnati Reds. Rumors of alleged betting on baseball by manager Pete Rose had begun to circulate in the commissioner's office.

On February 20, 1989 Pete Rose was summoned from the Reds spring training camp in Plant City, Florida to a meeting in New York with Peter Ueberroth, the commissioner of baseball, his soon-to-be successor commissioner-elect, National League president A. Bartlett Giamatti, and assistant commissioner Fay Vincent. Rose took two lawyers with him, Reuven Katz and his partner Robert Pitcairn. The commissioner's agenda was a discussion of Rose's gambling habits. First and foremost on the commissioner's list of questions for Rose was if he had bet on baseball. According to Rose, Ueberroth asked him, "Do you bet on baseball?" Rose responded, "No, sir. I didn't bet on baseball. The last bet I made was the (1989) Super Bowl."[23] Ueberroth told Rose he wasn't concerned with betting on football, he wanted to know about betting on baseball. Again, Rose denied placing any bets on baseball. Ueberroth also asked Rose if he owed any money to bookies and Rose said that he did not.

Three days after meeting with Rose in New York on February 23, 1989, the Commissioner's office hired a Washington, D.C. attorney John M. Dowd to begin a formal investigation of Rose and his alleged gambling habits.

General Manager Murray Cook attempted to get Marge Schott to not act as nothing had happened. But there was no public comment by Marge. She was fond of Rose, and whether or not she was in denial or just hoping that the whole affair would just disappear is speculation. Meanwhile, others were advancing the notion that Marge was actually angry with Rose, acting as if he was purposely putting her and the Reds through all of this.

On February 24, 1989 Paul Janszen, who was then serving six months in a halfway house in Cincinnati for tax fraud and calling in bets, was the first witness to be interviewed by Dowd. The Dowd Report states that Paul Janszen had been placing bets for Pete Rose during the period of April through July 1987. Janszen told Dowd that during that time he placed bets of $2,000 per game on various Major League Baseball teams, including the Cincinnati Reds.

Also, Paul Janszen stated in his testimony with John Dowd that he had taped recorded conversations in regard to Pete Rose's betting activities on April 4, 1988 and December 27, 1988. In addition, Janszen gave Dowd copies of his personal notebook, in which he recorded bets for Rose during the period of April 8, 1987 through May 13, 1987.

On March 20, 1989 Commissioner Peter Ueberroth issued a formal announcement that his office "has for several months been conducting a full inquiry into serious allegations"[24] about Cincinnati Reds manager Pete Rose.The first real comprehensive news of what was going on in the Rose investigation was reported in *Sports Illustrated* on March 22, 1989.

On April 1, 1989 A. Bartlett Giamatti formally took office as the sixth Commissioner of Major League Baseball and he took control of the Rose investigation.

At that time, Ron Peters, a Franklin, Ohio bookie, was awaiting sentencing in Cincinnati after pleading guilty to charges of cocaine trafficking and making false statements on an income tax return. On April 5, 1989 Peters gave a deposition in the Rose matter to John Dowd, at which he agreed to give full and truthful cooperation in exchange for an acknowledgement by the Commissioner's office to U.S. district judge Carl Rubin in Cincinnati that he had lent assistance. If anything, the testimony of Ron Peters was nothing more than icing on the cake for John Dowd in his investigation of Rose. The critical damage to the reputation of Pete Rose had already been done by Paul Janszen. The emphasis of the Peters's testimony was that he had accepted bets for Rose in 1985 and 1986 through an intermediary and in 1987 through Paul Janszen.

On April 21, 1989 it was Pete Rose's opportunity to set the record straight with baseball as he met with John Dowd. His statements would be included in a 358 page deposition, but he was aloof and not very cooperative in his statements. In his deposition, Rose denied under oath that he ever bet on Major League Baseball or of associating with anyone who placed bets on his behalf.

Still there was no response from Marge Schott.

On May 9, 1989 John Dowd presented his 225 page report, accompanied by seven volumes of exhibits to the commissioner. The Dowd Report detailed 412 wagers on baseball allegedly made by Rose between April 8 and July 5, 1987, including fifty-two wagers on the Cincinnati Reds. The Dowd Report stated that Pete Rose won 228 bets and lost 184 on baseball games during a two-month period in wagers with bookmakers. Evidence presented in the report included betting slips alleged to be in Rose's own handwriting, along with telephone and bank records. Major League Baseball stated that it was keeping the Dowd Report under tight security, but somehow a freelance writer got hold of a copy and began to peddle it to news organizations.

Marge Schott was disappointed with Rose, but in no mood to fire him. She feared the backlash of Rose's die-hard fans and even more the possibility of the entire City of Cincinnati coming after her head in a display of public discontent not seen since the arrest of Marie Antoinette during the French Revolution. How could she fire a guy who had a street named for him running right in front of Riverfront Stadium? Making circumstances even more complicated for Marge was that at the time the media began to break the story of Rose's shady associations and gambling habits, the Reds were in first place.

Bill Bergesch had been fired as the Reds general manager by Marge following the 1987 season and replaced by Murray Cook. As Rose was Marge's manager, Cook attempted to get her involved with the investigation but to no avail. Marge Schott wanted to distance herself from the controversy. Cook told Schott, "You can't stick your head in the sand and pretend that nothing happened. She wanted to hide," said Cook. "She wanted to separate herself from it."[25]

On June 5 the Reds were in first place, three percentage points ahead of the San Francisco Giants in the National League West Division. Reporters were now numerous in the Reds clubhouse, and suddenly there was a new group of visitors in the Reds clubhouse, lawyers standing by Rose as he answered questions from the press.

According to Rose, the pressure was becoming enormous and that at one point he considered going to Marge Schott and asking that he be permitted to show up at the ballpark just before game time to avoid the media. But after thinking about it, he came to the conclusion that the manager had to be front and center and take full responsibility for his actions and the team's.

On June 19 Pete Rose decided to fight back and filed suit against the charges being made against him. From that point on, the legal maneuvering by both Rose's attorneys and the commissioner's office would go on all summer long with suits being filed in Hamilton County Pleas Court, the Ohio Supreme Court, and the U.S. District Court.

As the Rose legal siege continued, it took a toll on the Reds in the pennant race. By July 23 the Reds had fallen to fifth place. On July 27 they suffered their thirty-second loss in the past forty-two games.

By late July, the Rose affair had cost both sides a tremendous amount with legal fees approaching $2 million dollars. Finally, by August 18 it was clear that as far as the legal sparring was going, Bart Giamatti had Pete Rose in a corner, and it was only a matter of time before he had to face the inevitable—he was going down. Consequently, negotiations began between the parties.

On Monday August 21 Pete Rose, in his last game as Cincinnati Reds manager, saw his team beat the Chicago Cubs 6-5 in ten innings at Wrigley Field. Tommy Helms was appointed to manage the Reds for the remainder of the season and the ball club lumbered along finishing fifth in the National League West Division with a record of 75-87 (14-21 under Helms).

On August 23 an agreement was reached between Rose and Giamatti that would permit the matter between the two to be resolved without a hearing. In the agreement, the commissioner would not make any determination that Rose had bet on any Major League Baseball game. In exchange, Rose would have to accept a lifetime ban, being declared permanently ineligible in accordance with Major League Rule 21 and placed on the Ineligible List. The agreement, however, did not preclude Rose the right under Major League rule (15 (c) to apply for reinstatement. It would be noted in the agreement that by signing it Rose was not making an admission or denial of the allegation that he had bet on any Major League Baseball game. Finally, there was to be no gag order in the agreement and both Rose and Giamatti were free to make any public statement they deemed necessary as long as it did not contradict the terms of the agreement. The agreement was signed by Pete Rose and Reuven Katz, as his witness, and by Bart Giamatti and Fay Vincent, as his witness.

So on that fateful day of August 24, 1989 the storied career of Pete Rose, a.k.a., Charlie Hustle, came to an abrupt end in one more head first slide into infamy with a lifetime ban from baseball. At 9:00 a.m. in Manhattan, Major League Baseball Commissioner Bart Giamatti held a news conference to announce the outcome of the Rose matter and stated in part, "The banishment for life of Pete Rose from baseball is the sad end of a sorry episode. One of the game's greatest players has engaged in a variety of acts which have stained the game, and he must now live with the consequences of those acts. The matter of Mr. Rose is now closed."[26]

Then at 10:00 a.m. at Riverfront Stadium in Cincinnati, Pete Rose held a news conference. Clenching his hands and fighting back tears for the second time in his career, Rose told the assembled media, "I made some mistakes, and I am being punished for those mistakes. As you can imagine, this is a sad day. Regardless of what the commissioner said, I did not bet on baseball. I did not bet on the Reds. It's something I told the commissioner in February and it's something I've said to you (the media) for four months."[27] Of course, in an interview with CBS news anchor Charlie Gibson in January 2004, Rose finally admitted he had bet on baseball.

Marge Schott was non-committal on her feelings in the matter of Rose. Although, behind closed doors she had referred to Rose as "that son of a bitch"[28] and disliked his taking the spot light from her. Most observers speculated that Marge was relieved by Giamatti's action having done what she didn't have the guts to do. Still, some insiders believe that had Rose not been suspended, she would have continued to employ him as manager of the Reds, just giving him heart-felt warning to change his ways.

In the end, it may have been Marge Schott's frugality that provided Major League Baseball with a smoking gun in the investigation of Pete Rose's gambling being connected to baseball more than the testimony of Ron Peters or Paul Janzen. Marge didn't like the players using the clubhouse telephone for free. So she put a policy in place that mandated that telephone operator at Riverfront Stadium keep records of all telephone calls. According to Fay Vincent, "We found that Pete made regular calls to a bookie,"[29] and the calls were listed in the Dowd Report. According to Ron Peters, some of those calls had been made to him from the phone in the Reds dugout at Riverfront Stadium.

Nine days following the banishment of Pete Rose on September 1, 1989, Commissioner Bart Giamatti suffered a fatal heart attack and died. Giamatti was fifty-one years old. He was succeeded as commissioner by Deputy Commissioner Fay Vincent.

Marge Schott knew she had a good team and they should have finished higher in the standings in 1989 than fifth, but the Pete Rose controversy had been a distraction. Going forward, Marge wanted to start the 1990 season with a clean slate. She perceived a connection between Rose and general manager Murray Cook and fired him. Marge had never been comfortable with Cook, and he did not fit in with her conception of marital values. She felt betrayed after hiring Cook and finding out that he had been fired in 1987 as the general manager of the Montreal Expos for having an extra-marital affair with Pamela Brochu, wife of Expos president and CEO, Claude Brochu. Murray Cook was replaced by Bob Quinn, former general manager of the New York Yankees.

Then Marge hired Lou Piniella as manager to replace Rose and Tommy Helms. Piniella was recommended to Marge by her old verbal sparring partner George Steinbrenner. Bob Quinn also knew Piniella well and agreed with Steinbrenner's recommendation. Piniella, who had worn the number 14 with the Yankees, reversed the digits on his Cincinnati uniform to 41 to avoid any conflict with the fans over using Pete Rose's uniform number.

The Reds team that Piniella would inherit for the 1990 season was basically the same one that Rose managed with a couple of changes. Before being fired, Murray Cook had made a trade with the Los Angeles Dodgers to bring infielder Mariano Duncan and pitcher Tim Leary to the Reds. Duncan would play second base in 1990 and have a career year. Also, relief pitcher Randy Myers was acquired from the New York Mets in a trade for relief pitcher John Franco. Myers combined with Reds relief pitchers Rob Dibble and Norm Charlton to form a flame-throwing trio of stoppers known as the "Nasty Boys" that would provide the Reds with the best bullpen in the National League in 1990.

The 1990 Reds under Lou Piniella won their first nine games and proceeded to go wire-to-wire in first place to win the National League West Division Championship. The closest that any team came to catching them was in September when the Dodgers pulled within three games.

The Reds then defeated the Pittsburgh Pirates four games to two to win the National League Pennant. In the 1990 World Series the Reds surprised the baseball world when they swept the favored Oakland A's four games to none.

In the first inning of Game Four of the World Series in Oakland, centerfielder Eric Davis dove after a ball and tore a kidney. Davis then attempted to get the attention of shortstop Barry Larkin to call a time-out, but Larkin didn't hear him, so he finished the inning. Then Davis went to the clubhouse and proceeded to urinate a cup full of blood.

Hospitalized in Oakland, Davis required a special airplane staffed with medical personnel to transport him back to Cincinnati. Davis would allege that Marge Schott had ignored him and forced him to rent his own plane to fly home to receive further treatment at Cincinnati's Christ Hospital. He felt that Marge Schott treated him horribly and told the press, "If I were a dog I would have gotten more care, and that's the truth,"[30] said Davis.

The Davis incident was a public relations nightmare for Marge Schott, who attempted to blame the circumstances on her general manager Bob Quinn as some sort of mix up. To attempt to smooth things over with Eric Davis and the fans who were outraged, Marge arranged a meeting with Davis at his Cincinnati home with the media present, and as the cameras rolled, professed her affection for him and stated that she would gladly pay all Davis's travel and medical expenses.

Any other owner in the history of the game would have been delirious with joy over their ball club's sweep in the World Series, but that wasn't the case with Marge Schott.

Revenue from the first four games in a World Series is split 60 percent to the players and 40 percent to the owners. When Marge learned that by the series ending in four games it would mean that she lost a lot of money by it not going to five, six, or seven games, she was furious. When her discontent with the length of series became public, she attempted to smooth the matter over by stating she was hoping that the Reds would win the series at home.

Following the Reds World Series sweep of Oakland A's, there was no formal celebration for the players or the staff. Marge just didn't want to foot the bill. So Jack Maier, one of the limited partners that represented Frisch's Restaurants, came forward and got the management of the hotel in Oakland where the Reds were staying to close off the restaurant and setup an open bar. Marge finally agreed, but with the caveat of no food. So some of the players went out and brought back sacks of hamburgers. Marge attended the impromptu victory party at the hotel, but got so drunk she had to be helped back to her room by the team's executive vice president Steve Schott (no relation to Marge).

Even though he had just won a world championship, Lou Piniella wanted to leave Cincinnati. But after Marge gave him a new contract nearly doubling his 1990 salary, he signed. While Piniella's Reds had won the 1990 division championship in such a convincing style, in 1991 they could do no better than fourth place.

Eric Davis had a subpar season in 1991 hitting .235 in eighty-nine games. Davis says he needed additional time to recuperate from his injury in the 1990 World Series, but he played anyway and that when the Reds failed to repeat as division champions, Marge Schott wanted a scapegoat, so he was traded to the Los Angeles Dodgers for the 1992 season.

The year 1991 included personal tragedy for Marge as Schottzie died. So Marge promoted another Saint Bernard to the position of Reds mascot and called it Schottzie 02. The dog's name would grace a $500,000 athletic field that Marge gave to St. Ursula Academy in Cincinnati. When Schottzie 02 died in 2001, Marge buried the dog with a

Reds cap on, and she tossed a replica of the 1990 World Series ring in its grave.

Lou Piniella stayed on for one more year, but with an injury plagued roster, the Reds finished in second place in 1992. Following the 1992 season Bob Quinn was not rehired as general manager and was replaced by Jim Bowden.

Prior to the 1992 season in an uncharacteristic display of spending, Marge Schott, whose front office financial cutbacks included counting paper clips, ensuring that copy machines were turned off at night, mandating that any purchase order over fifty dollars have her approval, and cutting the number of scouts, whom she claimed did nothing but watched ball games, gave her approval to signing All-Star shortstop Barry Larkin to a new five year $25.6 million contract. The contract prevented Larkin from becoming a free agent and making him one of the games top five paid players.

By 1991 big troubles had begun for Marge. She had fired Tim Sabo (no relation to Reds player Chris Sabo), the team controller on August 23, 1991. Sabo felt that he had been wrongly dismissed and decided to sue Marge in Hamilton County Common Pleas Court for $2.5 million. The central issue of Sabo's discontent was that he felt he had been wrongfully fired in retaliation for giving a court-ordered deposition to the Reds limited partners, who settled a lawsuit out of court in May 1991 over the distribution of $17.7 million in profits. In short, Sabo was alleging that Schott had ordered him to doctor the Reds books. Among other allegations made by Sabo in his deposition was that Marge fired him because he opposed her policy of not hiring blacks for front office positions.

Marge denied the charge and counter-sued stating, Sabo wrote himself checks totaling $6,894 without her authorization. Marge also charged that Sabo owed $52,571 for health-insurance premiums negligently paid to retired front office employees, and wanted $25,000 from him for defaming her.

However, things soon got very unsettled for Marge when the Reds former marketing director Cal Levy, who had been fired in 1989, stated in a deposition that Schott had called both Eric Davis and Dave Parker her "million dollar niggers."[31] In addition, Levy stated that he had heard Marge say, "Sneaky Goddam Jews are all alike ..."[32] Levy also stated that while at Marge's home for a Christmas party in 1987, he had found an armband with a Swastika on it in a drawer she had asked him to go into to get a dinner bell.

Soon after, Sharon Jones, a former executive with the Oakland Athletics, claimed that in a 1987 conference call, she had heard Marge saying she would "never hire another nigger. I'd rather have a trained monkey working for me than a nigger."[33]

According to the testimony of Roger Blaemier, the former Reds vice president of business operation, Eric Davis was referred to by Marge as the "trouble making nigger." He wanted red baseball shoes, and at the time, the Reds shoes were black. Blaemier stated as a result, "They ended converting over to red shoes the next year."[34] Marge Schott, when asked by lawyer Stephen Imm if she realized "nigger" was an offensive term to blacks, answered, "Yes. I think it is an offensive term to blacks. I don't know; I've never really asked them. I would think it would be offensive. Maybe it's not offensive to them. I don't know."[35]

As for her possession of the Nazi armband, Marge stated that she didn't know why she was given the armband. Perhaps it was because she is German—a lot of people collect memorabilia. She received it from a man who worked for her at her brick company in St. Louis.

The suit by Tim Sabo against Marge Schott was dismissed in mid-November 1992. The judge threw out some of the counts in Sabo's lawsuit, and then his attorney withdrew the others. So in effect, Marge was found not guilty of discrimination.

Although Marge had just dodged a bullet, almost immediately she put her foot back in her mouth. News of the depositions in the Sabo lawsuit had circulated in the press. In December 1992, *The New York Times* dubbed Marge Schott as "Baseball's Big Red Headache." In an interview with the paper she said, "Hitler was good in the beginning, but he went too far."[36] She also said that her use of the "N" word was a joke.

The other Major League team owners were starting to worry that some sort of backlash against Marge would damage their business interests. Major League Baseball still had a cloud hanging over it from the Los Angeles Dodgers general manager Al Campanis's interview on *Nightline* where he stated that blacks didn't have the necessities for certain jobs in baseball. The last thing that baseball needed with Schott's comments was for the world to think that racism was tolerated in MLB front offices. The owners were concerned that black activists such as Jessie Jackson and Al Sharpton might organize boycotts of fans and perhaps even players. Among others, Hank Aaron, then a senior vice president with the Atlanta Braves, called for the commissioner's office to investigate Marge Schott.

So Major League Baseball and the acting-commissioner, Milwaukee Brewers owner Bud Selig, felt it was in their best interest to appoint a four-person committee to investigate Marge. As a precursor, Selig asked National League president Bill White to meet with Marge in preparation for review at the next executive council meeting.

At that meeting with Bill White, Marge referred to her thirty-one-year-old new general manager Jim Bowden as "my boy." "They got mad at me," said Marge. "They told me honey's no good either. I can't remember anyone's name. I call them all honey."[37]

On February 3, 1993 acting-commissioner Bud Selig, representing MLB's executive council, announced that effective March 1, Marge Schott would be suspended from day-to-day operations of the Reds for one year and fined $25,000. But she would be able to maintain financial control. Also, she would be ordered to undergo multicultural training programs. In a ten-page report released by Selig, it outlined a pattern of language her fellow owners termed as "the most base and demeaning type of racial and ethnic stereotyping."[38] In November 1993 Marge Schott was reinstated to full operational control.

A week after Marge was suspended by MLB, although she was advised by her attorney Bob Bennett to not do so, on February 11 she appeared on ABC's *Primetime Live* with Dianne Sawyer. Her appearance was abominable. During her interview with Sawyer, Marge called the MLB investigation of her a "witch hunt" and repeated her belief that everyone uses the word "nigger." Marge even asked Sawyer if she had ever used the word. In addition, Marge stated that she didn't think the Swastika is a symbol of evil.

While everyone in the media was condemning Marge Schott for her racially insensitive remarks, Ira Berkow of *The New York Times* boldly raised the issue of if the owners had suspended Marge for the right reason or were just trying to avoid a storm of protests from fans. It was the opinion of Berkow that, in regard to the racial and ethnic slurs made by Schott, while not defending them, he pointed out that she made those comments in private and had the right of free speech, despite how reprehensible the comments were. In Berkow's opinion, the correct reason to have suspended Schott should have been over her hiring practices. In his column, Berkow wrote, "What Marge Schott should have been reprimanded for was that, as principal owner of the Reds, she did not hire minority employees in her front office at Riverfront Stadium. Since she took over as the leading light of the Reds in 1984, she hired exactly zero black or Hispanic employees in the front office."[39]

Nonetheless, the troubles continued to mount for Marge. In January 1994 she told manager Davey Johnson that if he didn't marry his live-in girlfriend she would fire him. So Johnson complied. Also that same year, Marge told the *Cincinnati Enquirer* that she wouldn't allow her players to wear earrings "because only fruits wear earrings."[40]

In early April 1996 Marge was back on the hot seat after a shocking and very sad incident occurred on opening day in Cincinnati. Home plate umpire John McSherry dropped dead on the field from a heart attack two minutes and seven pitches into the game. Marge hesitated before calling off the game. As the fans began leaving Riverfront Stadium she stated, "I feel cheated. This isn't supposed to happen to us, not in Cincinnati. This is our day. This is our history, tradition, our team. Nobody feels worse than me."[41] Marge said that she felt sorry for all the fans that had traveled so far to see the game. She asked if McSherry would not have wanted the game to be played. She said it could have been played in his honor. The fact that she had suggested that the game continue to be played with two umpires brought immediate scorn from the baseball world. Later, she sent flowers to the umpire's dressing room. But they turned out to be recycled flowers, ones given to her that day by someone else.

A month after the McSherry incident on May 3, 1996, Marge was interviewed on ESPN by Sal Paolantonio, and she sealed her fate with her fellow owners with more senseless comments. The interview was a fair list of questions in regard to the controversy surrounding her and ones that Marge had answered several times before, but when Paollantonio asked her about Adolph Hitler, she still seemed totally oblivious to the context of her response. As it turned out, it sounded like Marge was once again praising the virtues of Hitler. "Everything you read, when he came in he was good. They built tremendous highways and got all the factories going ... but then he went nuts. He went berserk, I guess," said Marge. "I think even his own generals tried to kill him, didn't they? Everybody knows that he did good at the beginning, but then he went too far."[42]

With the McSherry tragedy and her reaction to it and now the ESPN interview on record, Marge Schott became fair game for every sportswriter in the country. They all wanted to get on the bandwagon and take their shot at Marge Schott, because she had a huge target on her back and was very news worthy. So a deluge of negative articles appeared in every newspaper in the country blasting Marge Schott.

On May 20, 1996 an article written by Rick Reilly titled "Heaven Help Marge Schott" was published in *Sports Illustrated*. The article portrayed Marge as a quintessential buffoon, who had millions of dollars, but pinched pennies in the Reds front office, lived a life of isolation and loneliness, drank cheap vodka, and the only friend she had was her dog. The writer had clearly baited Marge in getting her to agree to the interview. The published article should have invoked some sympathy from Bud Selig and the other owners. Instead, they hid behind a shield of artificial embarrassment, smug in the knowledge that they knew they had her right where they wanted her. They knew that the press had done what they had been unable to do—strike the fatal blow on Marge Schott as a Major League mogul.

About the only person past or present from the baseball world who expressed any sympathy for Marge Schott was Pete Rose. "If the owners are going to get rid of Marge, they ought to take a couple other guys into consideration," said Rose. Marge isn't the only owner who's off-color and says things that don't come out right. People have to remember that Marge is really two people. She's the celebrity who owns the Cincinnati Reds, signs autographs, and does interviews before the game. But when the lights go out, she goes home and becomes another lady—with no close friends."[43]

On June 12, 1996 Marge Schott, for the second time in three years, was forced by Major League Baseball to give up day-to-day operations of the Cincinnati Reds—this time through 1998. John Allen, the team's controller, took over operations. During her suspension, she was not permitted to act as a spokesperson for the Reds or attend league meetings. However, she was still allowed to come to the ballpark and sit in her private box.

It took a long time for it to sink into Marge's head that she had limited speaking skills and shouldn't speak to the media, but suddenly she got it and declined to speak. After her return as the Reds CEO in 1998, Marge kept a low profile. But she was still being pressured by Major League Baseball to sell her majority shares in the Reds. With mounting health problems, on April 21, 1999 Marge relented and sold five and a half of her six and a half shares to three limited partners for $67 million. Then eighty-year-old billionaire Carl Lindner was named the new CEO.

Marge Schott did indeed love the Cincinnati Reds. But between the years following the Reds World Championship in 1990 and her final season as CEO in 1997, the Cincinnati Reds were a marginally competitive team. The Reds were in first place in the National League Central Division in August 1994 when the balance of the season schedule was cancelled by MLB due to the players' strike. So it is impossible to know how that season would have turned out. However, the 1995 Reds, under manager Davey Johnson, won the Central Division then were swept by the Atlanta Braves in the playoffs. The Reds finished third the next two seasons.

Marge Schott had considerable influence on the Reds' lack of success in the 1990s. First, Marge had decimated the Reds scouting system in an attempt to cut back on player contract expenses and ignored the farm system. Then she allowed Jim Bowden, a very inexperienced and somewhat naive young general manager, to operate without proper oversight. Consequently, Bowden made some very bad trades such as the Paul O'Neill for Roberto Kelly swap with the New York Yankees and sending catcher Dan Wilson to Seattle for Bret Boone. At the same time, with Marge's approval, Bowden was spending a lot of money signing other players to contracts that jeopardized the long term stability of the team.

After selling her majority control in the Reds, Marge appeared infrequently in public, usually at news conferences to announce donations to the Cincinnati Zoo and other local charities.

Marge Schott had been a heavy smoker, and on February 9, 2004 she was admitted to Cincinnati's Christ Hospital with breathing difficulties. She died three weeks later on March 2. She was seventy-five years old.

7

JOAN B. KROC

SAN DIEGO PADRES

Joan Beverly Mansfield was born in St. Paul, Minnesota on August 27, 1928. Her father, Charles Smart Mansfield, worked at various jobs: store keeper, railroad telegraph operator, salesman, just to name a few. Her mother, Gladys Bonnebelle Mansfield, was an accomplished violinist trained at the MacPhail School of Music in Minneapolis. She started teaching at the age of fifteen.

Joan followed in her mother's footsteps and also studied music to become a pianist. Following her training in music school, she began to teach and play the piano in a local music store. In 1945 at the age of seventeen, Joan married a returning Navy veteran named Roland F. Smith. A baby girl named Linda would be born to the couple a year later.

Joan first met Ray Kroc in 1956 in a restaurant in St. Paul where she was playing the piano and organ. Kroc was in St. Paul selling fast food franchises. He played the piano for her, and it was instant mutual attraction. At the time, both she and Kroc had other spouses. Ray Kroc was later to remark, "I was stunned by her blond beauty."[1] Soon after their meeting Kroc got a divorce. The two proceeded to have a secret relationship. Eventually, Joan divorced and they married in 1969.

At the time they met, Ray Kroc was twenty-six years Joan's senior. Joan said, "I didn't see him for six of those 12 years and only spoke to him three times during the other six. I ate my heart out. I wasn't terribly mature at 28. Beautiful maybe, but not mature. I had a teenage daughter. I just chickened out. I couldn't get divorced."[2]

Raymond Albert "Ray" Kroc was born in Chicago in 1902, the son of Bohemian immigrants. A high school dropout at the age of fifteen, he served in World War One with the Red Cross Ambulance Corps in France. Following the war, Kroc was employed in several positions. He first became a traveling jazz pianist. But he gave it up to marry at the age of twenty; he then held a few different jobs before becoming a paper cup salesman. Soon after, he gave up that vocation to become musical director at station WGES in Chicago. Still later, he moved to Florida to sell real estate and quickly went broke.

In 1926 Ray Kroc returned to Chicago and returned to selling paper cups for the Lily Tulip Company where he remained employed until 1937. It was during that time that Kroc met young Bill Veeck, Jr., who was the commissary manager for the Chicago Cubs. Kroc became a huge Cubs fan and began attending games almost every day when the team was at home. His favorite player was catcher Gabby Hartnett

By 1937 Ray Kroc had become the exclusive distributor for a soda fountain machine that was capable of mixing five milkshakes at a time. It was this device that would lead to making Ray Kroc one of the richest men in America.

In 1955 Kroc would take notice that a short order restaurant in San Bernardino, California had purchased eight of his machines. This was an unusually high number. So he went to California to observe the operation. He was thunderstruck to learn that people were standing in line waiting to buy milkshakes and clamoring for more. The stand was owned by two brothers, Dick and Mac McDonald.

Instantly, Ray Kroc saw an opportunity to cash in and approached the brothers about becoming a partner. He was sure that he could make money selling his milkshake machines to additional hamburger stands. The McDonald brothers didn't want to leave San Bernardino but agreed to let Kroc franchise their restaurant into a small chain of hamburger stands for 0.5 percent of the profit.

That same year at the age of fifty-two, Ray Kroc opened the first McDonald's franchise hamburger stand in Des Plains, Illinois. Later that year, he opened two more franchises in California and founded the McDonald's Corporation.

The hamburger stand franchise continued to grow throughout the late 1950s, and in 1961, Kroc borrowed $2.7 million and used it to buyout the McDonald brothers. That same year, McDonald's grossed more than $6 million. While Ray Kroc fought off critics and nutritionist who blasted his fried burgers as unhealthy, business at the McDonald's hamburger restaurants boomed throughout the 1960s, and by early 1973 stock in the corporation was trading at $71 a share. Investors who had bought the stock in the mid-1960s had seen their wealth increase more than sixtyfold. By 1977 McDonald's was grossing more than $3.7 billion a year and outselling its primary competitor Pillsbury owned Burger King by four to one.

Quality was paramount on Ray Kroc's operational agenda, and to establish continuity in his products, he established Hamburger University in Elk Grove, Illinois to train McDonald's franchise owners on how to clean grills, how to flip burgers, and tell when they were done. His training course led to achieving a "Bachelor of Hamburgerology" with a minor in French fries.

Ray Kroc had always been a baseball fan. Or course his favorite team was his hometown Chicago Cubs, and in 1970, Kroc approached owner Philip K. Wrigley with an offer to buy the team—but was turned down.

Four years later on January 31, 1974 Kroc bought the struggling San Diego Padres for $12 million from C. Arnolt Smith. Since entering the National League in 1969 as an expansion team, the Padres had been a bust at the gate. Their peak year for attendance had been 1972 when 644,273 fans came out to San Diego Stadium. Furthermore, in the Padres' first five years in the National

League West Division, they had finished in sixth place (last) every year.

Ray Kroc's intervention into the bidding for the team saved it from being transferred to Washington by Joseph Danzansky, a supermarket magnate. Former Padres general manager, Buzzy Bavasi, remarked that when a lawyer called him and said that he had a client, McDonald's, who was interested in buying the team, he thought it was the aircraft corporation. Remarking on how close the transfer of the San Diego franchise to Washington came, Bavasi said, "I'll tell how close it was. We had to unpack so many things that had been packed, we had a moving-van bill for $6,500."[3]

Upon buying the Padres, Ray and Joan Kroc moved from Chicago to San Diego. At the Padres home opener in 1974 Ray Kroc quickly established himself as an owner that wanted to improve the ball clubs performance. The Padres were losing to the Houston Astros 9-2 in the ninth inning when their leadoff batter walked. John McNamara, the Padres manager, sent in a pinch runner that was picked off first base. Before the next batter stepped in, Ray Kroc had sprinted from his box into the public address announcer's booth, identified himself, and commandeered the microphone.

Kroc began to blurt out of the P.A. system "I suffer with you"—then a streaker bolted out of the stands and ran across the outfield naked. "Get that streaker," bellowed Kroc. He paused while the exhibitionist was apprehended, then began again, "I have some good news," he said. "The good news is that we've outdrawn the Dodgers. They had 31,000 for their opener, and we had 39,000 for ours. The bad news is that I've never seen such stupid ball-playing in my life."[4]

Through tireless promotion in his first year as owner of the Padres, Ray Kroc was able to attract 1,075,399 fans into the ballpark to see a team that finished in last place in the Western Division with a record of 51-111. Kroc immediately began to attempt to build the San Diego Padres into a competitive team. When the free agent era began following the 1976 season, Kroc's hamburger money was spent freely to attract quality players. When the results did not pay dividends in the standings, Buzzy Bavasi was fired, as was John McNamara.

By the early 1980s Jack McKeon had been appointed vice president for baseball operations, and in 1982 Dick Williams took over as manager and the Padres started to emerge as a contender. On July 19, 1982 future Hall of Fame player Tony Gwynn made his debut with the Padres getting two hits against the Phillies. In December the Padres signed free agent, first baseman Steve Garvey, who played for fourteen years with the rival Los Angeles Dodgers, including four World Series.

Nonetheless, there had been some bumps for the Padres on the road to competiveness. In 1980 the Padres lost free agent and future Hall of Fame outfielder Dave Winfield to the New York Yankees. But the most notable faux pas was the Padres' contract squabble with future Hall of Fame shortstop Ozzie Smith, who had come up in 1978 and by 1980 had established himself as one of the best in the game.

Going into the 1980 season, Ozzie Smith and his agent, Ed Gottlieb, had demanded that Ray Kroc increase his salary from $65,000 to $150,000. To press the issue, Gottlieb took out a classified advertisement in the San Diego newspapers that stated, "Padre Baseball Player wants part-time employment to supplement income. College education, willing to work, prefer PR-type employment. Need hours tailored to baseball schedule, but would quit baseball for the right opportunity."[5] Smith's demands fell on deaf ears.

Joan Kroc then entered the fray and suggested that Ozzie Smith could work at $3.25 as an assistant to Luis, her gardener. The issue was resolved when, on December 10, 1981, Smith was traded to the St. Louis Cardinals for shortstop Garry Templeton.

During the late 1970s attitudes among the medical community in regard to treatment for alcoholics and drug abusers was changing. In 1980 Joan Kroc set precedence when she created the first employee assistance program by a major sports team for the San Diego Padres.

On January 14, 1984 Ray Kroc died. His health had started to decline in December 1979 when he had a stroke.

Soon after, he entered into an alcoholism treatment center in Orange, California. He said at the time in regard to his entry into the facility, "I am required to take medication which is incompatible with the use of alcohol."[6]

Kroc's fifty-six-year-old, blond, stylish widow took over as chairwoman of the Padres. According to *Forbes Magazine*, the heiress was worth $525 million, she drove a Rolls-Royce and sported a diamond on her finger that looked like it had fallen out of an ice cube tray.

Ballard Smith, a former prosecutor from Pennsylvania, had married Joan's daughter Linda in 1971. He was appointed club president. Joan readily admitted that she knew nothing about baseball, but she applied herself and began to quickly learn the fine points of the game.

At that point in time, Joan Kroc was best known for having been the co-founder of Operation Cork (Kroc spelled backwards), a national program to help the families of alcoholics. Started in 1976 and financed by McDonald's revenues through the Kroc Foundation, Operation Cork included a grant of $800,000 to Dartmouth Medical School to develop modern curriculum for the study of alcohol misuse and alcoholism.

Joan had grown tired of the opera, symphony, and zoo. She began looking for personal fulfillment. Joan admitted that buying a baseball team as her late husband had done would have been the last thing she would have done—although she gradually became a real fan. So she started Operation Cork in an attempt to create something that would benefit others.

Ray Kroc had been a staunch Republican, but Joan was a Democrat. When President Ronald Reagan offered her an opportunity to join a national businessman's group she turned him down. She was of the opinion that she was called because she was a woman. "I'm not going to be a token,"[7] she remarked.

On October 15, 1974 the first Ronald McDonald House was opened in Philadelphia by Dr. Audrey Evans; Philadelphia Eagles player Fred Hill (whose daughter, Kim, had leukemia); Leonard Tose, owner of the Eagles; Jim Murray, the Eagles' general manager; and Ed Rensi, the McDonald's regional manager. The McDonald's owner/operators in Philadelphia made the House possible, donating proceeds from the sale of Shamrock Shakes.

Upon the death of Ray Kroc in 1984 Joan Kroc established Ronald McDonald House Charities in memory of her late husband, who was a strong advocate for children. The mission of the charity is to provide a facility for parents who cannot afford to pay for hotel accommodations while their child is hospitalized.

In 1993 Joan Kroc established gifts of $500,000 in stock to each Ronald McDonald House open and operating in the U.S. That act of philanthropy by Joan was followed in 2003 by her bequeathing more than $60 million to Ronald McDonald House Charities. By 2011 there were 309 Ronald McDonald Houses operating worldwide.

As the 1984 season approached, over the winter the Padres acquired a couple of former New York Yankees. Third baseman Gregg Nettles came to San Diego in trade with the Yankees for two players, Dennis Rasmussen and minor leaguer P. Darin Cloninger. Then reliever Richard "Goose" Gossage, a free agent, signed a five year contract for $10 million, half of which was deferred. The day that Gossage signed his contract on January 12, he was taken by Padres officials to the hospital where Ray Kroc laid ill. Within a few days, Kroc died. For the 1984 season the Padres would wear the initials RAK on their uniform sleeves in memory of Raymond A. Kroc.

The San Diego Padres opened the 1984 season by winning their first four games with two victories over the Pittsburgh Pirates and two victories over the Chicago Cubs. In the first four games Goose Gossage had two saves.

In mid-July, led by newly acquired Gregg Nettles and Goose Gossage and the steady play of veteran Steve Garvey and two talented young outfielders, Tony Gwynn and Kevin McReynolds, the San Diego Padres maintained a comfortable lead in the National League Western Division race.

On Wednesday afternoon on July 18 at Wrigley Field, the Padres lost to the Chicago Cubs 4-1. But their division lead was still seven games over the Atlanta Braves. However, back in San Diego it would be a horrific day for the city and Joan Kroc.

That morning in San Ysidro, California, a border community near San Diego, forty-one-year-old James Oliver Huberty, an unemployed man that had recently relocated to California from Ohio, took his wife Etna and two young daughters with him to traffic court in San Diego. Then they had breakfast at a McDonald's and visited the San Diego Zoo. When they came home that afternoon, Huberty, dressed in combat fatigues, kissed his family and told his wife he was "going hunting humans."[8] What followed was the worst single-day massacre by a lone gunman in United States history.

Armed with a 12-gauge shotgun, an automatic rifle, and a 9-millimeter Browning pistol, at 4:00 p.m. Huberty arrived at a McDonald's about a half a block from his family's apartment and began firing point blank at persons both inside and outside the restaurant—even through the windows. Before he was fatally shot by the police ninety minutes later, twenty-one people had been killed and nineteen injured. The dead, eight men, seven women, and six children, included restaurant workers, customers, and passers-by. Eleven-year-old Joshua Coleman played dead for an hour after being shot in the restaurant's parking lot. Three of the victims were members of a young family about to enter the restaurant. Huberty coldly monitored reports of his deadly actions over an AM-FM radio he carried in an ammunition bag.

"He turned around and started shooting everything insight," said Police Chief Bill Kolender. "The guy fired just eight million times."[9]

The initial call that a man was shooting a gun inside a McDonald's went out a 4:04 p.m. A policeman on routine patrol arrived at the McDonald's at 4:06 p.m., but was immobilized by Huberty's gunfire at his car. A bureaucratic snafu delayed the assembly and initial action of a SWAT team with the proper command authority. Consequently, the fully authorized team did not arrive on the scene until 4:55 p.m. Inside the restaurant, Huberty paced the floor stepping over victims of his gunfire. Finally, at 5:17 p.m. a second green light order was given, and police sharpshooter Charles Foster fired one round from the roof of the U. S. Post Office next door, striking Huberty in the chest and killing him instantly.

The police claimed that the SWAT response was complicated by the shooting rampage taking place during rush hour and by the fact that San Ysidro is separated by fifteen miles from the rest of San Diego. Also, the San Diego SWAT unit's sixty members were all regular patrolmen that had to be called into SWAT service.

Joan Kroc was at home when she heard the first reports of the massacre on the television. Feeling a sense of frustration, she immediately called a press conference and announced that she was donating $100,000 of her own money to help with burial costs, counseling for survivors, and financial aid for relatives of the dead. Then she called the McDonald's corporate offices and told them she would like the board to come up with at least $25,000. The next day, McDonald's donated $1 million for assistance to the victims' families. Then the residents of San Diego raised an additional $1 million.

Joan told the press that she hoped to meet with the wife of James Huberty. "I hope to be able to give her comfort," Kroc said. "She is an innocent victim, overridden with guilt feelings. She must understand that the community holds nothing against her and her children."[10]

Later, she was to remark that San Ysidro is a needy community. "The people are poor. People don't plan where they're going to bury their kids. It was the worst possible tragedy. I thought maybe I could be a catalyst again."[11]

Etna Huberty stated that her husband started to lose his mind after he had lost his house and a series of jobs in Ohio. "I think he wasn't in his right mind: he was hearing voices. He told me God was 10 feet tall and had a long gray beard."[12]

The San Diego Padres went on to become 1984 National League Western Division champs and meet the Chicago Cubs winner of the Eastern Division crown in their first post-season series play in franchise history. During the season, the Padres drew an amazing 1,983,904 fans at Jack Murphy Stadium.

Prior to the National League Championship Series beginning in Chicago, Goose Gossage threw a party at his new home in San Diego for the whole team, including the woman that signed his paychecks—Joan Kroc. Gossage showed his appreciation for his boss lady by throwing her in the swimming pool. Why not? It was her turn.

The Chicago Cubs won the National League East Division title by six and a half games over the New York Mets. Facing the Padres in the National League Championship Series at home in Wrigley Field, the Cubs got off to a fast start, winning the first two games.

The series then moved to San Diego with the Padres needing to win all three remaining games or face elimination. On the evening of October 4, 1984 prior to game three of the National League Championship Series, the first home post-season game in San Diego Padres history, Joan Kroc decked out in a designer Padres uniform, from a few feet in front of the mound threw out the first ball at Jack Murphy Stadium. Her toss landed up along the third base line where catcher Terry Kennedy handled it on a hop. Then she reminded the 58,346 fans on hand that her late husband Ray Kroc had saved the team for their city.

The Padres won game three by a score of 7-1 on a home run by Kevin McReynolds in the sixth inning. In the ninth inning Goose Gossage made his first appearance in the series and blazed his fast ball past the Cubs.

The next night the Padres won game four by a score of 7-5 as Steve Garvey knocked in five runs with four hits in five at bats including a two run walk-off home run in the bottom of the ninth inning that broke a 5-5 tie. So now the series was tied two games apiece.

In game five the Cubs entered the bottom of the seventh inning with a 3-2 lead. Then Leon Durham made an error that allowed the tying run to score. That was followed by three straight singles that capped a four run rally by the Padres. Goose Gossage entered the game in relief for the Padres and shutdown the Cubs in the eighth and ninth innings to win the series. The San Diego Padres became the first National League team to ever come back from being two games down in the championship series to win.

But the 1984 World Series resembled a miss-match as the San Diego Padres lost to the Detroit Tigers four games to one. The Tigers battered the Padres pitching staff for a 13.94 ERA. For the Tigers, shortstop Alan Trammel hit .450, Jack Morris pitched two complete game victories, and Sparky Anderson became the first manager to win a World Series in both leagues.

Goose Gossage had been rocked for a three-run homer by the Tigers Kurt Gibson that put the final game out of reach. Alluding to George Steinbrenner's apology to New York when the Yankees lost the 1981 World Series, Gossage stated that Joan Kroc would not apologize. "I'm proud of the way she treated us,"[13] said Gossage.

Following the World Series, Joan Kroc made an attempt to assist Padres general manager Jack McKeon strengthen the team for the 1985 season by acquiring free agent pitcher Rick Sutcliffe. After being traded by the Cleveland Indians to the Chicago Cubs in June 1984, Sutcliffe was instrumental in leading the Cubs to the Eastern Division Championship with a record of 16-1.

Joan invited Sutcliffe and his agent, Barry Axelrod, to have dinner with her and Padres first baseman Steve Garvey in La Jolla. While Sutcliffe said he was impressed with Joan Kroc, the Padres, the people, and the area, he eventually resigned with the Chicago Cubs. To acquire another starting pitcher, the Padres arranged a trade with the Chicago White Sox for Lamar Hoyt.

In the 1985 season the Padres started off strong and held a five game lead in the Western Division on July 4, but in the second half they faded, finishing in a tie for third place with the Houston Astros.

Alan Wiggins had been the second baseman for the 1984 National League Champion Padres, hitting .258 with 154 hits; a speedster, he stole seventy bases and scored 106 runs. In the National League Championship Series Wiggins hit .316, and in the World Series he hit .364.

In February 1985 Alan Wiggins signed a four year contract with the Padres calling for $2.8 million. But he wouldn't finish the season with the club. Wiggins had a history of drug abuse. In 1982 he had been arrested for possession of cocaine. The Padres sent Wiggins to Orange

County for treatment and continued to pay his salary and stand by him. However, he was warned by Ballard Smith that the Padres would only do this once.

On April 25, 1985 Wiggins was hitting .054 with two hits in twenty-seven at bats when he failed to show up for a night game in Los Angeles. Alan Wiggins was once again using drugs. Ballard Smith said, "I thought he had been in an accident. I never thought about drugs. I'd talked to Alan for 45 minutes the day before and he seemed fine. When he disappeared, I called the Player's Association, but I was told I should not talk to Alan, that they would handle it."[14]

Well Ballard Smith talked to his mother-in-law, Joan Kroc, who in 1976 had founded Operation Cork to promote awareness of drug abuse. Joan Kroc issued an order that Alan Wiggins would never again wear a San Diego Padres uniform. Subsequently, the Padres sent Wiggins to their minor league affiliate in Las Vegas, and on June 27, 1985, he was traded to the Baltimore Orioles.

Wiggins' once promising Major League career came to end following the 1987 season when he was released by the Orioles. On January 6, 1991 Alan Wiggins died at the age of thirty-two in a Los Angeles hospital from complications with AIDS. He was the first Major League ball player to die from AIDS.

In December 1985 Joan Kroc and Ballard Smith were at loggerheads over a report that Smith had attempted to persuade Padres manager Dick Williams to resign, offering him a contract buy out for $250,000. Williams had become upset when Smith fired his friend, third base coach Ozzie Virgil. According to Virgil, his dismissal was a tactic to force Williams out.

Joan Kroc issued a vote of confidence for Dick Williams. But on February 24, 1986, the first day of spring training, Williams resigned.

With the approval of Joan Kroc and the vice president for baseball operations, Jack McKeon, Steve Boros, a forty-nine-year-old director of the San Diego Padres minor league instruction, was named the new manager. Under Boros's leadership, the 1986 San Diego Padres would finish in fourth place.

On August 29 with the Padres in last place, Ballard Smith announced that Goose Gossage had been suspended without pay ($167,033) for the rest of the season. Gossage had been openly critical of the team's management and Joan Kroc. Smith told the press that while the Padres acknowledged a player's right to speak out, they expected a player to do so in a professional manner. Ballard felt Gossage had crossed the line. So he decided to invoke Major League Rule 13 that permits owners to take disciplinary action for repeated and continuing insubordination and similar player behavior not in the best interest of the club.

Goose Gossage always maintained that the only reason he played the game was for the love of it. In an article published in *Newsday*, Gossage had been quoted as saying Smith was more concerned about the team's image than winning. "He wants choirboys and not winning players," said Gossage. "What are we in this game for, to show what good people we are or to win games? I never sang in a choir. I didn't know you had to go to church before you could play baseball."[15] Gossage was also quoted as saying that Smith "just listens to what Mom says," a reference to Joan Kroc.

In a reference to his old boss George Steinbrenner, owner of the New York Yankees, who Gossage often disagreed with, he stated, "George wanted to win. I couldn't say that about Joan Kroc."[16]

Earlier in the season, Gossage had said that Joan Kroc was poisoning the world with her McDonald's hamburgers. Gossage also disliked that Joan Kroc had banned beer from the San Diego Padres clubhouse and that Ballard Smith had stated that he was not interested in signing soon-to-be free agent Tim Raines. "If we don't sign some free agents, we'll be worse next year than we are now. And who's going to sign here for a one-year contract with no beer in the clubhouse? The attitude here is the worst I've ever seen"[17]

The reason for Joan Kroc's ban on beer in the clubhouse was based on notifications that liability insurance had gone up 3,000 percent in eight years, and the Padres could be liable for injuries or accidents that could be connected to beer.

Ballard Smith had stated the reason he was not interested in signing Tim Raines was because of his treatment for drug abuse several years before. The fact was, following his rehab treatment, Tim Raines not only became a highly productive offensive player, but also a strong advocate for drug rehab programs. Smith eventually wrote a letter to Raines stating that he should not have referred to him in that manner. The Kroc family and McDonalds Corporation have had a very good record for promoting rehab programs among its fast food employees.

Regardless of the fact that Goose Gossage had made some rather sever and potentially libelous comments in regard to Joan Kroc and McDonalds, notwithstanding the bad taste demonstrated in his comments about the Padres, the Player's Association under Donald Fehr was contending that management did not have a right to suspend a player for speaking his mind and filed a grievance on Gossage's behalf.

The matter had been scheduled to be heard by an arbitrator on September 19. But on September 18, the Padres lifted the suspension on Goose Gossage after he agreed to make an apology and give $25,000 to charity. Joan Kroc directed the donation should be made to the San Diego Ronald McDonald House.

In a prepared mea-culpa read by Padres spokesman Bill Beck, Gossage stated, "I apologize to Joan Kroc and Ballard Smith for my comments about them. I was wrong to make personal remarks about them, and I regret having done so. I also apologize to McDonald's. My family and I have been and will continue to be regular customers of McDonald's."[18]

Donald Fehr held the opinion that Gossage should not have made any statement and instead went before the arbitrator. In Fehr's opinion, the Padres action was unsupportable.

After just three years, Joan Kroc decided that she had enough of baseball and on November 22, 1986, decided to put the Padres up for sale. The asking price was $50 million. She assured everyone that the team would remain in San Diego. By 1987 the San Diego Padres had only made money in two of the franchise's eighteen-year history. Nonetheless, Joan stated that her reason for wanting to sell the team was that she and her son-in-law, Ballard Smith had lost interest in running the team. Furthermore, she wanted to devote her full-time efforts to various philanthropic and social causes she was involved with.

Among parties expressing an interest in buying the Padres were real estate mogul Donald Trump, who owned the New Jersey Generals in the United States Football League and a group of investors headed up by Steve Garvey.

In late March 1987 Joan Kroc agreed to sell the San Diego Padres to George Argyros, owner of the Seattle Mariners. Immediately, Argyros put the Seattle team on the market. According to Argyros, he wanted to sell the Mariners and buy the Padres so that he could keep a closer watch on his real estate development interests in Southern California and spend more time with his family in their Newport Beach home.

But George Argyros was facing serious obstacles in making the franchise switch. First, there were the formalities; he needed approval of three quarters of the National League team owners and a simple majority of the American League owners to make the franchise shift. Also, Argyros had to be free of his involvement with the Mariners before completing the purchase of the Padres.

By early June George Argyros had done the math and was fairly certain that if the matter of the franchise shift came to a vote with the National League team owners, he would be turned down 11-0. So both Argyros and Joan Kroc called separate news conferences and announced that the deal was off. Joan said she was taking the Padres off the market at least until the end of the season.

There were just too many issues for the deal to be made; Argyros wanted to renegotiate the stadium lease in San Diego, and local authorities were against it and there still had not been any buyer for the Mariners. Baseball Commissioner Peter Uberroth suggested putting the franchise in trust. But the owners were totally against that idea. Also, the National League owners had learned that

Argyros had a reputation as being difficult to work with in meetings and felt his personality would be bad for the collegiality of the league. The Mariners were not competitive and had the lowest payroll in the majors. So it was apparent to the National League moguls that Argyros was going to run the Padres in the same manner he ran the Mariners—a barebones operation.

Meanwhile, as the Padres cruised toward a last place finish in the National League West Division in 1987, Ballard Smith bailed out and resigned as president. Later in the year, Ballard Smith and Linda Smith would file for divorce.

Joan Kroc replaced Smith with Chub Feeney, who had been president of the National League for seventeen years (1970-1986) before resigning at the end of the 1986 season. The Padres finished in third place in 1988, and the season had been one filled with frustration by Chub Feeney. He was not liked by the Padres' fans, who criticized him for not re-signing key players who would become free agents and for frequent travels to his San Francisco home and elsewhere. Feeney's frustration was never more evident than during a night game at Jack Murphy Stadium in late September. Two fans paraded along the walkway during the seventh inning stretch with a banner urging Joan Kroc to "Scrub Chub."[19] Feeney's reaction to the incident from the club's box was to give the fans the finger. The two fans and their banner, which had drawn a large chorus of cheers, were quickly whisked away by stadium security guards. Soon after the incident, Feeney resigned.

On May 20, 1987 Joan Kroc received an honorary degree from Notre Dame. The Joan B. Kroc Institute for International Peace Studies was established at Norte Dame in 1986 through an endowment of $19 million by Joan. The **Kroc Institute for International Peace Studies** is one of the world's leading centers for the study of the causes of violent conflict and strategies for sustainable peace. From 1986 until her death in 2003, Joan Kroc would contribute $69.1 million to establish and support the institute.

Taking her concerns for world peace to the next level, in August 1987, Joan Kroc gave $1 million to the Democratic

National Committee. It was the single largest political contribution ever made. Joan said she "had become increasingly concerned by "an unwarranted and excessive increase of our military weapons" under President Reagan, and by "the use of military force as the priority in carrying out U. S. policy abroad."[20] In particular Joan cited military interventions in Lebanon, Libya, Granada, Nicaragua and the Persian Gulf.

In October 1988 Joan's daughter Linda would remarry to Jerry Kapstein, noted agent for Goose Gossage, Gregg Nettles, Steve Garvey, and Darrell Evans. The couple was married in a surprise ceremony at the La Jolla Beach Tennis Club. Friends of the couple and Joan thought they were being invited to a surprise party. But as the sun set over the Pacific Ocean, a clergyman appeared and the couple was pronounced man and wife.

On October 19, 1989, with Major League team owners facing a possible players' strike or lockout by the owners next spring, Joan Kroc put the Padres back on the market. The team was now valued at $85 million.

Joan Kroc had proposed giving the San Diego Padres to the City of San Diego. But the other Major League owners quickly quashed the idea. The old boys club (although it included three women) that ran Major League Baseball at that time tagged the idea of public ownership as inefficient. The owners, although mostly billionaires, were sweating bullets over the possibility that public ownership could present an opportunity for citizens of the community, notwithstanding the Player's Association to look at the financial books of a ball club at a time when they were attempting to develop strategies to minimalize free agency.

That same year, Joan Kroc purchased a letter written by Senator John F. Kennedy in 1959 to Jackie Robinson pledging support in fighting racial injustice. Joan purchased the letter in order to donate it to the National Baseball Hall of Fame.

On April 2, 1990 Hollywood producer Tom Werner signed a letter of intent to buy the San Diego Padres for $75 million. The following day the owners approved the sale.

Since February 1990 Jerry Kapstein had been acting as president of the Padres and the sales agent for Joan Kroc in selling the team. Subsequently, the Player's Association decertified Kapstein as an agent for players. Two weeks following the sale of the Padres, Joan's daughter Linda filed for divorce from Kapstein. The couple had been married eighteen months.

After his brief stint as chief executive of the Padres, Jerry Kapstein left baseball and worked with the homeless in San Diego. Later, he was named to the Board of the Padres new management.

Following her departure from Major League Baseball, Joan Kroc devoted herself tirelessly to philanthropic endeavors: she gave to causes promoting the fight against AIDS, cancer research, hospice care, nuclear disarmament, the arts, and education. She gave $15 million to flood victims in Grand Forks, North Dakota and $25 million to the University of San Diego to establish its institute for Peace and Justice. In 1998 she was ranked thirty-sixth among the top United States philanthropists by *Fortune Magazine.* That same year she gave $80 million to the Salvation Army in San Diego. All of Joan's gifts were monumental and the donation to the Salvation Army was the largest in the 133-year history of the organization.

In 1997 *Forbes Magazine* estimated Joan Kroc's wealth at $2.1 billion. When asked why she gave so much of her money away, Joan quoted her late husband Ray Kroc, who once answered a similar question stating, "Well, I've never seen a Brink's truck follow a hearse, have you?"[21]

On October 13, 2003 Joan Kroc died at her home at Rancho Santa Fe, California. The cause of death was brain cancer. She was seventy-five years old.

8

OTHER NOTABLE LADY MLB OWNERS AND CO-OWNERS

In addition to the aforementioned ladies there have been several other members of the fairer sex that have been or are a majority owner or co-owner of a Major League team that deserve historical notation in this work. Also, it should be noted that Jim Dunn left the Cleveland Indians to his wife in 1922, but she sold her interest.

The Brush Family Women:
Elsie Lombard Brush, Eleanor Brush Hempstead & Natalie Lombard Brush Gates de Gendron
• NEW YORK GIANTS •

When Major League Baseball pioneer John Tomlinson Brush died on November 26, 1912, in his will he left majority control in equal shares of the New York Giants to three women in his family; Elsie Lombard Brush, his second wife; Eleanor Brush Hempstead, a daughter by his first marriage, and Natalie Lombard Brush de Gendron, a daughter by his second marriage. At the time the New York

Giants were one of the premier franchises in Major League baseball. Unlike Helene Britton of the St. Louis Cardinals, the three women had no interest in running the Giants. Still they retained controlling interest in the franchise for six years until 1919.

The fact that none of the Brush women took an active leadership role in the operation of the team is irrelevant. From a historical perspective, the more salient point of their passive participation is that they as women were pioneers in Major League entrepreneurship. Their precedence in ownership would provide a foundation for other ladies that would follow.

John T. Brush was a classic rags-to-riches success story. Born in Clintonville, New York on June 16, 1845, he became an orphan at the age of four. Raised by his step-uncle on a farm, he was forced to sleep in an unheated barn with his brother George. At age seventeen he ran away and found employment in a country store in Utica. Eventually, he enrolled in a business school and having saved part of his salary, had the necessary capital to open a dry goods store in that city.

The business prospered, and Brush opened branch stores in Troy and Lockport. Eventually, Brush moved to Indianapolis where he opened another store. Along the way, John Brush had married. He divorced his first wife Agnes soon after the birth of their daughter Eleanor. To assist with the raising of Eleanor, Brush brought his two sisters Cora and Carrie to Indianapolis.

On June 6, 1894 Brush would wed for a second time. His bride was Elsie Lombard, a beautiful blond actress. Brush had become mesmerized by Elsie when he saw her perform in a production entitled *A Temperance Town.* At the time of their marriage, Brush was forty-nine years old and Elsie twenty-four. The couple would have a daughter they named Natalie. The lavish Brush home in Indianapolis was christened Lombardy in Elsie's honor at the suggestion of poet James Whitcomb Riley. It would become the hub of Indianapolis society and a haven for international celebrities traveling through Indiana.

Also in 1894, Brush's daughter Eleanor by his first marriage, only eighteen months younger than his second wife, would marry Harry N. Hempstead, a twenty-six-year-old vice president of the Morris European Express Company headquartered in New York. Soon after the marriage, the couple moved to Indianapolis where Harry would join John Brush's dry goods organization.

John Brush had always been a baseball fan and his entry into the game as an owner came as the result of a debtor paying him with stock in the Indianapolis baseball team. In 1884 Brush got an American Association franchise for Indianapolis, but the following year the team was dropped, and Brush moved to the Western League. However, the league soon folded.

In 1886 Brush bought the St. Louis team, and Indianapolis joined the National League. However, in 1890 both Indianapolis and Washington were dropped by the National League and replaced by Brooklyn and Cincinnati.

Nonetheless, John T. Brush had enough respect and stature in baseball to retain his league voting rights and was promised the option on the next available franchise if he would sell all his players. Almost of all Brush's players went to the New York Giants and he received about $67,000 and some Giants stock.

In September 1890 the Cincinnati National League team, in deep financial trouble, was sold to the Brotherhood, or Players League, for $40,000. This left an open National League franchise in Cincinnati. As a result Brush acquired the vacant Cincinnati Reds franchise for virtually nothing.

In 1891 the Cincinnati Reds were back in operation under the ownership of John Brush. However, going forward, John Brush's Cincinnati Reds teams were lackluster and operated on a slim profit margin. Also, as Brush lived in Indianapolis and also operated a minor league franchise in that city, he was an unpopular absentee owner with the Cincinnati fans.

By 1901 the rival American League had achieved Major League status and a fierce rivalry existed for players and fans between the National and American Leagues. As a result, New York Giants owner Andrew Freedman wanted to sell the team. John T. Brush had always wanted to own the Giants, so he set the wheels in motion for him to acquire the franchise. Skillfully, Brush convinced Andrew Freedman to take a young pitcher from the Cincinnati Reds organization in a trade that he wanted to protect—Christy Mathewson.

On July 28, 1902 Brush traveled to Cincinnati to meet with August Garry Herrmann, who was heading-up a group of buyers for the Reds that included yeast magnates Julius Fleischmann, his brother Max, and Cincinnati Republican Party political boss George B. Cox. Late that evening, Brush told Herrmann, "I will sell the Cincinnati Baseball Club for $150,000."[1] It was a done deal.

Then Brush traveled to Baltimore and convinced John McGraw to manage the Giants when he acquired control of the team. That event occurred on September 9, 1902 when Brush bought controlling interest in the New York Giants from Freedman for $200,000.

Brush wanted to make the Giants the greatest club in baseball. He had money and was willing to spend immediately in order to make money in the future. So Brush let McGraw get the players he wanted and didn't haggle with him over the costs.

Brush's business plan paid huge dividends. The New York Giants, with John McGraw at the helm and Christy Mathewson on the mound, became a dominating force in Major League Baseball in the first decade of the twentieth century. John T. Brush prospered and became a distinguished figure in the game. He was credited with developing the rules by which the modern World Series is played, among other contributions.

Brush's daughter, Natalie Brush de Gendron, recalled:

We use to spend our afternoons at the Polo Grounds. As we drove near the park the youngsters, recognizing the car, crowded around us cheering and asking for passes. Daddy had box 66 opposite first base which he preferred to the popular location behind the plate where he said you were bothered by the screen. I reveled in the proximity of actors and actresses whose complimentary boxes surrounded us. The only ballplayer I was allowed to meet was Christy Mathewson. He was a gentleman.[2]

By 1911 John Brush's health had been in decline for several years. He had long suffered from rheumatoid arthritis. Then he incurred a broken hip when hit by a U.S. Mail truck while being driven home from the Polo Grounds and became a virtual invalid. The injury would prove to be fatal.

John T. Brush had been diagnosed with a condition called locomotor ataxia. On the evening of November 26, 1912 Brush was en route by train to California where it was felt that the climate would be more conducive to his ailing body, when he fell unconscious and died at Seeburger, Missouri. He was sixty-seven years old.

On November 29 a funeral was held for John T. Brush in Indianapolis. At the time, it was believed to be the largest for a private individual in that city. More than fifty representatives from the Major and Minor Leagues attended as Brush was laid to rest in Crown Hill Cemetery.

John T. Brush left the New York Giants in a trust along with his estate valued at $1.5 million. He had appointed two trustees of his estate—his minority partner in the New York Giants, Ashley Lloyd of Cincinnati, and his forty-two-year-old son-in-law, Harry N. Hempstead, who was married to his daughter Eleanor by his first wife. For some unknown reason, Eleanor destroyed most of her father's personal papers soon after his death. There has been speculation that Eleanor, fiercely loyal to her father's legacy, feared that they might fall into the hands of an unfriendly journalist.

Brush's interest in the New York Giants, otherwise known as the National Exhibition Company of New Jersey was divided up in equal shares between his second wife Elsie, his daughter by his first marriage, Eleanor, and his daughter by his second marriage, Natalie. At the time, Natalie was still a minor, so her interests were under her mother's control, thereby giving her majority control of the New York Giants. However, this point is subject to debate, because in Brush's will, Eleanor and her husband Harry were given financial control of the estate, which meant they were actually in control of the New York Giants. Whatever the case, the value of the 1,306 shares of the New York Giants left to the Brush women were appraised at $348,702 or $267 a share.[3]

In his will, John Brush had stated that the trustees at their discretion should sell the New York Giants. Both Elsie Lombard Brush and Harry Hempstead wanted to sell the ball club, but Eleanor was totally against it.

Col Jacob Ruppert and Captain Tillinghast L'Hommedieu were both huge Giants fans and friends of John McGraw. So they approached McGraw and told him that they would like to buy the Giants. McGraw went to see Elsie about their interest, but was informed that the Brush women had decided to keep the ball club in the family. So in 1915 Ruppert and L' Hommedieu bought the New York Yankees.

It was informally communicated that none of the Brush women would be involved with making any policy or with running the ball club. In 1916 *The Sporting News* reinforced this edict in one of its editions featuring a picture of Eleanor with the heading, "She Plays Her Proper Part." The article stated, "Mrs. Harry N. Hempstead daughter of John T. Brush, who inherited a baseball gold mine, but turns over active control to capable hands of her husband."[4]

Harry Hempstead was appointed president of the Giants. The irony in the situation was that Harry Hempstead, although a decent man, had spent most of his professional life working in the Brush clothing business in Indianapolis and knew practically nothing about running a baseball club at any level.

In January 1913 Harry and Eleanor Hempstead, with their two sons, moved to New York. Harry Hempstead was well aware of the power that John McGraw wielded in the Giants front office. Harry was basically shy and felt uncomfortable around the monolithic McGraw and instead relied on the team's secretary John B. Foster for guidance. Still, upon settling in at the Giants offices located in the Fifth Avenue Building, one of Harry's first actions was to sign John McGraw to a long-term, five-year contract calling for more than $100,000 through the 1917 season. At the time, it was the most lucrative contract ever signed by a manager.

Still as time passed in that first year of Hempstead's tenure as president, McGraw began to feel that he and

Foster were starting to downplay his dominance and slowly nudging him from the spotlight in the Giants organization. It bothered McGraw to the extent that he would let go with an occasional public outburst. However, Hempstead and Foster knew that they had the support of the Brush women, Elsie, Eleanor, and Natalie, and continued to put McGraw in his place when they felt it necessary.

Harry Hempstead, with the support of John B. Foster, was able to avoid simply becoming a figure head. He represented the ball club at the league meetings competently, although he let John McGraw make the roster and game decisions. It all seemed to work as the New York Giants netted a profit in the 1912 season of $179,736 from winning the National League pennant and losing the World Series to the Boston Red Sox.

In 1913 the New York Giants won their fifth National League pennant under John McGraw, but lost the World Series to the Philadelphia Athletics.

Following the World Series, the New York Giants and Chicago White Sox made a world tour. Between late October 1913 and early March 1914, the two teams played thirty-one games and netted $97,240. Had not three games in Rome and four in Paris been rained out as well as a doubleheader in Tacoma on the final day of the American leg of the tour, revenues would have well exceeded $100,000. Neither Eleanor nor Harry Hempstead, nor any of the Brush women accompanied the team on the tour leaving the entire junket administratively to John McGraw.

The Giants didn't win another pennant until 1917, and by this time Elsie felt that there were safer investments than baseball and was once again pressing Eleanor to sell the ball club. Word started to circulate in New York that the Giants were for sale, and immediately, offers started to be made. However, the Brush women were not satisfied with any of them.

Finally, in 1919 Harry Hempstead, representing the Brush estate, sold part of the Brush women's controlling interest in the Giants to a group headed by Charles A. Stoneham that included Francis X. McQuade, a local judge, and John McGraw. However, Eleanor refused to sell her shares out of respect for her father.

According to Natalie Brush de Gendron, there were three reasons why she and her mother Elsie sold their controlling interest. "World War One was upon us players were being drafted and attendance was falling off. Mother was advised that hard times were ahead and, in any case baseball was no business for a woman."[5] In short, Elsie and Natalie wanted financial security, and they were not sure that Major League Baseball, with its revenue peaks and valleys, could provide that.

Harry N. Hempstead died at the age of sixty-nine-years-old on March 26, 1938 in New York. Following his days as president of the New York Giants, he never again was associated with baseball. He retired from business in 1922.

Eleanor Brush Hempstead continued to retain her shares in the New York Giants until June 1924. She died at the age of seventy-one years old on January 8, 1943 in her estate in Irvington, New York.

Elsie Lombard Brush, although attractive and talented, never remarried following the death of her husband. She died at the age of eighty-eight years old in Ft. Lauderdale, Florida on December 28, 1957.

Natalie Lombard Brush Gates de Gendron later became a novelist, and under the pen name Natalie Gates, had two Cold War spy thrillers published. She died at the age of eighty-four years old on June 16, 1980 in New York.

Olivia Taylor
• INDIANAPOLIS ABC'S •

The Indianapolis ABC's, sponsored by the American Brewing Company and owned by C.I. (Charles Isham) Taylor, relocated to Indiana from Birmingham, Alabama in 1914. There were no organized professional Negro Leagues teams at the time, and the ABC's would claim the title as Colored World Champions in 1916 after defeating Rube Foster's Chicago American Giants in a championship series.

When the Negro National League was formed in February 1920 by Rube Foster, the ABC's became a charter member along with the Kansas City Monarchs, the

Dayton Marcos, the Giants, and American Giants (both Chicago based), the Detroit Stars, the St. Louis Giants, and the Cuban Giants (no hometown). The ABC's played host to the league's first game on May 2, 1920.

When C.I. Taylor passed away in early 1922 his request had been that his wife Olivia Taylor, a former school teacher and president of the Indianapolis branch of the NAACP, take control of 75 percent of the franchise and his brother Ben Taylor receive the remaining 25 percent interest. In the new administration of the ABC's, Olivia ran the business affairs of the team, while Ben managed the team. Ben Taylor was a brilliant ball player with a .334 lifetime batting average and considered to be the best first baseman in black baseball until the arrival of Buck Leonard.

The new management of the team proved to be less than harmonious as Olivia and Ben argued over profits and how they were being divided. Ben was concerned that Olivia was taking a larger share of the profits than she was entitled to and more money should be given to the ball players and himself. Still, the ABC's had a fine seasons in 1922 with a record of 46-33, led by Negro League icon Oscar Charleston, who hit .370.

Eventually, Ben challenged Olivia's authority by independently organizing an All-Star team using the name ABC's and playing an exhibition game in Muncie, Indiana. While Olivia was outraged by the game, she was ignored and didn't receive a cut.

Olivia continued to operate the ABC's until 1924. But faced with increasing competition by the formation of the Eastern Colored League in 1923, the loss of many key players to the new circuit, including Oscar Charleston to the Harrisburg Giants and others to Ben Taylor, who had become manager of the Washington Potomacs and too many unpaid bills, the ABC's were dropped from the Negro National League.

Rube Foster was concerned that Olivia "had too many unpaid bills and no revenue to make good on those debts."[6]

Following the 1924 season, Olivia Taylor sold the team to Warner Jewell and began to devote her efforts exclusively to civil rights, including bringing the 1927 NAACP conference to Indianapolis.

Florence Wolfe Dreyfuss
• PITTSBURGH PIRATES •

Florence Wolfe was born in Louisville, Kentucky on March 31, 1872. She was the youngest of thirteen children. Florence met her future husband Barney Dreyfuss as a result of them having a mutual interest in music. They were traveling independently on a Sunday excursion train from Louisville to Cincinnati for a band concert. In her younger years, Florence was an accomplished piano player and Barney liked to sing.

It also just happened that Florence was also a baseball fan. Barney Dreyfuss had been a part owner of the Louisville Colonels in the National League from 1892 to 1898. Although women spectators at ball games were rare in the 1890s, Florence began to attend games with Barney.

Florence and Barney Dreyfuss were married on October 16, 1894. The couple had two children: a son, Samuel Wolfe Dreyfuss, and a daughter, Fanny Dreyfuss.

In 1899 Barney Dreyfuss purchased controlling interest in the Louisville club for $50,000 from Harry Clay Pulliam. However, the National League at that time was a top heavy twelve team circuit, and at the urging of New York Giants owner Andrew Freedman, the league was downsized to eight teams for the 1900 season by eliminating some of the weaker franchises in Baltimore, Cleveland, Louisville, and Washington.

As payment for his defunct franchise in Louisville, Dreyfuss was given $10,000, and as part of the agreement, he was permitted to buy interest in the Pittsburgh Pirates and sell or trade his players, most of whom went to the Pirates.

Barney Dreyfuss had actually seen the writing on the wall before his Louisville club became extinct and began trading his players to Pittsburgh. In all, Dreyfuss traded or sold fourteen players to the Pirates including such notables as Honus Wagner, Fred Clarke, Deacon Phillipe, Rube Wadell, and Tommy Leach.

Dreyfuss then bought controlling interest in the Pirates and proceeded to operate one of the premier teams in the

National League during the early decades of the 1900s, winning six pennants (1901-1903, 1909, 1925, 1927) and two World Series (1909, 1925). Overall, between 1900 and 1932, the Pittsburgh Pirates finished in third place or better twenty-one times. During those years, the Pirates were to be led by such legendary Hall of Fame players as Honus Wagner, Pie Traynor, Lloyd Waner, and Paul Waner.

On February 5, 1932 Barney Dreyfuss died in New York City. He bequeathed nearly his entire estate to his wife Florence, including his baseball holdings.

At a meeting of the Pittsburgh Pirates board of directors in mid-February 1932, Florence Dreyfuss was elected chairman. At the same time, her son-in-law William E. Benswanger was chosen at her insistence as president of the ball club and Samuel E. Walters, who had been the team secretary for some years, was given the additional title of vice president.

William Benswanger had married Fanny Dreyfuss in 1925. In 1931 he had been made treasurer of the Pirates. In regard to being elected president of the Pirates in 1932, Benswanger stated, "I was in there just because I was the only man in the family. I literally got dumped into baseball. I didn't know a thing about it."[7]

The fact that Florence Dreyfuss was now the majority owner of the Pirates created a situation not experienced in the National League since the days of Helene Hathaway Robison Britton with the St. Louis Cardinals. Actually, Florence Dreyfuss had helped groom her son Samuel, a Princeton graduate, to succeed his father. But he died from pneumonia at the age of thirty-four in 1930, two years before his father.

Although Florence had a solid background of nearly forty years in the game through her close association with her late husband, it was decided that, Benswanger and Walters would be responsible for the operation of the ball club. While Benswanger called the shots on the Pirates, out of respect for Florence as chairman of the board, he immediately informed her of any trades. He didn't want her reading about them in the newspapers. Nonetheless, it did not preclude Florence from occasionally putting her stamp of approval on a proposed trade. In fact, when the Pirates were at home, she sat in a box in the second tier behind home plate with Benswanger and paid close attention to what was transpiring on the field. "Sometimes we make suggestions for the next day,"[8] Florence shyly admitted.

Winning the 1925 World Series against Washington had been Florence Dreyfuss's biggest thrill in baseball. While Fred Clarke had been Florence's favorite Pirates manager, Houns Wagner had been her favorite player. She often told people that she didn't believe that there would ever be another like him.

Honus Wagner retired from playing Major League Baseball after the 1917 season. He then worked as a manager of a sporting goods store and obtained a political job as Assistant Sergeant-of-Arms in the Pennsylvania State Legislature. Also, to make ends meet, he continued to play semi-pro ball until he was nearly fifty years old. Now that Florence Dreyfuss was in a policy making position with the team, she promised that Honus Wagner would have a lifetime job as a coach with the Pirates. So in 1933 Wagner returned to the Pirates as a coach and remained one for the next nineteen years.

Florence Dreyfuss saw the increased interest of women in baseball and attendance at games as a positive step forward in making the milieu of the ballpark more wholesome and fan friendly. In an article she wrote in 1936 Florence stated:

> Women, perhaps, more than men, or the mere development of science, have been responsible for the multitudinous comforts which now fill the large stands and which create such a different atmosphere than existed in earlier years. Ladies Days have become established institutions in all major parks, and the very existence of such days is an eloquent testimonial in itself to the recognition given the patronage of the women. There is no denying the fact that ladies have given an added impetus to the refinements the game has acquired, and perhaps to the higher general caliber of ball-player who plays today, as contrasted with the general run of player forty years ago.[9]

During the depression and World War Two the Pittsburgh Pirates were a good team, a first division team, but not good enough to win the pennant. By the end of the war the Pirates were rumored to be for sale. When asked if the Pirates were for sale, Florence Dryefuss stated, "We've never thought of selling the team. And, we've never set a price. But that doesn't mean that we never will sell. If somebody mentioned a fancy figure and we thought it sound, we might be interested. I wouldn't know what to do with myself if I did sell the team. It keeps me active. I go to all the games at Forbes Field and when the team is away, I listen to the radio."[10]

During the end of 1945 and beginning of 1946 William Benswanger had received a wave of offers for the Pirates. He told Florence, "You've wanted to sell for ten years. You either have to sell it now, once and for all, or keep it."[11]

So on August 24, 1946 Florence Dreyfuss sold the Pittsburgh Pirates for $2,225,000 to a group headed by Frank McKinney, John Galbreath, Thomas Johnson, Bing Crosby, and Warner Communications.

When told that Bing Crosby was a partner in the buying group, Florence Dreyfuss said, "Crosby? Bing Crosby? Now let me see. Where have I heard that name before? Oh, yes. He does have a lovely voice. And he is a good actor too. I've seen him in a couple of his pictures."[12]

For several years after selling the Pirates Florence continued to live in the Schenley Apartments where she and Barney had taken up residency in 1924. Florence Dreyfuss died in Pittsburgh on May 12, 1950 at the age of seventy-eight.

Marie (Dearie) McKeever Mulvey
• BROOKLYN DODGERS •

On March 7, 1938 Stephen W. McKeever, president and principle owner of the Brooklyn Dodgers died at the age of eighty-four from complications with pneumonia.

Stephen McKeever had been associated with the Dodgers for twenty-five years. In 1912 Charles Ebbets needed $750,000 to complete construction on a new concrete ballpark in Flatbush for the Brooklyn team, which was having financial difficulties. Stephen McKeever and his brother, Edward J., came to the rescue of Ebbets by loaning him $750,000. In return, Ebbets gave the McKeever's half interest in the ball club.

The stadium, Ebbets Field, was completed and opened in 1913. Stephen McKeever was elected vice president of the ball club and Edward the treasurer. The triumvirate of Ebbets and the McKeever brothers lasted thirteen years. But in April 1925 both Ebbets and Edward McKeever died within two weeks of each other. The half interest in the Dodgers owned by Charles Ebbets passed to his heirs, while quarter interest owned by Edward M. KcKeever passed to his heirs. The remaining quarter interest was still in control of Stephen McKeever.

Wilbert Robinson, known as "Uncle Robbie," who had been managing the team since 1914, was elected president. For a while, McKeever and Robinson worked together amicably. But then a rift occurred between the two, and for the next few years the administration of the Brooklyn Dodgers was in utter chaos. Matters escalated to a point where it was necessary for National League president John A. Heydler to intervene. In February 1929, with Heydler acting as the intermediary, a fifth member, William "Dutch" Carter, one-time pitcher for Yale University, was named to the board of directors. Nonetheless, Robinson hung on until 1931 when McKeever finally forced him out.

On October 12, 1932 Stephen McKeever was named the new Dodgers president. The team, which had been named the Robins since 1914 in deference to manager Wilbert Robinson, was changed permanently to Dodgers in 1932. In 1937 McKeever named his son-in-law, James A. Mulvey, vice president of the Dodgers. Mr. Mulvey was also president of Samuel Goldwyn Productions.

Upon the demise of Stephen McKeever in 1938, his 25 percent interests in the Dodgers were left to his daughter Marie McKeever Mulvey. As a result of his wife being left a 25 percent ownership in the Dodgers, James A. Mulvey became a defacto owner.

At that time, the Brooklyn Dodgers were in debt more than $1 million, and the franchise was on the verge of collapsing. New York Bell had discontinued service because the bill had not been paid. The Dodgers front office employees were seeking new employment opportunities and bill collectors roamed around the offices everyday seeking payment. Now to make things worse, Marie Mulvey, the Edward McKeever heirs, and the Ebbets heirs, who numbered more than twenty were unable to agree on anything.

Despite their sharp differences, the warring factions comprising the Dodgers ownership knew that they had to come together and do something to at least stabilize the operations of the ball club or it was headed for disaster. So they went to National League president Ford Frick and asked his opinion on who they should hire as general manager. They wanted a strong general manager who knew baseball well and that would not be taken for granted among his peers and not make bad trades.

In turn, Ford Frick turned to Branch Rickey for advice. His advice was to hire Larry MacPhail. It had been MacPail that had turned the fortunes of the Cincinnati Reds around when they were facing similar circumstances in the early 1930s. MacPhail had induced wealthy local industrialist Powell Crosley, Jr. to buy the team. He then used Crosley's fortune to get rid of old ball players and replace them with younger more talented ones, began night baseball, hired Red Barber to do radio broadcasts and built a competitive team in a relatively short period of time that would go on to win back-to-back National League pennants in 1939 and 1940. Then MacPhail, who was a notorious boozer, got drunk and punched-out Powell Crosley.

With the Dodgers near bankruptcy, Marie Mulvey, the Edward McKeever heirs, and the Ebbets heirs approved the hiring of Larry MacPhail.

MacPhail would spend lavishly: $45,000 just to buy first baseman Dolf Camilli from the Philadelphia Phillies and borrowed $200,000 to fix up Ebbets Field. But his moves would quickly pay dividends. By 1941 the Brooklyn Dodgers, under MacPhail, were playing night baseball, had hired Red Barber away from Cincinnati to do the games on radio, signed fifteen scouts, even hired Babe Ruth as a coach, signed Pee Wee Reese, Joe Medwick, Dixie Walker,

Hugh Casey, and prospect Pete Rieser for $100 after being freed from his Cardinals contract by the Commissioner and won a pennant in 1941 after a twenty-one year hiatus.

But by the end of the 1942 season Larry MacPhail was under pressure from some of the stockholders and resigned as vice-president and general manager of the Dodgers. He left the club with $300,000 in the bank and in a position to pay off the mortgage on Ebbets Field. MacPhail was replaced by Branch Rickey.

At that time, the Brooklyn Dodgers were earning a modest annual profit and the Edward McKeever heirs were ready to cash in and move on. So Walter O'Malley, an attorney who worked for the Brooklyn Trust Company and had been with the Dodgers since 1933, arranged to bring in Branch Rickey and John L. Smith, a chemical manufacturer, on the deal and they bought 25 percent of the team. Of course 50 percent of the Dodgers stock was still in control of the divided Ebbets heirs and 25 percent owned by Marie Mulvey, the daughter of the late Stephen McKeever.

But by 1944 the Ebbets heirs were tired of fighting each other and wanted to sell their stock. However, things became a little complicated when Charles Ebbets, Jr. died in a boarding house and left two-thirds of his estate to a former housekeeper and one-third to his legal wife.

Nonetheless, O'Malley, Rickey, and Smith arranged for the majority of the financing to be done through loans from the Brooklyn Trust Company, and they suddenly owned 75 percent of the team with Marie Mulvey stubbornly retaining her 25 percent ownership. Branch Rickey was installed as president and given a five-year contract to run the team.

All along, the only one of the former Dodgers owners who had any real interest in the pennant race had been Marie Mulvey. To tens of thousands of Brooklyn Dodgers fans, players, and others throughout the country, Marie was known as Dearie.

In 1942 Marie Mulvey was named Brooklyn's "Ideal Mother of the Year" by the Mother's Day Commemorative League. The league said of her: "When she isn't helping some Girl Scout, she's helping a Boy Scout. If she isn't taking care of a crippled girl, she's taking care of a crippled boy. She has the desire to make life happier for everyone who crosses her path, which in our judgment, is the mark of true motherhood."[13]

Marie "Dearie" Mulvey had been a lifelong resident of Brooklyn until she moved with her husband in 1952 to White Plains, New York. In fact, her home in Brooklyn at 39 Maple Street was located only five blocks from Ebbets Field.

She could be found at nearly every one of the Dodgers home games at Ebbets Field seated in Box 117 with her children. She also distributed hundreds of complimentary tickets to Brooklyn youngsters. Marie even went to spring training each year.

Seventeen days after Brooklyn Dodgers pitcher Ralph Branca served up the pennant winning home run to the New York Giants Bobby Thompson on October 3, 1951 at the Polo Grounds, Marie Mulvey's daughter Ann married Branca.

Marie Mulvey was also an accomplished horse-woman and had established a world's record in 1932 by driving a three-year-old trotter over a one-mile course in 2.09 ¾ at the Road Association of New Jersey.

In July 1950 John L. Smith died of cancer. For a few years prior to Smith's death Walther O'Malley had been attempting to squeeze Branch Rickey out of the Dodgers ownership picture. Rickey's contract was due to expire in October 1950, and with the maneuvering of Walter O'Malley, the Dodgers board of directors refused to offer him a new contract. O'Malley wanted to offer Rickey $346,667, the price he paid for his share of the Dodgers stock in 1943. However, Rickey had a clause in his original partnership agreement that stated if he ever wanted to sell to a third person, O'Malley would have to meet the price. Branch Rickey wanted $1 million for his stock. Subsequently, O'Malley had to meet Rickey's demand.

While Walter O'Malley went on to become a very rich man owning the Dodgers, he carried a grudge against Branch Rickey until he died.

When Walter O'Malley moved the Dodgers to Los Angeles in 1958, Marie "Dearie" McKeever Mulvey continued to hold her 25 percent ownership. She died on November 25, 1968 at her home in White Plains, New York still a minority owner of the Dodgers.

The Mulvey family continued to hold the stock until 1975 when they sold it to Walter O'Malley giving him 100 percent control of the Dodgers.

In 1968 the Dodgers began the Jim and Dearie Mulvey Award. The award is voted on by the coaches and is given annually to the top rookie in the Dodgers spring training camp. A few of the past recipients have been Ted Sizemore (1969), Bob Welch (1978), Orel Hershiser (1983), Eric Karros (1991), Mike Piazza (1993, Tony Abreu (2007), and Xavier Paul (2009).

Helen Ruppert Silleck Holleran, Ruth McGuire & Helen Weyant
• NEW YORK YANKEES •

In late February 1915 two New York millionaires, Colonel Jacob Ruppert and Captain Tillinghast L'Hommedieu Huston, bought the New York Yankees for $480,000 after turning down an offer to buy the Kansas City franchise in the Federal League.

A native of New York, Ruppert had made his fortune as a real estate financier and brewery owner. He got his nickname of Colonel by being a colonel in the National Guard. From 1899 to 1907, Ruppert served in the U.S. House of Representatives as a Democrat from New York. When first elected to Congress he was just thirty-one. Huston, a former Cincinnati contractor and a retired army engineer and captain, had made a fortune in public works projects in Cuba.

In 1920 Ruppert would acquire Babe Ruth from the Boston Red Sox. Then during the period of 1922-1923, he and Huston would build Yankee Stadium. On May 21, 1922 Jacob Ruppert would buy out the shares of Tillinghast L'Hommedieu Huston in the Yankees for $1.5 million. From that point on the New York Yankees became a dynasty in the 1920s and 1930s and Ruppert's investment in the ball club would return to him tens of millions of dollars.

On January 13, 1939 Jacob Ruppert died at the age of seventy-one. Ruppert's estate was valued at $40 million. The worth of his baseball holdings was placed between $6 million and $10 million. Never married, Ruppert's stock in the New York Yankees was held in a trust for two nieces, Helen Holleran and Ruth McGuire, along with a friend, Helen Winthrope Weyant.

Among the three heiresses, the best known was Helen Ruppert Silleck Holleran. In the late 1930s and early 1940s she was one of the leading women golfers in the United States, and she was the wife of Joseph Holleran.

Ruth McGuire was the wife of J. Basil McGuire.

Helen Winthrope Weyant was a former actress. Her brother Rex Weyant had been the Yankees assistant secretary for the past three years. Upon learning that she had been named an heir to Ruppert's Yankees, she stated that she had no idea of why he had left her so much money.

Jacob Ruppert's assets were divided into two trusts: the Yankees trust and a residuary trust embracing all the other assets such as the brewery. The Yankees trust was to be transferred to a trustee—the Manufacturers Trust Company of New York. Income from the trust was to be paid for the benefit of Ruppert's nieces and Ms. Weyant, as well as having ownership maintained. However, the ladies did not officially own the New York Yankees; they did not have any say in the management of the ball club either. Lastly, they were prevented from expressing any personal preferences that would prevent an eventual sale of the team.

Edward G. Barrow, the president and general manager of the Yankees since 1921, held 10 percent of the stock in the ball club. Barrow was named as one of three executors for the Ruppert estate. The other two trustees were Byron Clark, Jr., the attorney for the estate, and H. Garrison Silleck.

Eventually, it was discovered that Ruppert's estate did not have sufficient assets to pay the federal and state death taxes or his personal debts of over $1 million. These circumstances, compounded with the administration expenses of the Yankees, forced eventual sale of the team. Interest in the brewery had to be sold as well.

On December 26, 1945 the Yankees were sold on behalf of Ruppert's heirs by the Manufactures Trust Company to a syndicate, including Dan Topping, Del Webb, and Larry MacPhail, for the bargain price of $3 million.

Linda Alvarado
• COLORADO ROCKIES •

Linda G. Alvarado, who currently owns a minority share of the Colorado Rockies, is unique among co-owners of Major League teams. Not only is she a woman, but she is a Hispanic woman, the first of such ethnicity to be associated with ownership of a Major League team. Also adding to Linda's uniqueness is the fact that, historically, most of the women who have either owned Major League teams or where co-owners arrived at their position either through inheriting a ball club or inheriting the money that permitted them to buy one. But Linda Alvarado became a successful business woman on her own and bought shares of the Colorado Rockies with her own money.

Born Linda Martinez in Albuquerque, New Mexico in 1951, she was the only girl in the family, having five brothers. Her parents, Luther and Lilly Martinez, were Protestant missionaries in the area until they began a family. Her father, Luther Martinez, then went to work for the U.S. Atomic Energy Commission. Linda grew up in an Adobe house with no heat or indoor plumbing. Her mother took in ironing to help make ends meet.

Linda's parent stressed the importance of education and made sure their children studied hard. Not only did Linda excel in her studies at Sandia High School, but she also participated in athletics—serving as captain of the women's baseball team.

Linda Alvarado attended Pomona College in Claremont, California on a scholarship, where she majored in economics. When Linda needed money to supplement her expenses in college, she sought out employment opportunities on the campus. While traditionally women in such need at Pomona College took jobs in the cafeteria, Linda bucked the administration and applied for a job as a landscaper. Winning approval, she became the only woman on the job and began a lifelong battle fighting off the constraints of traditional roles for females. Looking back on the experience, Linda told Dan Mayfield of the Albuquerque Tribune how much she enjoyed that experience, "I got to wear Levi's, be outside in the Southern California sun and get a tan."[14]

Following her graduation, Linda took a job with a California development company. She quickly developed a strong interest in the construction industry and returned to school for additional training. She studied bid estimating and blue print reading. Returning to the job market, she now found herself confronted with overt sexism in the building trades. Often in the restrooms on job sites she would discover drawings of herself in various states of undress. Other times, she was regulated to office duties such as filing.

It didn't take long for Linda to become cognizant of the profits being made in construction, so she decided to set off on her own. She developed a business plan for a construction company of her own, but was turned down by six banks. Finally, her parents took out a mortgage on their home and loaned her $2,500 for start-up money.

With the money, Linda launched Martinez Alvarado Construction Corporation in Palo Alto, California in 1974 with a partner that she eventually bought out. The company would be incorporated in 1976 as Alvarado Construction Inc.

At that time, there were very few minority set-aside bid laws or programs in the nation's states to aid fledgling minority start-up companies compete against established white owned construction companies. Nonetheless, Linda's company began to get contracts for small jobs such as paving. But it wasn't long before her company began to build bus shelters for municipal transportation agencies.

To mask the fact that she was a woman and thereby prevent discrimination in submitting proposals, Linda began to sign documents with just her initials, rather than signing her name. The company grew into a general contractor, and she moved the operation to Denver, Colorado with her husband. Linda began to acquire a reputation for bringing jobs in on time and on budget, and the word spread. Within two decades of launching her company, she was building high rise office buildings, bus stations, airport hangers, and even a convention center in Denver.

Linda talked Taco Bell executives into putting a store in a strip mall she was constructing, and when she experienced high profit margins, she sold the mall and kept the restaurant. Linda says that she learned a valuable lesson from that experience, "She who owns the land, controls the deal."[15] From that experience, she launched a second company, Pal Alto, Inc. The company evolved into a franchise holder for 150 Taco Bell, Pizza Hut, and Kentucky Fried Chicken outlets. Her husband ran the company.

In 1991 Linda Alvarado was approached by a group of six Denver businessmen who were seeking to bring a Major League Baseball expansion team to Denver. The group met with the governor of Colorado and then prepared a bid for $95 million to win the franchise. Linda Alvarado told the IMDiversity website, "I was the first woman to write a check. It was high risk, since the sizeable deposit check would be lost if we didn't get the franchise."[16]

The group won the bid and the Colorado Rockies were born in 1993. Linda Alvarado's participation in the franchise acquisition was viewed as a ground breaking event and created a sense of pride for women and Hispanics in such a non-traditional role that she played.

The Rockies playing at Mile High Stadium drew an astounding 7,701,861 fans in the franchise's first two years, an average of 57,051 per game. The attendance figure could have been even larger if it were not for the strike-shortened inaugural season in 1993.

Linda then used her contractor experience to participate in the feasibility study and cost estimate for Coors Field. Originally, the Rockies administration was of the opinion that the new ballpark should have a seating capacity of about 42,000. But with the huge attendance figures for the Rockies' first two seasons, that number was increased to 50,000 plus (50,480 capacity in 2013). The new ballpark opened in 1995 and continues to enjoy high attendance figures.

NOTES

Chapter 1

1. "Mrs. Britton Tires Some Evidence That She Has Not Enthusiasm for Base Ball that Marked Her Entry into the Game," *The Sporting News*, 4.

2. B. McKenna, "Helene Britton versus Roger Bresnahan," Baseball History Blog.

3. Mrs. Britton Tires.

4. "My Experience as a Big League Owner – Early Recollections and Later Views on Baseball and Athletic Sports," interview with Mrs. Helene Britton, *Baseball Magazine* (February 1917), 13.

5. Steve Steinberg, "Cardinals Opening Day, 1912," *Gateway Heritage*, 46-53.

6. "Woman Like She Has Last Word," *The Sporting News*, 4.

7. Mike Eisenbath, *The Cardinals Encyclopedia*, 398-399.

8. James Cruisnberry, "Mrs. Britton Wonders Why Ump Fired Players," *Chicago Daily Tribune* (August 14, 1914), 7.

9. "My Experience as a Big League Owner – Early Recollections and Later Views on Baseball and Athletic Sports," 14.

10. "How Just One Word Kept Woman Magnate In Game," *The Sporting News* (January 6, 1916), 5.

11. Joan M. Thomas, "Helene Hathaway Britton," Baseball Biography Project, http://209.85.173.104/search?q=cache...Ink&cd+28gl=us.

12. Joan M. Thomas, Helene Britton/SABR, http://sabr.org/bio proj/person/ecd910f9.

13. Sid C. Keener, "Magnatinga a Major League Ball Club is More Than a Fad or Fancy of Mere Woman," *The Sporting News* (December 16, 1916) 5.

14. "Mrs. Bigsby, Owned Baseball Club, 71," *The New York Times* (January 10, 1950) 29.

Chapter 2

1. A. B. "Happy" Chandler Oral History Project, Effa Manley interview with William M. Marshall, October 19, 1977, http://www.nvnncenter.org.

2. George Vecsey, Sports of The Times, "Taking a Seat With the Guys Again," NYTimes.com (February 28, 2006).

3. Jim Overmyer, *Queen of the Negro Leagues - Effa Manley and the Newark Eagles* (Latham, Md. & London: The Scarecrow Press, Inc., 1998).

4. Mark Ribowsky, *A Complete History of the Negro Leagues – 1884-1955.* Carol Publishing Group (A Birch Lane Peeks Book 1995).

5. *A Complete History of the Negro Leagues – 1884-1955.*

6. *Queen of the Negro Leagues - Effa Manley and the Newark Eagles.*

7. Dan Burley, "Manleys Threaten 'Player War' Over Paige," *New York Amsterdam News* (June 15, 1940), 20.

8. Neil Lanctot, *Negro League Baseball: The Rise And Ruin of A Black Institution* (University of Pennsylvania Press, Philadelphia, PA, 2004).

9. *Negro League Baseball: The Rise And Ruin of A Black Institution.*

10. Dan Burley, "Biggest Crowd In History (50,000) Sees East Beat West, 8-3," *New York Amsterdam-Star News* (August 2, 1941), 19.

11. Geoffrey C. Ward and Ken Burns, *Baseball – An Illustrated History,* Alfred A. Knoff (New York, 1994).

12. Peter Gollenbock, *Bums – An Oral History of The Brooklyn Dodgers,* G. P. Putnam's Sons (New York, 1984).

13. "Dan Burley, Big Leaguers Make Negro Star Team Look Like Sand Lotters," *New York Amsterdam News* (October 20, 1945), 24.

14. *Queen of the Negro Leagues - Effa Manley and the Newark Eagles.*

15. A. B. "Happy" Chandler Oral History Project.

16. Lawrence D. Hogan with forward by Jules Tygiel, *Shades of Glory – The Negro Leagues and the Story of African-American Baseball* (Washington, D.C.: National Geographic, 2006).

17. Ed McAuley, "Paging Satchel Paige," Cleveland News published in *Sports World,* vol. 1, no.4 (September 1949).

18. *The Negro Leagues and the Story of African-American Baseball.*

19. A. B. "Happy" Chandler Oral History Project.

20. *Negro League Baseball: The Rise And Ruin of A Black Institution.*

21. A. B. "Happy" Chandler Oral History Project.

22. Leigh Montville, *Ted Williams – The biography of An American Hero,* (Broadway Books: New York, 2004).

23. Claire Smith, "Negro Leagues Enshrined at Last," *The New York Times* (August 13, 1991), 9.

24. "Negro Leagues Enshrined at Last."

Chapter 3

1. Jimmy Banks, "Bibb Falk: Mixes Wit With Baseball," *Austin Bureau of The News* (date unknown).

2. Irving Vaughn, "Bank To Run White Sox For Eight Years," *Chicago Daily Tribune* (July 26, 1939), 17.

3. "Bank Files Petition Today To Sell Sox," *Chicago Daily Tribune,* (January 18, 1940), 21.

4. Doris Lockerman, "Comiskey's Widow Tells Plans to Fight Bank on Sale of Sox," *Chicago Daily Tribune* (January 19, 1940), 21.

5. "Comiskey's Widow Tells Plans to Fight Bank on Sale of Sox."

6. "Court Denies Plea for White Sox Sale," *New York Times* (March 1, 1940), 28.

7. Charles Bartlett, "Comiskey's Win In Court: Keep White Sox," *Chicago Daily Tribune* (March 1, 1940), 29.

8. "Comiskey's Win in Court: Keep White Sox."

9. "Comiskey's Widow Tells Plans to Fight Bank on Sale of Sox."

10. Associated Press, "Baseball Men Beware! Women Prove They Can Run a Team," *Chicago Daily Tribune* (April 20, 1941), 3.

11. Associated Press, "Young Comiskey, 21 Maps Climb to Presidency of the White Sox," *New York Times* (November 19, 1946), 1.

12. Irving Vaughan, "Grace Comiskey Says Sox Will Back Chandler," *Chicago Daily Tribune* (December 17, 1950), A1.

13. Jerome Holtzman, "Red's new owner is a real go-getter," *Chicago Tribune* (December 30, 1984), C2.

14. Irving Vaughan, "Comiskey Quits Sox in Family Row," *Chicago Daily Tribune* (January 15, 1952), B1.

15. Irving Vaughan, "Comiskey Out; Sox Leave Door Open," *Chicago Daily Tribune* (January 19, 1952), B1.

16. "Comiskey Out; Sox Leave Door Open."

17. Robert Creamer, *The Comiskey Affair, SI Vault* (February 24, 1958), http://cnnsi.printthis.clickability.com/pt/cpt?expire=&title=The+thrid-gneration+owners+o

18. Edward Prell, "Comiskey Blasts Lane, Backs Frick," *Chicago Daily Tribune* (September 2, 1955), C1.

19. "Comiskey Blasts Lane, Backs Frick."

20. Edward Prell, "Peace Settle On Sox Family," *Chicago Daily Tribune* (September 3, 1955), B1.

21. "Lane Hits Showdown," *New York Times* (September 14, 1955), 44.

22. "Lane Tires of Chuck's Moves," *Chicago Daily Tribune* (September 12, 1955), C1.

23. "Lane Tires of Chuck's Moves."

24. "Mrs. Comiskey: No Lane Date," *Chicago Daily Tribune* (September 19, 1955), B1.

25. David Condon, "Comiskey: Sox Will Win," *Chicago Daily Tribune* (March 11, 1956), 133.

26. "The Comiskey Affair."

27. "Veeck Closes Deal for Sox; May Sell Park," *Chicago Daily Tribune* (January 2, 1959), 4.

28. "Chuck Loses as Court OK's Sale of Stock," *Chicago Daily Tribune* (March 6, 1959), C1.

Chapter 4

1. Jospeh Durso, "Lady Linda Takes a Grip on Mets' Reins," *The Sporting News* (March 17, 1979), 34.

2. Joseph Durso, "Joan Whitney Payson, 72, Mets Owner Dies," *New York Times* (October 5, 1975).

3. Sidney Fields, "When Mrs. Payson's Mom Tossed an Egg at The Babe," *The New York Daily News* (January 8, 1968).

4. David Dempsey, "Says Mrs. Payson of the Mets, 'You Can't Lose Them All,'" *New York Times Magazine*, (June 23, 1968), 70.

5. "When Mrs. Payson's Mom Tossed an Egg at The Babe."

6. Rita Reif, "Van Gogh's 'Irises' Sells for $53.9 Million," NYTimes.com (November 12, 1987).

7. "When Mrs. Payson's Mom Tossed an Egg at The Babe."

8. "Robert Moses ran the Giants out of NY," (Archive) – Baseball Fever, hhtp://www.baseball-fever.com/archive/index.php/t-93395.html.

9. Peter Golenbock, *Amazin': The Miraculous History of New York's Most Beloved Baseball Team* (New York: St. Martin's Press, 2002), 58.

10. "Mets Just a $3,000,000 Hobby," *Chicago Daily Tribune* (April 1, 1962), 2.

11. Jimmy Breslin, *Can't Anyone Play This Game?* (Viking Press, 1963).

12. *Can't Anyone Play This Game?*

13. "Mrs. Payson Tosses Party for Her Mets" (April 6, 1963).

14. Whitney Tower, "Upstaged by Upstart Johnny," SI Vault (June 10, 1968), http://sportsillustrated.cnn.com.vault/article/magazine/MAG108125 7/index.htm.

15. M. J. Wilson, "Nobody Loves Mets More Than Owner, Joan Payson," *The Observer-Dispatch* (October 6, 1969), 6.

16. Joseph Durso, "Mrs. Payson Says Heartbreak Game Gave Way to Her Tears of Joy," *New York Times* (October 6, 1969).

17. Gene Ward, Joan Payson, "What a Beautiful Bunt, and That Beautiful Run," *Daily News* (October 16, 1969), 109.

18. "What a Beautiful Bunt, and That Beautiful Run."

19. Skip Myslenski, "Those Amazin' Mets," *Chicago Tribune* (June 8, 1979), C2.

20. Dick Young, "Some Things on My Mind," *Daily News* (December 6, 1975).

21. "Mets Now Really Become A-Mays-ing," *Chicago Tribune* (May 12, 1972), C1.

22. "Safety Valve or Time Bomb," *The Sporting News* (October 27, 1973), 12.

23. *Amazin': – The Miraculous History of New York's Most Beloved Baseball Team.*

24. Joseph Durso, "Mets Open With Old H," *New York Times* (March 12, 1978).

25. "Lady Linda Takes a Grip on Mets' Reins."

26. "Lady Linda Takes a Grip on Mets' Reins."

Chapter 5

1. David Cataneo, "So Long to Red Sox Grande Dame, Jean Yawkey," *Boston Herald* (February 27, 1992), 43.

2. Edgar J, Driscoll, "Yawkey Dies of Leukemia – Club Owner, 73, was Last of a Baseball Breed," *Boston Globe* (July 10, 1976), 23.

3. Susan Trausch, "They Call her Mrs. Yawkey," *Boston Globe* (April 6, 1988), 76.

4. Jack Sullivan, "Harrington Rose to Front Office on Good Fortune," *Boston Herald* (March 17, 1999), 34.

5. Mike Barnicle, "The Day of the Massacre at Fenway," *Boston Globe* (October 27, 1977), 27.

6. Marvin Miller, *A Whole Different Ball Game – The Inside Story of Baseball's New Deal* (New York: Simon & Schuster, 1991).

7. Associated Press, "Owners of Red Sox Wage a Power Struggle."

8. "Yawkey Speaks, but not to LeRoux" (United Press International, July 14, 1983).

9. Charles P. Pierce, "The Yawkey Way," *Sports Illustrated*, ed. Steve Wulf (March 16, 1992).

10. "Yawkey Speaks, but not to LeRoux."

11. "They Call her Mrs. Yawkey," 27.

12. Joe Fitzgerald, "Mrs. Y Held on to Sox for Best Reasons," *The Boston Herald* (February 25, 1992), 69.

13. Will McDonough, "Yawkey's Death Ends Era," *Boston Globe* (February 27, 1992), 41.

14. Joe Murphy, "Mrs. Yawkey, We'll Miss You," (February, 1992).

15. Tim Hogan, "Make No Mistake: Yawkey's in Charge," *Boston Herald* (July 31, 1988), 12.

16. Art Davidson, "Yawkey Death Shocks Sox," *Middlesex News* (February 27, 1992), 2.

17. Will McDonough, "Yawkey Never Won the Big One – But She Never Wasted Time Complaining Either," *Boston Globe* (February 27, 1992), 46.

18. Nick Cafardo, "End of An Era – Jean Yawkey's Passing Brings Sorrow To Organization, Baseball Community" (March 1992), 3.

19. Sean McAdam, "Red Sox mourn death of team owner Yawkey," *Providence Journal-Bulletin* (February 27, 1992), C4.

Chapter 6

1. Jerome Holtzman, "Reds' new owner is a real go-getter," *Chicago Tribune* (December 30, 1984), C2.

2. Judy Klemesrud, "Marge Schott, Cincinnati Booster, Is Rooting for Her Home Team," *The New York Times* (Mach 8, 1985), B8.

3. Gregg Hoard, "Marge Schott Acquires the Reds," *The Cincinnati Enquirer* (December 22, 1984), 1.

4. "Marge Schott, Cincinnati Booster, Is Rooting for Her Home Team."

5. "Marge Schott, Cincinnati Booster, Is Rooting for Her Home Team."

6. Richard Goldstein, "Marge Schott, Eccentric Owner of the Reds, Dies at 75," *The New York Times* (March 3, 2004), C14.

7. Mike Bass, *Marge Schott Unleashed* (Champaign, IL: Sagamore Publishing, 1993.)

8. *Marge Schott Unleashed.*

9. Cliff Radel, "Schott: Woman of the people," *The Cincinnati Enquirer* (March 3, 2004), 8.

10. "Schott: Woman of the people."

11. *Marge Schott Unleashed.*

12. Rick Reilly, "Heaven Help Marge Schott," Sports Illustrated (May 20, 1996), 77.

13. John Kiessewetter, "Bittersweet memories for Eric Davis," retro. Cincinnati.com (April 13, 2012)

14. *Marge Schott Unleashed.*

15. Earl Gutskey, "Drug-Use Suit Filed by Pirates: Dave Parker Sued: Breach of Contract," *Los Angeles Times* (April 22, 1986), http://articles.latimes.com/print/1986-04-22/sports/sp-1516_1_dave parker.

16. *Marge Schott Unleashed.*

17. Terry Flynn, "Schott Steams Listening to Rose on Radio," *The Cincinnati Enquirer* (September 9, 1985), C1.

18. Tim Sullivan, "Pete Played It His Way; He Hit," *The Cincinnati Enquirer* (September 9, 1985), A1.

19. Pete Rose and Roger Kahn, *Pete Rose: My Story* (New York: Macmillian Publishing Company, 1989).

20. *Pete Rose: My Story.*

21. Rosemary Munsen, *The Cincinnati Enquirer* (September 12, 1985).

22. *Pete Rose: My Story.*

23. *Pete Rose: My Story.*

24. Craig Neff, *Sports Illustrated* (March 27, 1989), vol. 70, no. 19.

25. *Marge Schott Unleashed.*

26. A. Bartlett Giamatti, AP, *The Home News* (August 25, 1989).

27. Al Salvato, *The Cincinnati Post* (August 24, 1989).

28. *The Cincinnati Post* (August 24, 1989).

29. Michael O'Keeffe, *Daily News* (December 12, 2002).

30. "Red's Davis Takes Shot as Schott," *Chicago Tribune* (October 28, 1990), 3, http://articles.chicagotribune.com/keyword/eric-davis/recent/3.

31. Howard Wilkinson, "Insensitivity Defined Reign Over Reds – and Ended It," *Cincinnati Enquirer* (March 3, 2004), 8.

32. John Hopkins, "Reds," *The Cincinnati Enquirer* (November 11, 1992), A8.

33. "Insensitivity Defined Reign Over Reds – and Ended It."

34. "Reds"

35. "Schott Said She Didn't Mean to Offend," *The New York Times* (November 21, 1992), 28.

36. Charles McGarth, "Big Mouth," *The New York Times* (December 26, 2004), 55.

37. Murray Chass, "Schott Sees Bill White, Then Defends Conduct," *The New York Times* (November 24, 1992), B11.

38. "Baseball Bans Cincinnati Owner for a Year Over Racial Remarks," *The New York Times* (February 4, 1993), A1.

39. Ira Berkow, "Schott Punished for Wrong Thing," *The New York Times* (February 4, 1993), B11.

40. "Insensitivity Defined Reign Over Reds – and Ended It."

41. Richard Green, "Schott: 'I can't Believe This Has Happened,'" *The Cincinnati Enquirer* (April 2, 1996), 1.

42. "The Schott ESPN Interview," http://content.usatoday.com/sports/baseball/sbbw0804/htm.

43. Bob Klapisch, "Owner Schott continues to put Reds in a no-win situation," *The Home News Tribune* (May 26, 1996),

Chapter 7

1. Anne Adams, "Joan Kroc Philanthropist, History's Women," http://www.historyswomen.com/historyinthemaking/JoanKroc.html.

2. Murray Dubin, "Joan Kroc: 'Madre' of the Padres Takes on Social Ills," *Chicago Tribune* (October 17, 1984), D4.

3. Dave Anderson, "The Cubs Fan Who Owned the Padres," *The New York Times* (October 5, 1984), A23.

4. "The Cubs Fan Who Owned the Padres."

5. "Scorecard" SI Vault (May 5, 1980), http://sportsillustrated.cnn.com/vault/article/magazine/MAG1123420/2/index.htm.

6. Eric Pace, "Ray A. Kroc Dies at 81; Built McDonald's Chain," *The New York Times* (January 15, 1984), 28.

7. "Joan Kroc: Madre' of the Padres takes on social ills."

8. Michael Wright, "Richard Levine and Caroline Rand Herron, Day of Killing in California," *The New York Times* (July 22, 1984), E2.

9. "Day of Killing in California."

10. UPI, "$1 Million Given to Massacre Survivors," *Chicago Tribune* (July 21, 1984), 2.

11. "Joan Kroc: Madre' of the Padres Takes on Social Ills."

12. "$1 Million Given to Massacre Survivors."

13. George Vecsey, "No Apologies For Gossage," *The New York Times* (October 15, 1984), C3.

14. Dave Anderson, "Yanks Mulled Wiggins Deal for Randolph," *The New York Times* (June 24, 1985), C3.

15. UPI, "Padres' President Suspends Gossage," *The New York Times* (August 30, 1986), 13.

16. Ira Berkow, "The Goose in His Old Nest," *The New York Times* (June 4, 1988), 52.

17. George Vecsey, "The Goose: Country Hardball," *The New York Times* (September 5, 1986), D16.

18. "Gossage and Padres Reach Settlement," *The New York Times* (September 19, 1986), D17.

19. AP, "Feeney Quits Padres Post," *The New York Times* (September 26, 1988), C6.

20. "Happy McDemocrats," *The New York Times* (August 14, 1987), PB4.

21. "McDonald's Heir Gives $80 Million to Salvation Army," *The New York Times* (September 24, 1998), A12.

Chapter 8

1. *Cincinnati Times Star* (July 29, 1902), 1.

2. "The Forgotten Indiana Architect of Baseball," *Indianapolis Star Magazine* (May 4, 1975), 47.

3. "Brush Stock Put at $500 a Share," *The New York Times* (March 24, 1915), 15.

4. "She Plays Her Proper Part," *The Sporting News* (December 7, 1916), 7.

5. "The Forgotten Indiana Architect of Baseball."

6. Leslie Heaphy, "Ladies of the Negro Leagues," *BSTM* (October 2008), vol. 10, 22.

7. "Benswanger, Out of Game, Relaxes by Writing History of Baseball," *Pittsburgh Post-Gazette*, http://news.google.com/newspapers?nid=1129&dat=19470102&id=nvEnAAAAIBAJ&sjid.

8. "Baseball Men Beware! Women Prove They Can Run a Team," *Chicago Daily Tribune* (April 20, 1941), B3.

9. "Florence W. Dreyfuss. Baseball Today," *The Sport* (July 1936), 3.

10. Les Biderman, "Right Price Can Buy Any Business, But Pirates Lack Bona Fide Offer" (1945).

11. "Benswanger, Out of Game, Relaxes by Writing History of Baseball."

12. "Right Price Can Buy Any Business, But Pirates Lack Bona Fide Offer."

13. "Mrs. James A. Mulvey, 70 Dies; Heiress to Share of the Dodgers," *The New York Times* (November 25, 1968), 47.

14. Linda Alvarado: Biography from Answers.com, http://www.answers.com/topic/linda-alvarado.

15. Linda Alvarado: Biography from Answers.com.

16. Alvarado, Linda: 19523-: entrepreneur – FREE Alvarado, Linda: 1952, http://www.encyclopedia.com/doc/1G2-3433900010.html.

BIBLIOGRAPHY

Alexander, Charles C. *Rogers Hornsby – A Biography*. New York: Henry Holt and Company, 1995.

Allen, Lee. *Cooperstown Corner – Columns from the Sporting News 1962-1969*. Cleveland, OH: A SABR Publication.

Ardell, Jean Hastings. *Breaking into Baseball – Women and the National Pastime*. Carbondale: Southern Illinois Press, 2005.

Bass, Mike. *Marge Schott Unleashed*. Champaign, IL: Sagamore Publishing, 1993.

Schott, Marge. *Cincinnati Reds Official Yearbook/Program: 1991*.

Creamer, Robert. "The Comiskey Affair – The third-generation owners of the Chicago White Sox are fighting among themselves." *SI Vault* (February 24, 1958). http://cnnsi.printthis.clickability.com/ptccptexpire=&title=The+third-gneration+owners+o.

Dempsey, David. "Says Mrs. Payson of the Mets, 'You Can't Lose Them All,'" *New York Times Magazine*, June 23, 1968.

Eig, Jonathan. *Opening Day – The Story Of Jackie Robinson's First Season*. New York: Simon & Schuster, 2007.

Elfers, James E. *The Tour to End All Tours*. Lincoln and London: University of Nebraska Press, 2003.

Graham, Frank. *McGraw Of The Giants*. New York: G. P. Putnam's Sons, 1944.

Golenbock, Peter. *Amazin' – The Miraculous History of New York's Beloved Baseball Team*. New York: St. Martin's Press, 2002.

Golenbock, Peter. *Bums – An Oral History of The Brooklyn Dodgers*. New York: G.P Putnam's Sons, 1984.

Heaphy, Leslie. "Ladies of the Negro Leagues." *BSTM* 10 (October 2008).

Hogan, Lawrence D., forward by Jules Tygiel. *Shades of Glory – The Negro Leagues and the Story of African-American Baseball*. Washington D.C.: National Geographic, 2006.

Lanctot, Neil. *Negro League Baseball – The Rise and ruin of a Black Institution*. Philadelphia: University of Pennsylvania Press, 2004.

Maneley, Effa. "A. B. "Happy" Chandler Oral History Project: Interview with Effa Manely." By

William J. Marshall. *Baseball Commissioner Oral History Project* (October 19, 1997), http://www.nunncenter.org.

Montville, Leigh. *Ted Williams – The Biography of an American Hero.* New York: Broadway Books, 2004.

Neft, David S., Richard M. Cohen, and Michael L. Neft. *The Sports Encyclopedia – Baseball 2000, 20th Edition.* New York: St. Martin's Press, 2000.

Overmyer, James. *Queen of the Negro Leagues - Effa Manley and the Newark Eagles.* Lanham, Md., & London: The Scarecrow Press, Inc., 1998.

Ribowsky, Mark, *A Complete History of the Negro Leagues – 1884 to 1955.* A Birch Lane Press Book, 1995.

Ribowsky, Mark. *The Man, The Myth, and the Transformation of American Sports.* New York: W.W. Norton and Co., 2012.

Riechler, Joesph L. editor, *The Baseball Encyclopedia – The Complete and Official Record of Major League Baseball, Eighth Edition.* New York: Macmillian Publishing Company, 1990.

Reilly, Rick. "Heaven Help Marge Schott," *Sports Illustrated,* no. 20, vol. 84 (May 26, 1996).

Ronald McDonald House Charities. "Our History." www.rmhc.com/who-we-are/our-history/.

Rose, Pete, and Roger Kahn. *My Story.* New York: Macmillian Publishing Company, 1989.

Trausch, Susan. "They Call Her Mrs. Yawkey," *The Boston Globe* (April 6, 1989).

ABOUT THE AUTHOR

William A. Cook is the author of numerous book on major league baseball and true crime. He has appeared in productions on ESPN2 and the MLB Network. A former health administrator and township councilman in North Brunswick, NJ, he currently lives in Manalapan, NJ.